Tom Paine

America's Godfather

THOMAS PAINE

From the portrait painted in 1792 by George Romney. This portrait is considered the best likeness of Thomas Paine.

TOM PAINE:

AMERICA'S
GODFATHER
1737–1809

By W. E. WOODWARD

ILLUSTRATED

LONDON
Published by Secker & Warburg
1946

Published in Great Britain by
Martin Secker & Warburg, Ltd.,
7 John Street, London, W.C.1

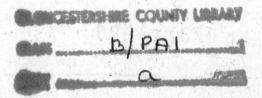
Printed in the United States of America
by American Book—Stratford Press, Inc., New York

Preface

For about a hundred and fifty years Tom Paine has been a target for abuse. Much of it has come from ignorance, and the clods of mental dirt that are flung when Paine's name is mentioned are often cast by people who have never read anything that he wrote, and who know nothing about him except his name. He has been called an atheist, a hater of Christ and a man steeped in sin. These lying epithets have become so deeply imbedded in the minds of men and women that they may never be wholly effaced, for popular hate—like popular esteem—furnishes its own nourishment and grows with the passage of time.

"An eminent man in an age of conflict must be, to the folk imagination, either wholly good or bad," says Dixon Wector. "After his death this legend continues to expand, helped by orators, poets, biographers and interested groups for or against him. If he is soon accepted by the mass as its saint or hero all his faults are forgotten; but if he proves unacceptable he becomes a villain, and whatever services he rendered are canceled out. . . . Hero worship read backwards is like the Black Mass." [1]

The purpose of this biography is to present a true picture of Tom Paine and his place in American history. This means that both his good and bad qualities should appear, and as I had no prejudice in the matter and no predetermined opinion of Paine and his accomplishments, it would seem, on first consideration, that the preparation of the book would not be a very difficult task. But it has turned out to be extremely complicated, for the reason that the data concerning Paine have been overlaid by such an accumulation of lies, false impressions, twisted remarks, and untrue and slanderous episodes that the most intensive research has been required.

[1] From an article in *The Virginia Quarterly Review*, 1942.

It has been worth the labor, for it has revealed the truth. Consider the matter of religion. As a figure in our history Paine has been cloaked by his enemies, from head to heels, in the false mantle of atheism. He has been so well disguised that his true features cannot be readily seen, and most of our fellow-citizens simply classify him as a dirty infidel and godless blasphemer, and file him away in the pigeonhole of things to be despised.

That he inspired the Declaration of Independence and is the godfather of the free American nation is either unknown or disregarded. That he was the most potent advocate during the whole of the eighteenth century for human freedom, equality of men, free education, universal suffrage, and rights of women is also a neglected fact.

I shall feel well repaid for my work if, through the medium of this book, the men and women of our country acquire a clearer conception of Paine's true life and character than they have had in the past.

I have received considerable assistance from admirers of Paine in furnishing sources of information and suggestions.

The title of the book, *Tom Paine: America's Godfather*, was suggested by Franchot Tone, an admirer of Paine. Among the many others who have been helpful I may mention, with gratitude, Joseph Lewis, head of the Freethinkers; and Frank Ewing, president of the Paine Historical Association.

W. E. WOODWARD

New York City

Contents

Illustrations

Tom Paine

America's Godfather

Tom Paine

America's Godfather

CHAPTER I

The Little Quaker Boy

I

THE AMERICAN people are hero-worshippers by nature and training. We give to our cherished national figures a respect —and, indeed, an adoration—which would have turned them into demigods in the days of pagan Rome.

Patrick Henry, a small-town lawyer in Virginia, shouted his defiance of King George III and said, "Give me liberty or give me death." At that time only a few people knew who he was; today everybody has heard of him, and almost every schoolboy has been made to memorize his famous speech and recite it on special occasions.

Paul Revere, a silversmith, rode along a country road one fateful evening to warn the people that the British troops were coming. There was really nothing remarkable about his ride except its laudable purpose. He was never in any danger, even though a British patrol held him up for a few hours, and he was not a bit tired when he had reached the end of his journey. No doubt he would be astounded if he came back to earth right now and learned that books and poems had been written about him and his wonderful achievement.

But public approval is as changeable as the wind, and it may be deflected or set in reverse by clever and unscrupulous persons and organizations who know how to control it. Consider Tom Paine. At the time of the American Revolution and for several years thereafter he was held in high honor. He was truly the godfather of the American nation, for he did more than any other individual to bring about the Declaration of Independence. This statement carries no detraction of the work of such men as Jefferson, Hancock, Samuel Adams and other Revolutionary leaders. It means that through his writings Paine brought all diverse revolutionary activities together and gave them a common aim, which was the establishment of American independence.

His *Common Sense,* in which he urged the Colonies to sever their relations with Great Britain and to create a nation of their own, was the most widely read book of that time. Men quoted from it daily; it was the subject of orations and sermons; the regimental officers in the Continental Army read *Common Sense* aloud to their soldiers drawn up in formation. George Washington wrote that "the sound doctrine and unanswerable reasoning contained in the pamphlet *Common Sense* will not leave numbers at a loss to decide upon the propriety of separation." And John Adams, despite the barbed-wire texture of his views on most men and measures, said, "History is to ascribe the Revolution to Thomas Paine."

To Paine, also, belongs the honor of naming our country the "United States of America." He was the first to use the name in print, and it was his own creation.

Elbert Hubbard said, in his simple succinct manner, that Tom Paine "was first of all men who proposed American independence; suggested the Federal Union of States; proposed the abolition of Negro slavery; suggested protection for dumb animals; proposed arbitration and international peace; advocated justice to women; pointed out the reality of human brotherhood; suggested international copyright; proposed the education of children of the poor at public expense; suggested a great republic of all the nations of the world, and urged the purchase of the great Louisiana Territory."

During the American Revolution the name of Tom Paine was known to every man and woman in the struggling Colonies, and it was looked upon with respect and reverence. While the struggle with the mother country was going on all Americans, of every class, were occupied with the war. There was no time to think of other matters, for the minds and muscles of the colonial people were strained to keep up the military enlistments, to supply the fighting patriots with food, clothes and arms. Toward this end Paine's writings were an inspiration of tremendous vitality. We are beginning only now, in our present generation, to realize the full extent of his influence and to accept the historical fact that he kept the American Revolution from breaking down under the weight of defeat, hunger and discord.

With independence won, and the Colonies free of the mother country, the great landowners, the aristocrats, and their henchmen applied themselves to the formation of a new nation. What they had in mind was a republic of aristocracy and wealth, with all the power in the hands of the upper class. Paine soon found himself out of favor as an outsider whose ideas were unacceptable. He was so much concerned with the condition of the underdog in the political and economic scheme, and so outspoken about it that he was looked upon as a dangerous disturber, a jackass who did not have enough sense to keep still, but kept up his braying in season and out of season. There is a time for everything, they said, and while Paine had accomplished a great deal in the movement for independence, he should not attempt to interfere with things which did not concern him.

It was not easy to smear this outspoken, eloquent and brilliant advocate of the common man, for his career was an open book. He had nothing to conceal in his public or private life; there was nothing about him that was deceitful, or wicked or dishonest. The profits earned by his books, which ran into such huge editions, would have made him rich if he had kept them, but he turned them over to the cause of liberty. He was a poor man. He had no love affairs, no secret amours. He did not engage in dubious business transactions. He was so utterly outspoken and unafraid of the truth that he never dreamed of lying about anything, though a little diplomatic playing with genteel and social lies would have been very helpful to him in his career.

What could be done to destroy the reputation of a man of this type? By what form of skillful disparagement could the public be led to consider Thomas Paine a disreputable, worthless nobody? These questions ran in the minds of men like Gouverneur Morris, Fisher Ames, and other well-to-do notables who looked upon Paine and his views as dangerous. To bring him into disrepute was one of their practical problems and they handled it in a practical way.

They encouraged and, in some instances, actually hired experts in defamation—mud-slingers of the press and unprincipled public speakers—to destroy Paine's reputation. The first thing these specialists in the art of slander did was to create a general impression that Paine was a slobbering drunkard who mumbled in his speech and reeled when he walked.

It is true that he drank whisky, wine and beer, like every other man of the period. A teetotaler, if one could have been found in that liquorish era, would have been considered hardly human. Men got drunk as a matter of course, and that includes preachers as well as laymen, professors as well as students, bankers as well as paupers, senators and voters, mechanics and their employers, sailors and soldiers.

But the experts in the art of slander seized upon Paine's drinking and depicted him as a filthy sot who did not keep himself clean. He stank, they said; his clothes were rags; he was drunk all the time—morning, noon and night—not just in the evening when a gentleman was supposed to be tipsy.

If Thomas Paine had drunk even half the liquor that they said he drank he never could have written anything, but would have died of delirium tremens before he had reached middle age.

His detractors succeeded in destroying his reputation both before and after his death. For a hundred years, or thereabouts, his memory was held in contempt by most Americans. The young people were brought up either in ignorance of what Paine did to help in the War for Independence; or, on the other hand, they were taught all the slanders that have been tacked on to his memory. Public speakers and candidates for office made it a point never to quote from his writings in making their orations, even when such a quotation would be illuminating, for mention of the disreputable Paine would have brought boos and sneers from their audiences. Histories of the American Revolution that did not contain even a mention of Thomas Paine were actually printed and circulated.

Paine should be in the Hall of Fame, of course, with Washington, Jefferson, John Adams and other founders of the republic, but his name was voted down. Theodore Roosevelt characterized him as a "filthy little atheist," a three-word phrase in which not one word is correct, for he was not filthy, nor little, nor an atheist.

Will this patriot and fighter for human rights ever be restored to his proper place in the reverence and affection of the American people? No one can say for certain, for no one knows, but it is a fact that during the past decade much of the fog of slanders that dimmed his reputation has been dissipated by the sunlight of truth. Our grandfathers seldom mention him without some expression of contempt, but today men of understanding know better. Consider the words of Thomas A. Edison, who said, "I have always regarded Paine as one of the greatest of all Americans. Never have we had a sounder intelligence in this republic."

He said further:

It was my good fortune to encounter Thomas Paine's works in my boyhood. I discovered a set of the writings of Paine on my father's bookshelves when I was thirteen. It was, indeed, a revelation to me to read that great thinker's views on political and theological subjects. Paine educated me then about many matters of which I had never before thought. I remember very vividly the flash of enlightenment that shone from Paine's writings, and I recall thinking at that time "What a pity these works are not today the schoolbooks for all children!" My interest in Paine and his writings was not satisfied by my first reading of his works. I went back to them time and again, just as I have done since my boyhood days.

There can be no question that the national memory of Paine is being slowly lifted in our time from the mire of unjust obloquy and disrepute in which it has lain for more than a hundred years. Nevertheless, as late as 1942 the Fairmount Park Commission, of Philadelphia, refused to give the Thomas Paine Bicentennial Committee permission to erect a statue of Paine, by Jo Davidson, in Fairmount Park. Many Philadelphians, the commission declared, would find this statue objectionable because of Paine's "reputed religious views."

Prejudice can be refuted only by facts, and the purpose of this book is to present the facts concerning Thomas Paine, his life and works, and to do it properly we had better begin with his birth.

2

Joseph Paine (or Pain), father of Thomas, was a commonplace person. He was placid and pious, industrious and poor.

Born in 1708, he lived for nearly eighty years in his native village of Thetford, in the English county of Norfolk. In religious belief and practice he was a Quaker. He wore the drab garments of that sect, and his speech was sprinkled with *thees* and *thous*. His voice was never raised in anger or dispute, for he believed in the power of meekness and felt that in the course of time the meek shall inherit the earth.

By trade he was a staymaker, which means a maker of corsets, and his shop was part of his small cottage on Bridge Street, which is now called White Hart Street. In the eighteenth century the cumbersome, heavy stays worn by women were made by hand. Every community had one or more staymakers who were on the same social level as the tailors, the shoemakers and the blacksmiths.

In Thetford there resided a spinster lady whose name was Frances Cocke. Her father was an attorney of excellent reputation, but Frances appears to have been rather thoroughly disliked on account of her "sour temper and eccentric character." There is a lack of precision in these comments, for the term "eccentric character" might cover almost anything from a refusal to milk the cow on Sunday to a habit of staying up till midnight in a village where everybody was supposed to be in bed an hour after sundown. And the meaning of "sour temper" has the same latitude, depending to a large extent on the person who makes the characterization. Few people are sour to everybody.

But in the case of Frances Cocke this comment seems to have considerable justification, for it does not come from one person but from several. Moreover, the lady was thirty-seven years old and unmarried which, at that time and place, was a fact of much significance. In the eighteenth century an old maid was a curiosity and every woman who could get a man in her early twenties made haste to marry him. There were no careers open to unmarried women except as servants or teachers or nurses, and most spinsters dragged out their days as household drudges or as dependents in the families of well-to-do relatives.

Despite her vinegary repute Frances Cocke attracted Joseph Paine. Why and how this happened is one of the minor mysteries. Perhaps he made her a pair of stays and fell in love with her face and figure, and in his new-found ardor did not care if she had the tongue of Xanthippe and the eccentricities of the Lady Who Lived in a Wood. Such bursts of emotion do occur, though they seldom happen to Quakers. It is more likely that he paid court to her just because she was sour-tempered and eccentric. Men who are deeply religious do have such preferences now and then. They look upon their bitter-tongued wives as a form of penance for their sins. The principle is that every man should provide his own purgatory.

Joseph's advances were welcomed by the lady, and they were married on June 20, 1734, in Euston parish, near Thetford. In the parish register Joseph's age is set down as twenty-six, and that of his bride as thirty-seven.

Besides the striking difference in their ages, there were other odd circumstances connected with this marriage. Joseph was a dyed-in-the-wool Quaker, and Frances—like her father—was a member of the Church of England. This means that their respective religious convictions were very dissimilar, one from the other. The English no longer persecuted Quakers; the Toleration Act of 1689 had put an end to that; but they were nevertheless considered a tribe apart from the general run of civilized beings. In other words, they were usually looked down upon and mildly despised. They refused to serve as soldiers, to fight in any war, or to take an oath in court, and these various refusals caused the patriotic subjects of the King to have bitter thoughts about them.

There was also a rather definite social distinction between the daughter of an attorney and a workingman. Frances Cocke must have felt that she was marrying beneath her own class. It was obviously an ill-assorted marriage, but in spite of its discordant elements it lasted fifty-two years or until the death of Joseph Paine in 1786.

3

Their son Thomas was born in Thetford on January 29, 1737. His parents lived in the small house on White Hart Street. A photograph of this cottage exists, but the building was torn down in the 1880's. In its place there stands a pretty garden and a fountain. The house had four or five rooms, one of which on the street level was used by Joseph as a shop.

We know only a few facts about Tom's early years and shall never know more, for the sources of information have long since dried up. He had no brothers or sisters to keep him company. His mother gave birth in August, 1738, to a daughter—christened Elizabeth—but this little girl died in early infancy. So Tom grew up as an only child in a home that was morbidly depressing. His father's solemn personality, filled to the brim with a sense of sin and an abhorrence of every kind of frivolity, was matched by the cantankerous fault-finding of his mother. In that family no games were played, no funny stories told, and no jolly parties gathered to pass the evening.

We may picture young Tom, repressed and silent, moving about the somber rooms and in and out of the garden, hardly knowing what to do with himself. Many years later he wrote of Quakers in *The Age of Reason*:

Though I reverence their philanthropy, I cannot help smiling at the conceit [notion] if the taste of a Quaker had been consulted at the creation, what a silent and drab-colored creation it would have been! Not a flower would have blossomed its gaieties, nor a bird been permitted to sing.

It is a curious fact that Paine never said anything concerning his youth in Thetford. He seemed to have had no reminiscences of his school days, no funny stories about his chums—the sort of memories that almost everyone acquires. He seemed, when he had reached maturity, to live only in the present and the future. In his writings, and in conversation, he made a few brief and kindly references to his father, but he never mentioned his mother to his friends or to his reading public. Notwithstanding this obvious attitude of coolness he contributed to her support in her old age, giving her a weekly sum through a third person. There are to be found many unusual circumstances in the life of Thomas Paine, but this silent antipathy between himself and his mother is one of the most extraordinary. Most men have an affection for their mothers which is strong enough to stand a great deal of friction without wearing out.

For six or seven years he was a pupil of the local grammar school. Apparently he made no close friends among his fellow-pupils, nor did he take part in any of their sports. A writer of that period, a contemporary of Paine, went to Thetford after Paine had become famous and made inquiries about him. This inquisitive visitor learned very little that is worth while. He wrote that Paine was deemed "a sharp boy, of unsettled application; but he left no performances which denote juvenile vigor or uncommon attainments."

This characterization leads one to think that they expected little from such a mediocrity. But he became famous throughout the world, and today the town of Thetford's one claim to celebrity is that it was his birthplace. For many years, before and after his death, the citizens of Thetford did not like to be reminded that it was Paine's home town. They were in the habit of saying that Thetford should not be blamed; that a child might be born anywhere. If the discussion ran on any further the Thetfordites usually reminded the visitor that Tom Paine left the village when he was about seventeen, before he had acquired his maturity.

Paine has now been dead nearly a hundred and fifty years and Thetford has become proud of having been his home. Inquiring visitors are shown the site of the Paine cottage, the school he attended, the playing field on which he occasionally kicked a ball; and the little bookshop has all of Paine's books in stock.

In 1943 the members of the American air force stationed in England joined the citizens of Thetford in subscribing funds to purchase a handsome bronze plaque in memory of Thomas Paine.

The plaque carries this inscription:

THOMAS PAINE, 1737–1809,
*Journalist, Patriot and Champion
of the Common Man.*

THOMAS PAINE, SON OF A HUMBLE THETFORD STAY-MAKER, WAS BORN NEAR THIS HOUSE. FROM HIS TALENTED PEN CAME THE VOICE FOR THE DEMOCRATIC ASPIRATIONS OF THE AMERICAN REPUBLIC THROUGH SUCH SPLENDID WRITING AS "COMMON SENSE," "CRISIS," AND "THE AGE OF REASON." BURIED IN NEW YORK, THIS SIMPLE SON OF ENGLAND LIVES ON THROUGH THE IDEALS AND PRINCIPLES OF THE DEMOCRATIC WORLD FOR WHICH WE FIGHT TODAY. IN TRIBUTE TO HIS MEMORY AND TO THE EVERLASTING LOVE FOR FREEDOM EMBODIED IN HIS WORKS, THIS PLAQUE IS GRATEFULLY DEDICATED THROUGH THE VOLUNTARY CONTRIBUTIONS OF SOLDIERS OF AN AMERICAN AIR FORCE GROUP.

Paine was nearly forty before he accomplished anything worthy of attention. It may be that he was an example of arrested development, though the more probable supposition is that his precocious talents were suppressed when he was a boy. Whatever the cause, he personifies an unusual case of delayed achievement.

Psychologists tell us that children who have no brothers or sisters and are without playmates or sympathetic parents become introspective, and that introspection is the mother of introverted personalities that depend upon their own thoughts for companionship. Strange projects and ideas come into their minds, all of them untempered by actual experience. These gifted and introverted children are mentally much older than their age.

Tom Paine may have been a gifted child without any opportunity at home or at school to show his quick perception, originality and unusual abilities. In the 1740's these qualities would have been looked upon with dislike in an English village. Their possessor would have been called pert and saucy and "too big for his breeches." The schoolmaster would have repressed any such upstart exhibitions with the strokes of a cane laid on the boy's back. In that early day there were no special classes for gifted children, and no recognition even that such children were in existence.

It is wholly possible that if Paine was unusually gifted as a boy his superior qualities were crushed so completely at school and in his home that they took a good long sleep and did not awake until his life began anew on another continent.

4

The master of the Thetford school spent the greater part of his time in teaching Latin to the pupils, but young Paine did not take the Latin course and his instructor was Reverend William Knowles, an assistant, or usher, in the school. Long after his school days, Paine wrote, in the *Rights of Man*, Part II:

I did not learn Latin, not only because I had no inclination to learn languages, but because of the objection the Quakers have against the books in which the language is taught. But this did not prevent me from being acquainted with the subjects of all the Latin books used in the school. The natural bent of my mind was to science. I had some turn, and I believe some talent, for poetry; but this I rather repressed than encouraged, as leading too much into the field of imagination.

It is quite certain that he had no knack for languages. He lived ten years in France, from 1792 to 1802, took part in the French Revolution and met thousands of Frenchmen, yet he never learned enough French to make a speech in that language, or to say anything at all except the few sentences that were needed in ordering food and commenting on the weather. He could read French slowly and fairly well, however, and could understand it if it were spoken clearly.

He says his "natural bent was to science," and he intended no doubt to include mathematics in this classification. He was indeed an excellent hand at calculations of all kinds that involved mathematical conceptions.

He thought, as he says above, that he had a talent for poetry, but he seems to have been mistaken, for the poems that appear in his collected works are mere doggerel. The first of his verses, written when he was only eight years old, was an epitaph for a crow which he buried in the garden. It runs in this fashion:

> Here lies the body of John Crow,
> Who once was high, but now is low;
> Ye brother Crows, take warning all,
> For as you rise, so must you fall.

In 1750, when Thomas was thirteen, he was taken from school to be taught the trade of staymaking. It was a handicraft that required a fairly long apprenticeship. One had to learn the qualities of various fabrics, such as silk, linen, calico and linsey-woolsey. Cutting the cloth was an operation that called for skill, for each pair of stays was an individual product. Tape measurements of the customer were made in the first place, and a pattern was laid out. This pattern was kept in the shop and the stays were fashioned according to it. The garment was strengthened by strips of whalebone. It had to be strong enough to hold the body in shape, yet sufficiently flexible to permit the wearer to bend.

As a staymaker Tom Paine was entirely out of place. He was an intensely masculine person who felt that the making of women's garments ought to be done by women and not by men.

His mind always worked—both as youth and man—with a startling directness, and he was likely to make the most abrupt and disconcerting remarks. Whenever he had anything to say applicable to the matter in hand, he spoke out tersely without frills or flowers. That would be all right in a revolutionary committee, or in a debating society, but it is not an admirable quality in those who follow such occupations as ladies' tailors, floorwalkers and headwaiters; nor in those who sell stays to women.

Why then did Tom Paine become a staymaker? Because his father was a staymaker who had built up a small business and did not expect to live forever. Who would take over the shop and carry on after his death? His son, of course. That is the immediate answer to the question of why Tom went into the staymaking trade, but another and deeper answer lies in the character of English civilization in the eighteenth century.

During this period the social pattern of England was becoming static under the leadership of the noble families and rich landowners. The powerful influence of this aristocracy of birth and wealth extended over the whole of the economic and social life of the nation. It was an essentially snobbish civilization in which the ruling upper class not only wanted everything for itself but was actually offended by evidence of unusual ability on the part of anyone who belonged to the common people.

This spirit of exclusion was not limited to those who strove to rise in the fields of commerce, law, the Church, or the armed forces. It gave no encouragement whatever to poor and obscure persons who hoped to accomplish anything in the fields of literature or art unless these achievements were produced under the patronage of a social superior.

From these prevailing ideas arose the general principles of a static society where each one followed the occupation of his family. The children of servants became servants in their turn; a cabinetmaker or a blacksmith was expected to train his son to follow the paternal trade; the sons of army officers went into the army; the heads of departments of the government were selected from about two dozen noble families.

The social structure was not as completely rigid as it might appear from this brief description, for there was no law to prevent a laborer's son from becoming an architect, let us say, but the whole invisible yet powerful weight of social custom almost automatically placed obstacles in the path of those who endeavored to rise.

Thetford, in the 1750's, was a dull and uninviting village. Like most English towns of that period it was as colorless as a mud pie. It was also as dirty as a hog wallow, and there was a permanent unpleasant smell in the air, owing to the lack of a sewage system. Although it was a country town of only two thousand inhabitants the houses were built close together, city fashion, so each side of the street presented the appearance of an unbroken wall.

The houses of the common people were simply stone boxes with a roof over them. Porches and verandas were unknown; the fronts of the houses ran right up to the street, without an inch of space for a front yard; but most of the houses had back yards or gardens. There was no running water; wells stood here and there in the streets. After nightfall the village was almost totally dark, though lanterns holding candles were set at the street corners. The only illumination anywhere was candlelight.

The village, with others in the neighborhood, formed a "pocket borough" of the Duke of Grafton. This means that he had the borough in his pocket, figuratively speaking. He named all the officials as well as the representatives of the borough in the House of Commons. There were only thirty-two men in the community who had the voting franchise, and they cast their votes according to the instructions of the Duke of Grafton. The people of the town had no interest in politics; it was all above their heads. Any such interest, if it led to criticism of those in power, would have got the simple townsmen into a good deal of trouble.

The Duke of Grafton was a Whig and, for the whole period of Paine's youth, the Whigs ran the government. The nobles and wealthy landowners who were at the head of the party formed what we call in America a corrupt ring or a "bunch of grafters." But in those days such terms were unknown and people in general looked at the whole subject from a different standpoint. In these matters there were hardly any differences between the Whigs and the Tories. The leaders of both parties, when they came into power, treated the national treasury as their private property. They robbed the revenues in a frank, openhanded way. These lordly looters were men of Oxford and Cambridge, they had excellent taste, they read Latin and Greek, they patronized the arts, and they had mastered the punctilio of elaborate Court etiquette. They would have been genuinely and deeply astonished if anyone had accused them of stealing just because they put their sons and relatives into lucrative positions which had no duties, or because they sold offices for cash, or awarded government contracts to their friends at fanciful prices.

5

After nearly five years in his father's shop Tom Paine ran away. In later life he never told what caused him to leave his parents and his native village, for he refused to talk about it at all, but one may guess that he was bored and fed up, and that he wanted to see a little of the world. His teacher at the Thetford school —the Reverend William Knowles—had served, in his youth, on board a man-of-war. He liked young Tom and he told the boy many wondrous tales of life on board a fighting ship, with the usual embroidery of imagination which goes with such yarns.

The boy remembered these sagas and by the time he had reached the age of seventeen the dark little shop, the women customers, the eternal piety of his father, and the sharp, upbraiding tongue of his mother had become so unendurable that he ran away from home to go to sea. England and France were then carrying on an undeclared war. At the port of Harwich, about thirty miles from Thetford, the privateer *Terrible* was about to sail for the purpose of raiding French commerce. The captain of the *Terrible* bore the incredible name of Death.

Seventeen-year-old Tom slipped out of the house with a little bundle of clothes and made his way to Harwich to unite his fortunes with those of *Terrible* and Death. He had not been long on his way before his father learned about it and set forth in pursuit.

Tom reached Harwich, volunteered, was accepted and had a square meal which was hardly over before his father arrived. Captain Death gave him up and Joseph and his son left for home and more staymaking.

The ship sailed on her cruise. In the course of time she encountered a French warship, and in the ensuing battle the *Terrible* was disastrously defeated, losing one hundred and seventy-five of her two hundred men. When Paine heard of it he called himself lucky, and thereafter when he found himself in a desperate situation he relied on luck to save him. And luck did just that, on several occasions.

Two years later, in 1756, he went away again without his father's permission and joined the privateer *King of Prussia*, commanded by a Captain Mendez. Of this adventure nothing whatever is known except the bare fact that he went to sea on that ship. Paine would never say anything about it, but his attitude in respect to this particular exploit is not at all remarkable. He was as reticent about it as about everything that concerned his personal life.

The tendency to falsify the facts about Paine is so well-established and deep-seated that it may be described as a literary disease. It was started by Paine's enemies while he was still living and its purpose was to destroy his influence upon the people by casting aspersions upon his character and his motives. To do that it was necessary to make Paine appear despicable. Today this tendency is still active, and one of its curious features is that it appears frequently in the utterances of Paine's ardent admirers, as well as in the attitude of his enemies. As late as 1943 an author who is undoubtedly an enthusiastic believer in him and his works wrote a novel in which Paine is the central figure. In the course of the narrative the author describes young Tom's life aboard the privateer. The account is purely fanciful and without any factual authority to support it. He declares that the captain of the vessel caught Tom stealing his rum and that thereafter he gave the boy so many beatings that his body was a livid mass of bruises.

Then he goes on to say that Tom swam ashore when the ship arrived in the Thames and became a thief, drunkard and alley cat in the London slums. He is portrayed as living in the hut of a garbage collector and finding daily food in the garbage buckets, until "one day he took hold of himself, left Gin Row, and apprenticed himself to a staymaker." The facts are that Tom got a job with a staymaker almost at once, and his evenings were spent in studying the sciences. He was a well-behaved, studious youth.

In the same novel the author gives what he calls an account of the first meeting of Paine and Benjamin Franklin, who was at that time the official representative in London of the American Colonies. His story of that occasion is a farce which is unpardonable in its reflections on Tom Paine. He depicts Paine as swaggering into Franklin's study with insolence in his manner —a filthy, ragged, unshaved slum vagabond with a you-can-go-to-hell tone in his speech.

The fact is that Paine went to a great deal of trouble to look well when he called on Franklin. He wore his best clothes, and was carefully shaved, combed and brushed. In conversing with Franklin his manner was respectful, and what he had to say was so intelligent that Franklin was impressed.

Invention is a privilege of the novelist, but even a writer of fiction has no right to libel a heroic character who has actually lived, and who has been already maligned and slandered in the past by his enemies.

The author of the novel, Howard Fast, professes admiration for Paine and shows him as an active force in the American Revolution, and one wonders what could be his motive in presenting such a false picture. My guess is that there may be two motives: One is the novelists' inclination to make everything dramatic and picturesque; the other is a tendency of many novelists of today to portray ability, dignity and courage in a coating of grime and bad manners. Take the Communist mind in America as an illustration. In a general sense it closely resembles the mind of a ten-year-old child, and a boy of that age would be pleased at the thought of a swaggering street urchin who tells somebody—the teacher, for instance, or that man at the bank— to go to the devil.

We do not know how long Paine was a member of the *King of Prussia's* crew, but it could not have been more than a year, for in 1757 he was working as a journeyman staymaker in the shop of Mr. Morris, who owned an establishment in Hanover Street in London.

He was certainly not sodden in dissipation, nor did he hang around taverns after his work at the shop. There is ample evidence that he was a studious young man, and that he spent his spare hours in acquiring knowledge. He was interested in astronomy, mathematics and philosophy. "As soon as I was able," he wrote long afterward, "I purchased a pair of globes, and attended the philosophical lectures of Martin and Ferguson, and became afterwards acquainted with Dr. Bevis, of the society called the Royal Society, then living in the Temple, and an excellent astronomer."

He left London in 1758, went to Dover, and got a job in the shop of a staymaker named Grace. In April, 1759, he went to Sandwich, which is a village in Kent, and opened a shop of his own on borrowed money. In September of that year, when he was twenty-two years of age, he married a young woman, an orphan whose name was Mary Lambert. She lived in Sandwich and was employed as a maid by Mrs. Richard Solly, the wife of a woolen draper.[1]

[1] On the marriage register, Paine signed his name "Thomas Pain," without the final "e." The name of his father was Pain, and it seems that his adoption of the name Paine was a matter of accident. He had the habit of ending his signature by a little flourish which somewhat resembled the letter "e," and was no doubt mistaken for it. In writing to him people, after looking at his signature, addressed him as Paine. He did not adopt the name with the final "e" until he came to America, and his first letters with that signature were written in 1775.

HOUSE INDICATED BY A CROSS IS THE BIRTHPLACE OF THOMAS PAINE.

The house stood in Thetford, England, but it no longer exists and a flower garden occupies the site.

Etching by E. T. Scowcroft

THE INDIAN QUEEN IN PHILADELPHIA

This roomy, colonial inn was Paine's favorite daily resort during his residence in Philadelphia in the 1770's and 1780's.

COMMON SENSE:

ADDRESSED TO THE

INHABITANTS

OF

AMERICA,

On the following interesting

SUBJECTS.

I. Of the Origin and Design of Government in general, with concise Remarks on the English Constitution.

II. Of Monarchy and Hereditary Succession.

III. Thoughts on the present State of American Affairs.

IV. Of the present Ability of America, with some miscellaneous Reflections.

Written by an ENGLISHMAN.

Man knows no Master save creating HEAVEN,
Or those whom choice and common good ordain.
THOMS
on

eten-
usurpa-

PHILADELPHIA, Printed

And Sold by R. BELL, in Third-Stree   It

59

TITLE PAGE OF THE FIRST EDITION OF *Common Sense*

Note that name of the author is not given. On later editions
Thomas Paine's name is set down as the author

Paine was inefficient in all commercial affairs, even in the conduct of a small shop. This should not be considered as a reflection on his intelligence and energy, for he had an abundant supply of both these qualities. He was simply not designed by nature to be a business man, just as others who are excellent as corporation executives would be lost and bewildered if they were expected to make their living by writing.

His little staymaking business was beginning to fail when he married Miss Lambert, and in a few months he moved his shop to Margate, where he hoped to do better.

There—at Margate—his wife died, in 1760. She had been married to Paine less than a year. Nothing whatever is known of her except that she was young, a native of Kent, and had been employed as a lady's maid. The cause of her death is equally unknown.

Francis Oldys (which is a pen-name for George Chalmers) was the first of Paine's lying biographers, and he hints that Mary Lambert died because of ill-usage by her husband. There is nothing whatever to support such a statement, not even the gossip of neighbors; it is a lie out of whole cloth without a thread of truth running through it. Like the rest of us, Paine had his faults, but cruelty was certainly not one of them. He was, in fact, extraordinarily kindhearted and generous.

Soon after his wife's death Paine gave up the staymaking business and applied for a place as an exciseman.[2] The father of his late wife had been in the excise earlier in life, and it may have been that her talk about her father suggested this occupation to Paine. The duties of the post required, apparently, some considerable study, and Paine went to London to prepare himself. About a year later, in 1761, he was given a place as supernumerary officer of excise, and on December first of the next year (1762) he was appointed gauger of brewer's casks. Two years later he was stationed at Alford on the lookout for smugglers. This was a post of danger, for there were heavy

[2] An exciseman was an inspector, or measurer, of taxable commodities. Every member of the excise had a regular round of taverns, brewers, distillers, grocers and other places, to measure the tax.

penalties for smuggling, and the daring fellows who followed that illegal trade were likely to fight back upon detection.

Paine's salary was fifty pounds a year, which was small pay for the work, but it became even less after the necessary expenses were deducted. He made a calculation which showed that the net yearly wage was only thirty-two pounds, or twelve and a half shillings a week. This stipend figures out to be about fifty cents a day in American money, but it probably had a buying power of four times as much at that time.

At that period the practice of "stamping" was common among the excisemen. Stamping meant taking the dealer's word for the amount of taxable goods that he had in stock, without going to the trouble of measuring them. His papers were then stamped and the entries in the exciseman's books were made out accordingly.

On one occasion it was found that Paine had taken the word of a victualer without making an examination of his stock. Upon being charged with this dereliction he confessed frankly, saying that the daily rounds he was expected to make were so long that he could not cover them.

For this offence he was discharged from office on August 27, 1765. He had then been about four years in the Excise Department. For three years he had served as a supernumerary officer, and one year—or thereabouts—as an excise officer of full rank.

CHAPTER II

A Life Without Motive

I

A<small>T THE</small> age of twenty-eight Thomas Paine found himself out of a job and out of money. His wages had always been small, and he had not saved a farthing. In his mind there was no vision of his own future; he never dreamed that he would become, during his lifetime, a world-famous figure; or that he would write books which would inspire millions of readers. He was at that period of his life a drifter without plan or purpose.

It was not long before he had a job in the shop of a Mr. Gudgeon, a staymaker in the tiny town of Diss, in the county of Norfolk. We do not know how much he received in wages, but if he was paid at the customary rate he earned eight shillings sixpence a week, or thereabouts, equivalent to two dollars and twelve cents in our money. These wages were considered fairly good for a workingman in the 1760's, when a shilling would purchase as much as a dollar in our time.

He did not remain long in Mr. Gudgeon's employment, for early in 1766 he was living in London and teaching English— which meant English grammar and composition—in the academy of a Mr. Noble, who is as dim in outline as the staymaker Gudgeon. As a teacher Paine was paid nine and a half shillings a week, or twenty-five pounds a year. The surprising thing about this school job is that Mr. Noble ever thought of employing a staymaker to teach English. Workingmen were not expected to possess scholarly knowledge of any kind, and a great many of them could not read. The common people, such as craftsmen, farm hands and laborers were purposely kept at a low educational level by the ruling classes that governed the country. These lords and masters could not understand why a man who is destined by the social order and his surrounding circumstances to lay bricks or plow the soil all his life should

33

have an education. It would be a complete waste of his time and the time of those who taught him. Besides, it would make him discontented with his lot, or so they reasoned. The village schools, or most of them, were therefore limited to a curriculum which included hardly anything but the A B C's and easy reading, the scrawling of poorly shaped letters, and a few simple rules of arithmetic.[1]

Though Paine left school at the age of thirteen and went to work, he had a burning desire for knowledge that continued all his life and he was a self-taught, lifelong student. When he was in his fifties he said to his friend Rickman: "I have seldom passed five minutes of my life, however circumstanced, in which I did not acquire some knowledge."

His mind was quick, lively and intensely curious. He was attracted by all sorts of things and occurrences which people generally disregard or accept as a matter of course. In this sense he resembled Benjamin Franklin, who was also a continual knowledge-seeker. But there the resemblance ends, for Franklin was a practical person who did not consider it worth while to fight hopeless battles for ideals, while Paine had the heart and soul of a martyr.

While he was teaching English in Mr. Noble's academy he was doing his best to be reinstated in the excise. He wrote letters to his former superior officers in the department and induced his friends to recommend his reinstatement. The job seems, from this distance in time, to have been hardly worth having, with its small pay, hard work and heavy responsibility. But, if one may judge from the circumstances, he had nothing else in sight. Staymaking had been definitely abandoned by him in 1765 when he gave up his job in the shop of Mr. Gudgeon, or so it appears, and teaching held no promise of a future.

[1] The grammar school at Thetford, where Paine was a pupil, was much superior to the schools supported by the parishes. It was founded on a legacy left by Sir Richard Fulmerston in 1566, and was not dependent on public funds. Some of the higher branches of knowledge such as history and the sciences, were taught there.

On July 3, 1766, he wrote this letter to the Board of Excise:

Honourable Sirs: In humble obedience to your honours' letter of discharge bearing date of August 29, 1765, I delivered up my commission and since that time have given you no trouble. I confess the justice of your honours' displeasure and humbly beg to add my thanks for the candour and lenity with which you at that unfortunate time indulged me. And though the nature of the report and my own confession cut off all expectations of enjoying your honours' favor then, yet I humbly hope it has not finally excluded me therefrom, upon which hope I humbly presume to entreat your honours to restore me. The time I enjoyed my former commission was short and unfortunate—an officer only a single year. No complaint of the least dishonesty or intemperance ever appeared against me; and, if I am so happy as to succeed in this, my humble petition, I will endeavor that my future conduct shall as much engage your honours' approbation as my former has merited your displeasure. I am your honours' most dutiful humble servant,

THOMAS PAINE.

Such a humble, pleading letter is very interesting in contrast to the letters that he wrote later in life. In this petition to the Board of Excise he shows that he lacks confidence in himself. The missive has no backbone or stamina; it is a begging letter. But it was effective. The board, meeting the next day, July 4, ordered that he "be restored on a proper vacancy."

No "proper vacancy" in the excise appeared for a year and a half. For a few months he continued to make his living as a teacher. His employment at the Noble school came to an end in December, 1766, but in the following month he found a position as teacher in the Gardiner school at Kensington. His connection with this school lasted only three months. In May he was offered the post of excise officer at Grampound, in Cornwall, but he declined it and "prayed leave to wait another vacancy."

What was his occupation meanwhile? He was no longer a teacher, and he had refused an offer for a place in the excise in a remote corner of England. It is hard to believe that he would have declined the job in Cornwall if he had not some other resource to fall back on.

Francis Oldys asserts that in 1766 Paine became an itinerant preacher, without regular orders and outside the church, although he preached the Christian doctrine. In other words, an evangelist. He declares that Paine preached in Moorfields and elsewhere in England "as he was urged by his necessities or directed by his spirit."

There is nothing but Oldys' word to support this assertion. Paine never even hinted at such an experience, nor did any of his friends in England. He says in *The Age of Reason*:

> From the time I was capable of conceiving an idea and acting upon it by reflection, I either doubted the truth of the Christian system or thought it to be a strange affair; I scarcely knew which it was, but I well remember, when about seven or eight years of age, hearing a sermon read by a relation of mine, who was a great devotee of the Church, upon the subject of what is called *redemption by the death of the Son of God*.

> After the sermon was ended, I went into the garden, and as I was going down the garden steps (for I perfectly recollect the spot) I revolted at the recollection of what I had heard, and thought to myself that it was making God Almighty act like a passionate man who killed His son when He could not revenge Himself in any other way, and, as I was sure a man would be hanged who did such a thing, I could not see for what purpose they preached such sermons.

Instead of making his living as a roving preacher it is probable that he worked here and there, during this waiting period, at odd jobs, such as part-time staymaking, coaching private pupils, and acting as an assistant exciseman without having his name appear on the rolls.

2

Eventually a place in the excise was found for Paine and he re-entered the service on February 15, 1768. He was stationed at Lewes in Sussex near Brighthelmstone, which is now known as Brighton.

Paine was then thirty-one. He would have been a very ordinary looking man except for his fine eyes. He was five feet nine inches tall, and slender. He must have been rather good-looking. His nose was prominent—of the combative type—but his delicate mouth and large, dark-blue eyes gave his face a sentimental, imaginative cast that one associates with a feeling for poetry. His complexion was ruddy. In his later years, when he was surrounded by enemies who magnified every quality that might serve to discredit him, the ruddiness of his face was ascribed to excessive drinking. This was not so; his pink complexion was of the ordinary English type, and he had possessed it all his life. Upon meeting him for the first time the piercing brilliancy of his eyes attracted immediate attention.

In his novel, to which reference has already been made, Howard Fast misrepresents Paine's personal appearance in a way that is startling, to say the least, and for which there seems to be no rational excuse. The Paine he describes is so vastly different from the actual man that one wonders at his purpose in creating such a caricature.

He writes of Paine's "oddly twisted eyes." As a matter of fact his eyes were large, sharp, clear and his gaze was direct. He was not cross-eyed. But this mention of "twisted eyes" occurs again and again in Mr. Fast's book.

Paine's hands, he says, were "meaty and broad," and he refers to them several times as the hands of a peasant. One man, in his book, speaking to another person, says of Paine, "He's a peasant. Have you seen his hands; like slabs of beef." But Paine's hands were slender, according to the evidence of his portraits. He was really tall and slim, but in the novel he is depicted as wide and squat, also as having a "large, sharp, hooked nose." It is true that his nose was large and sharp, but the "hook" in it is one of the novelist's inventions.

At Lewes Paine obtained lodgings in the home of Samuel Ollive, a Quaker who ran a tobacco shop. This building still stands in Bull Lane and is one of the show places of the town because it was once the home of Thomas Paine. One of the residents of the town at that time was Thomas Rickman, who became a devoted, lifelong friend of Paine. In his later years he wrote his recollections, with many reminiscences of his friend who, by that time, had become a person of world-wide renown. Paine seemed, according to Rickman, to be always in a hurry

when on his official rounds. He carried a stick covered with figures and an ink bottle hung from a buttonhole in his coat. That
was not out of the ordinary; all excisemen were equipped with
the figure-covered stick, to be used in measuring, and the ink
bottle for writing notes and signing receipts. His speech, Rickman says, was quick, incisive and often witty.

In Lewes at the time there was an informal club composed of
"a very respectable, sensible and convivial set" who gathered in
the evenings at the White Hart Tavern. Paine, a member of
the club, and called the "Commodore" on account of his former
service at sea, became famous among them for his clever arguments and for his tendency to take the unpopular side in most
of the discussions just to prolong the debate.

"In politics," according to Rickman, "he was at this time a
Whig and notorious for that quality which has been defined
perseverance in a good cause and obstinacy in a bad one. He was
tenacious of his opinions, which were bold, acute and independent, and which he maintained with ardor, elegance and argument."

Most of Paine's leisure time in the past ten years had been
spent in reading and making notes. Though he had been only
an artisan and a minor legal official and a petty instructor in a
school, his knowledge was much superior to that of the average
man. But his self-taught education had some queer gaps in it.
Of novels and plays, and of the whole body of what we call
belles lettres, he knew little or nothing. In science, history, philosophy and economics he was well-informed. Apparently he
did not read books for pleasure or amusement, but to get something substantial out of them.

His mind had a pronounced tendency to disregard authori-
tative opinions, including the views of famous writers who had
lived in the past. He tried, instinctively, to put all streams of
logic into their most primitive forms. He argued that if you
start out with a time-honored assertion which you accept as
valid just because it comes from Lord Bacon or Aristotle you
may be on the wrong road altogether, for Bacon and Aristotle
may be wrong.

The disputes at the White Hart Club often ran on for hours, though they were always tempered by good humor, good ale and good food. On a morning after a debate that had been vehemently maintained it was the custom of some of the jolly spirits of the club to send what they called the "Headstrong Book" to the most obstinate debater. This volume belies its name, as it was nothing more than an old Greek *Homer*, and why it was chosen as the "Headstrong Book" is a mystery. Perhaps some obscure and long-forgotten joke was connected with it. The recipient of the battered *Homer* kept it until the next meeting, when he brought it back to the White Hart. Rickman says it was sent more frequently to Paine than to anyone else.

One of the members of the club, a Mr. Lee, wrote a poem about Paine's skill as a debater. This piece of verse was read before the club and all members had copies of it. Its text follows:

> Immortal Pain, while mighty reasoners jar,
> We crown thee General of the Headstrong War;
> Thy logic vanquish'd error, and thy mind
> No bounds but those of right and truth confined.
> Thy soul of fire must sure ascend the sky,
> Immortal Pain, thy fame can never die;
> For men like thee their names must ever save
> From the black edicts of the tyrant grave.

One should not take the lofty praise of this poem too seriously, for the club was a jolly affair where praise and persiflage were inextricably mingled, but the verse does show that Paine stood high among its members.

The warm debates at the White Hart were almost invariably on political or economic subjects as shown in the state of English affairs. Paine, on account of his quickness of mind and ready wit and command of logic, was the lion of this little group. He became a local celebrity in a small way. Excisemen were constantly changing posts, going from one part of the country to another, and through them Paine's reputation for intelligence spread gradually throughout the whole body of the excise.

He had always been a rebel, but a silent and moody one, with his rebellious and democratic ideas unexpressed and festering in his mind. During the years he passed at Lewes he learned self-expression; he learned how to develop arguments so that they would carry conviction. He was there for six years, from 1768 to 1774, and they should be considered as among the more important years of his life, for in that period he ceased to be Thomas Paine the Shy and Timid and became Thomas Paine the Bold and Confident.

His natural talent for arousing men to action, which had been long suppressed, began to emerge in these White Hart gatherings. He had a distinct genius for inspiring people to think and to act.

3

Every civilization has its faults, as we all know, but the civilization of England in the eighteenth century was somewhat over-supplied with them.

In the development of his subsequent notable career as a rebel and a democrat Paine was profoundly influenced by memories of the overbearing lordliness, the iniquities, the cruelty and the poverty that he had seen in England.

The Hanoverian kings from George I to George IV were all ignorant boobies, so stupid that they never learned anything but the most rudimentary facts about the English people. Although they were British sovereigns they never forgot their German origin, and when circumstances called upon one of them for an important decision the question was referred to some deeply imbedded brain cell which had never emigrated from Hanover.

George III was given annually the prodigious sum of eight hundred thousand pounds to support himself and the royal family as well as to provide gifts and sinecures for a swarm of hangers-on, lickspittles and yes-sayers. Like all the Georgian monarchs, he detested the mere existence of public opinion and thought that something ought to be done to suppress it.

He was genuinely puzzled and, of course, deeply offended by adverse comments on his policies or the doings of his ministers. He understood autocracy, but the British form of government with its Parliament, and its Bill of Rights, and its *habeas corpus* was to him a kind of nightmare, or a machine out of order and running wild to its own destruction. Some are born to rule and others to be ruled, he thought and said, and those of the lower orders should accept gracefully the wisdom and the edicts of their superiors.

The King and his henchmen bought pocket boroughs with the nonchalance of one who buys a handful of roasted chestnuts from a vendor on the street. There was nothing secret about it; it was done quite openly. Where the number of voters was small a borough could be obtained at a bargain, for in such cases there were not many votes to be purchased. But even in large communities the total cost rarely exceeded five thousand pounds.

In Thetford, a town of two thousand inhabitants, only thirty-two residents could qualify as voters, but they sent two members to Parliament. The representatives of the Thetford borough were selected invariably by the Duke of Grafton, and the voters had no say in the matter.

The deserted village of Old Sarum had only seven voters; nevertheless it was a borough and had its two members in the Commons. It was a long-standing joke in English political circles that the members who represented Old Sarum did not know where their borough was located. On the other hand, Yorkshire had sixteen thousand voters, all belonging to one huge borough. They sent to the Commons only two members, just the same as Old Sarum and Thetford.

"A shop was publicly opened in the Pay Office," Horace Walpole wrote, "whither members [of Parliament] flocked and received the wages of their venality in bank bills." This was in 1763. A bond issue of three million pounds was floated in such a way as to give a clear present of three hundred and fifty thousand pounds to "ministers' friends" who were permitted to purchase the bonds at a low price.

The luxury among the ruling classes seems almost incredible. They built most of the vast, widespreading palaces, or so-called country houses, that one may see today in the English counties.

The present generation cannot afford to live in them, for they are too big. Some of them have hundreds of rooms to be kept in order and heated, and a multitude of servants to be fed and paid. In many cases the titled gentlemen and ladies of today have, as a measure of economy, closed up the whole of the ancestral mansion, with the exception of ten or twelve rooms, in which they live.

There was a pervading dissoluteness in all classes of society from the highest to the lowest. Among the aristocracy such vices as drinking, gambling and sexual immorality were so common that a Sir or Lord who did not practice them was looked upon as a peculiar person who deserved little or no respect.

It was a gambling age. The swaggering gallants in velvet and silk would bet on almost anything from the fall of dice to the fall of monarchies. Two men bet that Colley Cibber would outlive Beau Nash, but both the bettors committed suicide before the bet was settled. At a gambling table Charles James Fox lost two hundred thousand pounds in a single night, and on another occasion the Duke of Devonshire lost Leicester Abbey on a bet.

High living, with its enormous meals and prodigious drinking, led to such bodily ailments as gout and rheumatism, which were common among the upper class. Many of the celebrated characters of the time were gluttons who gobbled enormous quantities of meat at every meal, including breakfast. A gentleman who refused to get drunk was considered a freak. Dr. Samuel Johnson, speaking of his youth in the country, said, "All the decent people of Lichfield got drunk every night and were not the worse thought of." He himself once drank thirty-six glasses of port at a single meal.

The working people, the artisans, laborers and all those at the bottom of the social scale, were underpaid and overworked. This was not done as a matter of necessity, but as a matter of principle. The ruling class believed that, with decent, adequate wages the laboring people would become idle and shiftless and unmanageable. That they be kept at starvation wages was considered an economic imperative.

Witt Bowden, in his *Industrial Society in England Toward the End of the Eighteenth Century,* summarizes the opinions of eighteenth-century economic authorities in these words:

In the eighteenth century a practically universal distinction, explicit or implied, was made between those who have "surplus labor in store," that is, property, and those who "must labor for subsistence."

But without poverty necessitating work on the part of the laboring class, its usefulness to society would be lost: "there could be no riches, no refinement, no comfort, and no benefit to those who may be possessed of wealth."

Men possessed of no property, and capable of nothing but labor, are entitled to nothing but the means of daily subsistence. Were they possessed of more they would remit their daily labor.

This is the subsistence theory of wages stated in its rawest form.

In the 1770's there was much bitter comment among the people of property and substance because of the growing tendency of workingmen and their families to use tea, sugar and white bread. These extravagances, they said, showed that wages were too high, and such pampered laborers would soon demand even more luxuries. Arthur Young, who lived in Thetford, and was an authority on agricultural economics, wrote that the staple diet of farm laborers should be potatoes and rice.

The drinking of the poor was confined to beer and ale in the early decades of the century, but around 1750 gin appeared in all the plebeian drinking places. Within a few years it had become a national curse. Gin was drunk by everyone, even by little children. The ginhouses had signs which read, "You can get drunk here for a penny, dead drunk for twopence. Straw provided free."

Whole families of the slums—father, mother and children—were often found lying in the public streets, dead drunk. When the government laid a heavy tax on gin to prevent its consumption there were gin riots among the poor. The tax was ineffective, for the gin was then made secretly and bootlegged to its consumers.

People do not turn themselves into beasts without cause, and the cause in this particular case was malnutrition, fatigue, unsanitary surroundings, and hopeless poverty. The governing classes appeared to have no sensible idea whatever in the matter of human welfare. To raise additional funds the administration had a tax put upon windows, of all things. As a result, and to avoid the tax, most of the windows in the slums were bricked over by the landlords, so the poor sat in gloomy, dark dens like wild beasts.

The twisted and vicious social system produced paupers in luxuriant profusion. They sprang up like weeds in a neglected garden. The workers' pay was too low to permit anything to be laid aside, and the hours of labor—twelve to fourteen a day—coupled with poor food and unsanitary housing wore out these laboring people while they were still in middle age.

Swarms of beggars appeared on the country roads and in the streets of the towns.

Before workhouses were established, around the middle of the century, there were various forms of public relief administered by the parishes and by religious bodies. The workhouse was the result of an effort to handle the problem of poverty in a systematic way. These institutions—we call them almshouses—sheltered the indigent and jobless, gave them food and provided work for them when they were out of a job.

The workhouse soon became an integral part of the English economic system. It gave employers an additional excuse for paying starvation wages, for in case of illness or unemployment the worker would always have a home and food at the workhouse.

The lodgers at these charitable institutions were expected to work, if they were physically able. There were farms attached to all the workhouses, and in many of them there was some form of indoor employment.

Anyone who refused to enter a workhouse lost all claim to public relief, yet many of the poor did refuse. The workhouses were infested by vermin. They were indescribably filthy and jail fever was an ever-present scourge.

4

The legal code bristled with barbarous laws and cruel punishments. There were nearly two hundred so-called "crimes" which were punishable by death. Among them were such offenses as these: breaking the dam of a fish pond; taking a piece of linen from a bleaching ground; cutting down a tree on land that belongs to somebody else; stealing a sheep; picking pockets for more than a shilling.

One of Hogarth's drawings shows two women swinging from the gallows, side by side, for having passed a counterfeit one-pound note. Highwaymen—and there were plenty of them—were hanged at rural crossroads when they were tried and found guilty. Their bodies were left swinging in the wind until they rotted and fell to pieces.

As might be supposed, the political ring of aristocrats, royal favorites and toadies that controlled national affairs as well as the national treasury endeavored strenuously to muzzle or destroy any newspaper that dared to express an opinion adverse to the administration, and they usually succeeded.

But the case of John Wilkes and his weekly journal *The North Briton* was an exception. They suppressed the paper but they could not suppress Wilkes. During the whole of the 1760 decade he was before the public eye in Britain—as a shining hero, if you believed in democracy and free speech; or as a blackguard, vile wretch and fool if you believed in the ineffable wisdom and goodness of the King and his administration.

Wilkes, who was a member of the House of Commons, owned and edited *The North Briton,* which was an outspoken liberal, democratic newspaper. On April 23, 1763, this publication in its No. 45 printed some comments on the King's speech which had been delivered before Parliament on April 19. Wilkes attempted to anticipate any charge that he had intended to insult the King by disavowing it respectfully. He wrote, "The King's speech has always been considered by the legislature and by the public at large as the speech of the minister." Lord Bute was then Prime Minister, and was the special object of this attack by Wilkes.

Then he proceeded to characterize the members of the King's cabinet as "the tools of despotism and corruption." Further on he says, "They have sent the spirit of discord through the land and I will prophesy it will never be extinguished but by the extinction of their power." He described the King's speech, prepared by his ministers, as "the most abandoned instance of ministerial effrontery ever attempted to be imposed on mankind." The rest of his comments ran along in the same vein.

To Americans of today, or to the English of the twentieth century, there seems to be nothing in this political article that would justify calling out the troops, or the constables. It was merely a political editorial by an antiadministration editor. But in the England of 1763 Wilkes' comments sounded like treason, rebellion and the overturn of the social order. That a newspaper editor should be permitted to make such scathing comments on high officials of the realm seemed to the King and his ministers to be utterly preposterous.

Upon the appearance of this number of *The North Briton* a general warrant was issued on behalf of Lord Halifax, who was then the Home Secretary, against every person who had anything whatever to do with the publication. The round-up included forty-eight individuals. Among them were the printer's apprentices, the typesetters, and many of those who had ever written anything for the paper on any subject. Wilkes, being a member of Parliament, was sent as a prisoner to the Tower. He was released within a week by Lord Chief Justice Pratt on the ground that his arrest was a breach of the privilege accorded to all members of the House of Commons.

His enemies started another attack against him almost immediately. By theft and bribery they got hold of a pamphlet which had just come off the press at Wilkes' printing office. It was an obscene parody of Pope's *Essay on Man*, and was called an *Essay on Woman*. Only twelve copies of it had been printed. Wilkes fled to Paris and sent to the Speaker of the House, on

January 11, 1764, a certificate of ill-health to excuse his non-attendance.

The House took action in the matter and he was expelled on January 19. He did not return for trial and was outlawed. For the next four years he lived on the Continent. When he returned to England in 1768 he was again elected to Parliament. Then he surrendered to the court, was fined five hundred pounds and sentenced to a year's imprisonment.

His popularity was immense. He was elected to Parliament four times and was immediately expelled. This persecution of Wilkes caused riots among the common people—the workmen and artisans. In time his enemies gave in, and in 1774 he was again elected and took his seat. During that same year he was also elected Lord Mayor of London.

Wilkes was tall, homely and had a squint in his eyes that gave him an unearthly look. He was witty, and his remarks concerning his adversaries were long remembered throughout Britain. One of his bitter opponents was Lord Sandwich. In a public debate Sandwich declared that Wilkes would die either on the gallows or of venereal disease. Wilkes replied, "That depends, my lord, on whether I embrace your principles or your mistress."

Wilkes was a liberal, and far ahead of his time, but he was not an anarchist, a ruffian, or even a revolutionary. The four planks of his platform were:

1. Reform of Parliament.
2. Enfranchisement of the lower classes.
3. Suppression of rotten boroughs.
4. Protection of individual liberty.

There does not seem to be anything especially menacing, as we look at political movements today, in the Wilkes program. The ruling classes of England in the 1770's had a different view of the matter, however, and Wilkes' support of the American cause during the Revolution increased their antipathy against him.

In public speeches and in writing he argued, over and over
again, that there was no point of dispute with the Colonies that
could not be settled amicably. All he said on this most important
subject was sensible and to the point. But the wooden-headed
sovereign and his advisers were determined to treat the Colonials as enemies, and to put the controversy on a war basis. The
Americans were to be subdued and brought down to the level of
underlings and inferiors despite their English origin, their English speech and their English manners and customs. If the advice of Wilkes had been followed there would have been no
American Revolution.

Thomas Paine never met John Wilkes, but he was a reader
of *The North Briton*, and a silent spectator of Wilkes' fight for
reform. Years later he said that he had been deeply moved by
the ideas which Wilkes had expressed in his writings.

There is no doubt that Wilkes was a potent influence in
Paine's life—in the shaping of his ideas, and in the character of
his public activities.

5

Samuel Ollive, with whom Paine lodged in Lewes, died in July,
1769. He left a widow and three children besides a tobacco business that was on the down grade in sales and profits. In those
days a tobacconist made most of his own merchandise. Ciga-
rettes were unknown and cigars were such a rarity that they
were preserved as curiosities. Tobacco was smoked in pipes, or
chewed, or ground up to be used as snuff. Like all other tobac-
conists, Samuel Ollive bought leaf tobacco in casks, as it came
from America, and worked it up on the premises. In the base-
ment of his house he had a snuff mill and other devices belonging to his trade.

Mrs. Ollive and her daughter Elizabeth, who lived with her,
had a hard time making both ends meet, for the business was
too complicated for them to handle efficiently. In an effort to
help them Paine became a part owner of the tobacco shop, which
was thereafter carried on under his name. Before long the shop

was selling groceries and other household supplies as well as tobacco. As a business man Paine was always extraordinarily incompetent. His mind was swarming with ideas, but not one of them had to do with the problem of making money. He had no sense of possession and no conception of money value.

He was during this period busy daily in the excise, and the women ran the shop under his general direction, such as it was. Month after month the little business went more deeply into debt.

On March 26, 1771, he married Elizabeth Ollive. He was then thirty-four and she was ten years younger. We know nothing about Elizabeth except that she was considered pretty. She and her husband lived in the Ollive house in Bull Lane with her mother,

CHAPTER III

Paine Comes to America

I

Thomas Paine became spokesman for all the excise officers of England in 1772 in their plea for an increase in wages. It was an early labor movement in effect, though not in name. These minor officials were paid fifty pounds a year from which they met their own expenses. Most of them were mounted officers, as they had to carry on their inspections over several villages and towns. This meant that each man had to own a horse and pay for its keep, and also his own expenses at inns when he was away from home, which was most of the time.

The movement was a long time getting under way, for although the excise men were unanimous in wanting higher pay, there were many different opinions among them as to the best way of bringing it about. Finally it was decided to appeal directly to Parliament. The chief promoter of this plan was Thomas Paine, and the campaign was placed in his hands. A fund of five hundred pounds for expenses was raised by a voluntary contribution of three shillings from every excise officer in the kingdom.

During the summer of 1772 Paine spent many weeks in writing and revising a paper entitled *The Case of the Officers of Excise*, and in the winter of 1772–73 he was in London for months trying to influence members of Parliament and others in favor of his cause. He did not give up his position in the excise department while engaged in this project, but got an extended leave of absence. The paper that he had written was printed, but not published. It was distributed to the members of Parliament and to others who might be interested.

Paine's chief argument was that those who were entrusted with so much responsibility, and therefore subject to so many temptations, should be adequately paid as a means of safeguarding the revenue which they collected.

He wrote:

Poverty, in defiance of principle, begets a degree of meanness that will stoop to almost anything. A thousand refinements of argument may be brought to prove that the practice of honesty will be still the same, in the most trying and necessitous circumstances. He who never was ahungered may argue finely on the subjection of his appetite; and he who never was distressed, may harangue as beautifully on the power of principle. But poverty, like grief, has an incurable deafness, which never hears; the oration loses all its edge; and "To be, or not to be" becomes the only question.

Note that his style has a limpid simplicity. He never writes a long and involved sentence. After describing the privations of the families of excise men, he says:

The rich, in ease and affluence, may think I have drawn an unnatural portrait; but could they descend to the cold regions of want, the circle of polar poverty, they would find their opinions changing with the climate. There are habits of thinking peculiar to different conditions, and to find them out is truly to study mankind.

Though Paine spent the whole winter of 1772 in trying to get Parliament to take some action the campaign was a complete failure. Neither the Commons nor the Lords paid any attention to the subject. The Commissioners of Excise said there were so many applicants for places in the service that any officer who was not satisfied with his pay was welcome to quit, and they would be able to fill his place immediately.

While he was in London Paine met some notable persons. One of them was Benjamin Franklin, who was then in England on business of the Colonies. Franklin took a liking to Paine, who asked him many intelligent questions about scientific problems. It was Franklin who caused him to turn his eyes toward America. Another London acquaintance was Oliver Goldsmith. Paine introduced himself to the author and playwright by writ-

ing him a letter on December 21, 1772. He addresses Goldsmith, in this epistle, as "Honored Sir," and sends him a printed
copy of *The Case of the Officers of Excise* for his perusal. He
says further:

> The memorial before you met with so much approbation while in
> manuscript that I was advised to print 4,000 copies . . . I have received
> so many letters of thanks and approbation for the performance, that were
> I not rather singularly modest, I should become a little vain.

In his faint effort to disclaim vanity he succeeds in proving
the opposite. There is nothing remarkable about that, for authors create a product that cannot be weighed on the scales, or
measured in feet and inches. If they do not have a good opinion
of their own creations, they cannot expect others to admire
them. More than any other class of workers they need constant
reassurance, and that is certainly why Paine wrote to Goldsmith.
    The letter is rather long; at its close he says:

> I have some few questions to trouble Dr. Goldsmith with, and should
> esteem his company for an hour or two, to partake of a bottle of wine,
> or anything else, and apologize for this trouble, as a singular favor con-
> ferred on his unknown humble servant and admirer.

He went to see Goldsmith and that eccentric genius took a fancy
to him.

Not only was Paine's labor wasted in this effort to induce the
government to raise the salaries in the department, but his
leadership in this affair had drawn toward him the baleful glare
of the Commissioners of Excise. Thereafter they checked his
records and notes with a microscopic intensity and timed his
comings and goings by the clock. They considered him a trouble-
breeder and waited only for a good excuse to drop him from
the service.

2

Meanwhile the business of the shop on Bull Lane was going
from bad to worse. It was carried on by his wife and her mother

while he was absent from home, and the sales of tobacco products and groceries dwindled month by month.

On account of his debts judgments were issued against Paine, and in those days a judgment often meant a debtors' prison. He left Lewes suddenly to avoid his creditors—or maybe to borrow money elsewhere, and for a week or two his whereabouts was unknown. This departure without permission gave the Board of Excise its awaited opportunity to get rid of Paine for all time. On April 8, 1774, the Board issued this order of discharge:

Thomas Paine, officer of Lewes 4th O. Ride Sussex Collection having quitted his business without obtaining the Board's leave for so doing, and being gone off on account of the debts which he hath contracted, as by the letter of the 6th instant from Edward Clifford, Supervisor, and the said Paine having been once before discharged, ordered that he be again discharged.

To avoid being sent to prison he made over all his property to his creditors, and it was sold at public auction at Lewes on the fourteenth of April. Enumerated in the list of goods to be sold were household furniture, stock in trade (tobacco and groceries), a tobacco and snuff mill, with all the utensils for cutting tobacco and grinding snuff: and, also, two unopened crates of cream-colored stone ware.

It was a clean sweep. He had nothing left but his clothes.

This cataclysm was followed in a couple of months by the formal separation of Thomas Paine and his wife Elizabeth. The reason for this action is not clear. To the end of his life Paine refused to speak of the matter even to his close friends. When asked why he and his wife had parted, his invariable reply was, "It is nobody's business but my own; I had cause for it but I will name it to no one."

One of the peculiar features of his marriage to Elizabeth Ollive is that, although they lived together, properly married, for more than two and one-half years, there was never any sexual relation between them. This state of affairs in the Paine household was a matter of common knowledge in Lewes. It was the sort of information that would never be given out by Paine himself, so we can be sure that it became public because Elizabeth mentioned it to her cronies, and it was spread by them as a piece of gossip.

As to the cause of this extraordinary relationship there has been much conjecture among Paine's biographers, friends and enemies. The most obvious supposition is that Paine was sexually impotent. But he had been married before, and during his first marriage there had been no talk of his incapacity. While he was in America there was some gossip of one or two secret love affairs in which he played a part, but the stories are vague and probably untrue.

The weight of evidence, as far as there can be worth-while evidence in such a private matter, is that Thomas Paine was not greatly concerned over sex and the activities arising from the sexual urge. It is not an uncommon disposition among men and women and is the reason why some of them remain single for a lifetime, but this lack of sexual inclination does not imply impotency. It seems likely that he married Elizabeth for companionship, and learned after the marriage that she expected more than mere conjugal friendliness.

His friend Rickman wrote many years afterward that "Paine always spoke tenderly and respectfully of his wife, and sent her several times pecuniary aid, without her knowing even whence it came."

They were never divorced, but only legally separated. Elizabeth called herself Mrs. Paine for the rest of her life. She resided with her brother Thomas, who was a watchmaker in Cranbrook, Kent. In 1800 she was a party to some form of legal agreement concerning property, and in settling the matter she was called upon to state whether she was a maid, a wife or a widow. In reply she asserted that she had been married to a Thomas Paine; that in 1774 she and her husband separated; that thereafter her husband quitted the kingdom, "and resided (if living) in parts beyond the sea, but had not since been heard of by the said Elizabeth Paine, nor was it known for certain whether he was living or dead."

When Elizabeth gave that testimony the name of Thomas Paine was known throughout the civilized world; and in England itself there had been such a reverberating uproar over his *Rights of Man* that it is difficult to understand how any fairly intelligent person could have failed to catch some echo of it. It is quite possible that she had heard of a Thomas Paine whc was causing an angry commotion among the higher-ups but had no idea that he was her former husband.

3

Paine went up to London in June, 1774, and remained there about three months. As he was almost penniless and had no future in England his outlook must have seemed to him to be nearly hopeless. We do not know how he managed to exist during this period but it was probably on borrowed money. Paine was extraordinarily secretive about his personal affairs during the whole of his life. Today we have only scraps of information as to his manner of living, the names of his friends, his amusements, if any, and his income and expenses. His existence was almost wholly mental and any faithful delineation of him must necessarily be drawn chiefly from his writings.

He called, now and then, on Benjamin Franklin during this sojourn in London, and that philosopher's penetrating insight soon gave him a clear understanding of Paine's troubles. He realized that the former excise officer and bankrupt shopkeeper could never get a firm footing again in England, and he advised Paine to go to America and make a fresh start in life. He gave him a letter of introduction to his son-in-law, and may have advanced him the money to pay for his passage.

The ship *London Packet* that sailed for Philadelphia in the last week of September, 1774, carried Paine as a cabin passenger. The voyage took nine weeks; the vessel reached Philadelphia on November 30. There were only three or four passengers in the cabin, but she brought in her hold—which was the eighteenth-century equivalent of the modern steerage—one hundred and twenty indentured servants. A disease known as "putrid fever," which may have been typhoid, broke out among them, and five passengers died and were buried at sea. Paine contracted the fever and could not rise from his berth when the ship docked. But the fact that he bore a letter from Benjamin Franklin became known in a few hours, and Doctor Kearsley, a well-known physician, took it upon himself to drive down to the dock in his carriage and take Paine to quarters on Market Street. There he was nursed back to health, but he did not leave his room for three weeks.

The letter of introduction from Benjamin Franklin to his son-in-law Richard Bache ran in this fashion:

The bearer, Mr. Thomas Paine, is very well recommended to me as an ingenious, worthy young man. He goes to Pennsylvania with the view to settling there. I request you to give him your best advice and countenance, as he is quite a stranger there. If you can put him in the way of obtaining employment as a clerk or assistant tutor in a school, or assistant surveyor, of all of which I think him very capable, so that he may procure a subsistence at least, till he can make acquaintance and obtain a knowledge of the country, you will do well, and much oblige your affectionate father.

Paine had never seen any place outside of England until he landed at Philadelphia. It is true that he had served on the *King of Prussia* privateer for a short time, but it was not the custom of the privateers in the seafaring lanes around the British Isles to put into foreign ports.

When he arrived at Philadelphia near the end of 1774 it was a thriving town of about 35,000 inhabitants—the largest community in America and the wealthiest. It had the air of a large overgrown village. Shade trees grew in the streets and most of the houses stood in gardens. The houses were not numbered; strangers inquiring their way were told that the house they were seeking was close to this or that landmark. Some of the principal streets were paved in the middle for carriages and had narrow brick sidewalks, but most of them were as nature had made them. In wet weather these thoroughfares became puddles of sticky mud.

Some of the well-to-do went here and there in carriages, but sedan chairs were in more general use. Carriages were considered an evidence of snobbery. They were also detested by the common people because in rainy weather they splashed mud on those who were walking in the streets; and sometimes, for that reason, they were pelted with stones.

In common with the rest of the Colonials of the later eighteenth century the inhabitants of Philadelphia were fascinated by bright colors. The shop fronts were gaudy with paint and great signs of red, yellow, blue and green swung over the streets. A substantial part of the population consisted of Quakers, some of whom, on special occasions, appeared in their somber clothes, but for everyday wear had apparel which was smart, colorful and costly. Their silken knee breeches were likely to be of any shade of color. They wore silver buckles on their shoes and large silver coat buttons with the owner's initials engraved on them were one of the distinguishing marks of wealth. Swanky young men of fashion also wore swords, as in England, though the sword-wearing habit had been abandoned by the older men. Their cocked hats were decorated with gold lace. The wearing of wigs was going out of fashion, and most of the elegant gentlemen of the period had their hair curled and powdered. It was worn several inches long in the back and the "pigtail" was caught up in a silken net bag.

The ladies of society were resplendent in silks, velvets and brocades. Their stays were as stiff and hard as iron, and their hoop skirts did not extend an equal distance from the body all around, but on the right and left stretched out from six inches to two feet. The effect was to give the wearer a wide, flat appearance. To enter a room a lady had to come sideways through the door.

There were many taverns and coffeehouses, all of which served liquor, ale and wine as well as coffee. Among them was the London Coffee House on Front Street, and the Indian Queen Hotel on Fourth Street. The Indian Queen was renowned as a gathering place for members of the Continental Congress. These two houses of refreshment were frequented by

Paine, but he did not live at either of them. According to a local legend he took a room in a private house on Market Street the day he came off the ship and lived there for more than a year. But this is only a bit of hearsay without proof. The house, or houses, in which he lived in Philadelphia have never been clearly identified.

He must have been impressed by the prosperous appearance of the town and by the relatively small amount of poverty among its inhabitants. He had seen English cities in which a third of the population, at least, existed year after year in a state of utter destitution, in rags and filth. There was nothing like that in Philadelphia. The place had poor people but there were no slums. Land was not dear, and there was plenty of room for everybody. A laborer's family might live in a cabin, but around the flimsy dwelling there would be a garden where vegetables and fruit could be grown and a cow could be kept in a stall. The cattle were driven out to the common meadow every day and brought home at night. Everybody, however poor he happened to be, had sunlight, fresh air and enough to eat. In the city of London, which was a familiar ground to Thomas Paine, there were tens of thousands of people who lived in semi-darkness, in foul air, and who were always hungry.

Colonial civilization, like that of England, was an aristocracy based on money and land. But there was no wide, unbridgeable gap between the upper and lower classes in America as there was in England. American fortunes were new; all of them had grown from small beginnings in the past two to three generations, while the great fortunes of the mother country were encrusted with age and honors. The murders and robberies on which most of them were founded had passed out of the memories of men, and the living possessors of the titles, fortunes and lands were looked upon with profound respect and admiration.

The wealthy families of the Colonies did their best to surround themselves with the same worshipful atmosphere, but with little success. In many instances the greedy land-grabber or miserly skinflint who had founded the family fortune was too well remembered to evoke the veneration of the multitude; and in cases where the origin of the wealth was so far back that it could not be recalled by firsthand memory it was embalmed in tradition and passed around with the tea and cake at social gatherings.

The common people, unlike the poor of England, were not only lacking in obsequiousness but also in ordinary good manners. The meekness of the European peasant was left out of their rough and ready personalities. They were sturdy, brave, tough—and often rowdy and quarrelsome. They could use a hunting rifle with the deftness of a carpenter driving nails. If these plowmen, bear hunters, cattle drivers and mechanics had been properly trained and disciplined they would have driven the entire British Army into the sea during the first year of the American Revolution. But it was found impossible—as history shows—to organize them into effective units, or to keep them from deserting the army and going home whenever they pleased, or to arm them with effective weapons, or even to feed and clothe them.

4

A letter of introduction from Dr. Franklin meant something, for he was the most distinguished American, and the only one who was known by reputation all over Europe. Naturally there was a good deal of polite interest in Thomas Paine, and as soon as he had recovered his health Richard Bache [1] had a number of people meet him. One of these introductions led to his employment as editor of the *Pennsylvania Magazine*, a new publication which made its first appearance in January, 1775.

The proprietor of this thin little monthly was Robert Aitkin, who owned also a bookstore and a printing shop. The editorial job carried a salary of fifty pounds sterling a year. That does not seem much; it figures out to be about five dollars a week in modern currency, but the purchasing power of money was several times greater then than it is now.

[1] Richard Bache, who had married Benjamin Franklin's daughter Sarah, was at the head of an extensive importing and exporting business. He was a man of means and of excellent reputation.

Paine edited the magazine for about six months and wrote the greater part of its contents under such fanciful names as Atlanticus, Aesop and Vox Populi. He was evidently a success as an editor. The circulation of the magazine was six hundred copies monthly when he took charge of it; within three months it had fifteen hundred subscribers.

Around mid-year in 1775 he gave up his job to devote himself to the revolutionary cause. That was one reason for leaving the magazine; another was the attitude of Robert Aitkin, the owner of the publication, who objected to the outspoken radicalism expressed in Paine's articles. There were constant disputes between the editor and the proprietor and some of Paine's contributions to the magazine were slashed and eviscerated by Aitkin.

Hesketh Pearson says, in his *Tom Paine, Friend of Mankind*, that Paine was "probably the first person to display an entirely civilized attitude towards women," and credits him with starting the movement for woman's emancipation. He anticipated the single tax theories of Henry George, and foreshadowed Comte's religion of humanity. He was the first also to propose a toast to "world revolution," but he was not a Communist. Far from it. Like Jefferson, he believed in individualism. He regarded the state as a "necessary evil"; the less of it the better. His three stars in the heaven of ideas were Freedom, Reason and Kindness (which he called "Humanity").

In May, 1775, he wrote an unsigned article in which he condemned and ridiculed the practice of dueling. This article caused a great deal of comment. In another issue he wrote of the lessons to be learned from the life of Lord Clive, conqueror of India, whom he characterized as a cruel and vicious despot. Most of his contributions, like those here mentioned, were of a critical nature, but he was constructive also, and in the article entitled *Useful and Entertaining Hints* he urged his readers to encourage scientific pursuits and foster the inventive genius of the people. In that essay he suggested ways of making the soil more productive and advocated the use of labor-saving devices.

One of the articles written by Paine during this period was entitled *African Slavery in America*. It was published in the *Pennsylvania Journal* (not the *Magazine*) in March, 1775. He proposed the abolition of slavery altogether, and although he was not the first opponent of Negro slavery he was the first writer on the subject who was entirely outspoken before a fairly large audience. There is nothing in his article that would startle anyone today, but in 1775 it was considered revolutionary, to say the least, for Negro slavery was then looked upon as a part of the essential nature of things. Many kindly, generous people never doubted for a moment that slavery was a beneficent institution, for it took heathen Negroes away from their savage wilds and turned them into civilized workers—and Christians. Mr. Aitkin thought Paine's article somewhat too disturbing for his gentle-mannered *Pennsylvania Magazine*, so it was printed in the *Journal*. Within a month after it appeared the first anti-slavery movement was started in Philadelphia.

In the article called *Thoughts on Defensive War* (July, 1775) Paine wrote:

I am thus far a Quaker, that I would gladly agree with all the world to lay aside the use of arms, and settle matters by negotiation; but unless the whole will, the matter ends, and I take up my musket and thank heaven He has put it in my power.

He says further in the same article:

In the barbarous ages of the world men in general had no liberty. The strong governed the weak at will; 'til the coming of Christ there was no such thing as political freedom in any known part of the earth. The Jewish kings were in point of government as absolute as the Pharaohs. Men were frequently put to death without trial at the will of the sovereign. The Romans held the world in slavery, and were themselves the slaves of their emperors. The madman of Macedon, governed by caprice and passion, strided as arrogantly over the world as if he had made and peopled it; and it is needless to imagine that other nations at that time were more refined. Wherefore political as well as spiritual freedom is the gift of God through Christ.

Reflections on Unhappy Marriages, which appeared in June, 1775, does not throw much light, except indirectly, on the failure of his own marriage. He asserts, however, that after the ecstasy of the honeymoon has passed, affairs in the marital sphere may become rather sour.

Sure of each other by the nuptial bond, they no longer take any pains to be mutually agreeable; careless if they displease, and yet angry if reproached, with so little relish for each other's company that anybody's else is welcome, and more entertaining. Their union thus broke, they pursue separate pleasures; never meet but to wrangle, or part but to find comfort in other society.

That paragraph—quoted here—says to an imaginative mind, though not in plain words, that Elizabeth Ollive, before their marriage, appeared to have much interest in the same things that occupied Thomas Paine's attention. Like Mr. Paine, she thought the existence of a king in any country was a relic of barbarism; and the crushing injustice of the whole system was turning men into slaves. Men and women should own the land on which they toiled, and they should be freed from the ever-present fear of the workhouse in their old age. Just as Mr. Paine often said. She was interested in authors, too, the same authors that Mr. Paine read—like Defoe and Pope and Goldsmith.

It goes on to say, however—if we read between the lines—that after her marriage Elizabeth Paine yawned when her husband remarked that the British exports into the American Colonies had dropped because of the boycott brought on by the Stamp Tax; and that she had not read John Wilkes' last speech —no, not a line of it—and why in the name of God should she read it at all? It says, too, in the veiled language of the unconscious, that Elizabeth was furious when he went to London, and stayed there for months and did not take her with him, and she had not been to London in ages, and that he would have done better if he had stayed in Lewes attending to his business instead of gallivanting all over creation with his rum-drinking companions; and that she is ashamed of the look of the rooms for his books and papers are scattered all over the place, and he never thinks of putting away his things when he is through with them, but would rather live in a pigpen and he would have the house looking like one if she did not follow after him cleaning up until she is worn down to skin and bone, and he never sees anything close by, but just let a man that lives a thousand miles away write something that pleases him and he talks about that man as if he were a next-door neighbor.

5

In 1775, and the following year, Philadelphia was the center of attention in America. The second Continental Congress was in session there during the greater part of the year, and the leaders of the American people might be seen in the streets every day. Everyone wondered what would be the outcome of the controversy between Great Britain and her American Colonies. Most of the sessions of the Congress were held behind closed doors, and the reports of what was done or said at the meetings were garbled by hearsay. But all of them agreed that the Congress had no idea of asserting the independence of the Colonies.

The first Continental Congress, which met in September, 1774, had passed a "Declaration of Rights," which was a memorial to Parliament. This plea was permeated by a spirit of loyalty and friendliness. The Congress requested—but did not demand—the repeal of about twenty acts of Parliament that had to do with American affairs, and which the Congress considered unjust and oppressive.

The appeal to Parliament was ineffective. No, that term is too weak. It was not only ineffective; the rulers of England considered it insolent and provocative. The mere fact that the Congress had met at all was construed into an insult to the sovereign power.

Before the second Continental Congress was convened in May, 1775, the Battle of Lexington had taken place. The war had begun, and an extraordinary situation had developed, for the Colonies did not want to secede from the British Empire. They did not want to fight the mother country; they sought for nothing but a redress of their grievances. The Continental Congress had no power to raise armies—or, at any rate—it had been given no such authority. It was, in effect, a committee of all the Colonies assembled to consider their common problems.

The reluctance to secede went back much further. In October, 1765, the Stamp Act Congress, which was organized to protest against the taxing of the Colonies without their voice or consent, declared that the connection of the Colonies with Great Britain was their "great happiness and security" and that they "most ardently" desired its "perpetual continuance." In January, 1768, the Massachusetts Legislature said officially, "We cannot justly be suspected of the most distant thought of an independency of Great Britain. Some, we know, have imagined this . . . but it is so far from the truth that we apprehend the Colonies would refuse it if offered to them, and would even deem it the greatest misfortune to be obliged to accept it."

The first Continental Congress, in its solemn petition to the King, adopted October 26, 1774, said: "Your royal authority over us and our connection with Great Britain we shall always carefully and zealously endeavor to support and maintain."

In March, 1775, Benjamin Franklin said in London that he had never heard in America one word in favor of independence, "from any person, drunk or sober."

As late as May, 1775, George Washington had a talk with his friend Jonathan Boucher about the possibility of the Colonies separating themselves from the mother country. Washington said, in parting, according to Boucher, "that if ever [he] heard of his [Washington's] joining in any such measures, [he] had his leave to set him down for everything wicked."

More than two months after the Battle of Bunker Hill Thomas Jefferson, who became the author of the Declaration of Independence, wrote to a kinsman that he was "looking with fondness toward a reconciliation with Great Britain." On July 6, 1775, the second Continental Congress adopted a declaration which set forth the Colonial grievances. In this important document these words appear: "Lest this declaration should disquiet the minds of our friends and fellow-subjects in any part of the Empire, we assure them that we mean not to dissolve that union which has so long and so happily subsisted between us, and which we sincerely wish to see restored." In one year, less two days, after that declaration, the second Continental Congress parted company with the British Empire.

It may be clearly seen that the movement for American independence began reluctantly, and late. But when it was once on its way it gathered mass and momentum and went swiftly. It had its origin in many motives and currents of thought, some of them wholly unrelated to the others, and this possibly accounts for its tardiness.

CHAPTER IV

Paine Writes a Best Seller

I

IT WAS Thomas Paine who brought all these tangled revolutionary impulses to a head and sent them moving in the direction of independence. He wrote a thin book, or pamphlet, called *Common Sense* in which he pointed out the folly of a strong, self-reliant people taking orders from a nation across the sea; and he showed also that many of the British rules and regulations concerning the Colonies were utterly senseless, and could have been conceived only by stupid officeholders who lacked all sound ideas of America and its people.

Paine was the first author in our history to reach the whole American public. His book was an extraordinary best seller, and its keynote was American Independence.

During the first six months after its publication about one hundred thousand copies of *Common Sense* were sold; the price was two shillings. There was no copyright law at that time, and the immense popularity of the pamphlet inspired several pirated editions, and these were big sellers also. The total distribution of all the printings was at least three hundred thousand copies —maybe even more.

Paine never made a penny from its publication. He intended to turn over all his profits to the Continental Army as a contribution to the cause of independence. But his arrangement with the printer—who was also the publisher—was so loosely worded that Paine had no way of checking up costs and profits, and the printer claimed that the cost of publication had absorbed nearly the whole amount received from the sale of the pamphlet, so there was only a little dribble of profit remaining and that was given to the patriotic fund. Paine was swindled, as he was in most of his financial transactions.

His name did not appear on the title page of the first edition

when it was brought out on January 10, 1776. But its authorship was not wholly a secret. A few people had seen the manuscript. *Common Sense* was so thoroughly revolutionary in intent
and context that Paine anticipated difficulty in finding a publisher, and he asked some of his friends to look over the manuscript and suggest a printer. Among them was Dr. Benjamin
Rush, who knew all about Philadelphia and its people. He put
Paine in touch with Robert Bell, a Scotch bookseller and printer
who had been established in Philadelphia for some time. (In
those days the printers were the only publishers, and they
brought out books as a side line to their job-printing activities.)

Three years afterward, in 1779, in a spirit of reminiscence,
Paine wrote concerning the publication of *Common Sense* to his
friend Henry Laurens:

I gave Robert Bell the pamphlet to print on the following conditions:
That if any loss should arise I would pay it—and in order to make him
industrious in circulating it, I gave him one-half the profits, if it should
produce any. I gave a written order to Col. Joseph Dean and Capt.
Thos. Prior, both of this city, to receive the other half, and lay it out
for mittens for the troops that were going to Quebec. I did this to do
honor to the cause.

Bell kept the whole and abused me into the bargain. The price he set
upon them was two shillings. I then enlarged the pamphlet with an ap-
pendix and an address to the Quakers, which made it one-third bigger
than before, printed six thousand at my own expense and delivered them
ready stitched and fit for sale to Mr. Bradford at the Coffee-house; and
though the work was thus increased, and consequently should have borne
a higher price, yet, in order that it might produce the general service I
wished, I confined Mr. Bradford to sell them at one shilling each, or
tenpence by the dozen, and to enable him to do this, with sufficient advantage to himself, I let him have the pamphlets at $8\frac{1}{2}$ pence each,
Pennsylvania currency.

The sum of $8\frac{1}{2}$ pence each was reserved to defray the expense of
printing, paper, advertising, etc., and such as might be given away. The
state of the account at present is that I am thirty-nine pounds eleven
shillings out of pocket, being the difference between what I have paid
for printing, etc., and what I have received from Bradford.

He has a sufficiency in his hands to balance with and clear me, which is all I aimed at, but by his unaccountable dilatoriness and unwillingness to settle accounts I fear I shall be obliged to sustain a real loss exclusive of my trouble.

It may seem strange that Benjamin Franklin, who had recently returned from England (where he had been the representative of the Colonies) knew nothing of the pamphlet until it appeared in print. More than a month after its publication he was not sure that Paine was the author, as he wrote to General Charles Lee on February 19 that Paine "is the reputed and, I think, the real author of *Common Sense*." But it appears from a statement made by Paine in 1777 that he had meant the pamphlet to be a pleasant surprise to Franklin. He said:

"In October 1775, Dr. Franklin proposed giving me such materials as were in his hands toward completing a history of the present transactions and seemed desirous of having the first volume out the next spring. I had then formed the outlines of *Common Sense* and finished nearly the first part; and, as I supposed the doctor's design in getting out a history was to open the new year with a new system, I expected to surprise him with a production on that subject much earlier than he thought of; and without informing him of what I was doing, got it ready for the press as fast as I conveniently could, and sent him the first pamphlet that was printed off."

One may read *Common Sense* from cover to cover in three hours; it contains only twenty-five thousand words. Paine, who was always a most painstaking writer, spent the entire autumn of 1775 in writing and revising the pamphlet. Simplicity and force were two of the vital principles of his creative literary work. He reasoned that if an argument did not carry force and conviction there was no sense in printing it at all; furthermore, if it were so intricate in style and expression that only the learned could gather its full import most of its possible readers were thus excluded.

In the eighteenth century learning and literature were pompous. They were speckled with quotations from Greek and Latin authors. To prove his scholarship, and as a matter of self-respect, an author was moved to refer familiarly to Plato and Aristotle, to Catullus and Cicero, even if his argument concerned nothing more important than the right to catch fish in a pond.

But in *Common Sense* there is not even one quotation from the classics; Paine wrote in the English of the people, in the language that men use as they go about their daily business.

2

The first part of the pamphlet has to do with the nature of government in general, with its relation to human actions, and particularly with the origin of the British constitution. All this was laid down as the groundwork of what followed. The following is a characteristic paragraph:

I draw my idea of the form of government from a principle in nature which no art can overturn, namely, that the more simple anything is the less liable it is to be disordered, and the easier repaired when disordered; and with this maxim in view I offer a few remarks on the so much boasted Constitution of England. That it was noble for the dark and slavish times in which it was erected, is granted. When the world was overrun with tyranny the least remove therefrom was a glorious rescue. But that it is imperfect, subject to convulsions, and incapable of producing what it seems to promise, is easily demonstrated.

He has only contempt for a social system which sets up a king to rule over other human beings. "Male and female are the distinctions of nature," he says, "good and bad the distinctions of heaven; but how a race of men came into the world so exalted above the rest, and distinguished like some new species, is worth inquiring into, and whether they are the means of happiness or of misery to mankind."

On the next page he says:

Government by kings was first introduced into the world by the heathens, from whom the children of Israel copied the custom. It was the most prosperous invention the devil ever set on foot for the promotion of idolatry. The heathens paid divine honors to their deceased kings, and the Christian world has improved on the plan by doing the same to their living ones. . . . To the evil of monarchy we have added that of hereditary succession; and as the first is a degradation and lessening of ourselves, so the second, claimed as a matter of right, is an insult and imposition on posterity. . . . One of the strongest natural proofs of the folly of hereditary rights in kings is that nature disproves it, otherwise she would not so frequently turn it into ridicule by giving mankind an *ass* for a *lion.*

Concluding this first part of *Common Sense* Paine wrote:

In England a king hath little more to do than to make war and give away places; which, in plain terms, is to impoverish the nation and set it together by the ears. A pretty business, indeed, for a man to be allowed eight hundred thousand sterling a year for, and worshipped into the bargain! Of more worth is one honest man to society, and in the sight of God, than all the crowned ruffians that ever lived.

Throughout the long and bitter controversy between England and her American Colonies the movement for independence made so little progress that it was virtually negligible until the fateful year 1776.

The Colonies were the children of their mother England, and the Colonials realized it. Their natural feeling was one of affection for the mother country—affection and respect. They wanted to remain citizens of the British Empire, and subjects of the King, but they were made rebels by the stupidity of the English politicians. The British Parliament developed a fixed policy for regulating the internal affairs of the Colonies in a manner that was most distinctly unworkable.

Paine said, in *Common Sense:*

As to government matters, 'tis not in the power of Britain to do this continent justice; the business of it will soon be too weighty and intricate to be managed with any tolerable degree of convenience, by a power so distant from us, and so very ignorant of us; for if they cannot conquer us, they cannot govern us. To be always running three or four thousand miles with a tale or a petition, waiting four or five months for an answer, which, when obtained, requires five or six more to explain it, will in a few years be looked upon as folly and childishness. There was a time when it was proper, and there is a proper time for it to cease.

The governing class in England was obsessed by the wholly erroneous notion that the American Colonists had never grown up, that they were mere children in all matters of statecraft, that they were incapable of governing themselves wisely, that —as simple backwoodsmen—they lacked perception and vision, and should be told what to do in respect to the public welfare.

This attitude was a mistake, with far-reaching and disastrous consequences. The men of Massachusetts, the Carolinas, Virginia—and of all the Colonies—were quite as capable of sensible self-government as the men of Yorkshire or Devon.

There can be no doubt that these false impressions were planted and nourished by the swarm of British officeholders in the Colonies. They had a good thing in the way of fat salaries and perquisites and they wanted to keep it. The American Colonies were a sort of cashbox, kept perpetually open, for the scheming, impoverished and useless members of the British ruling class. The reports that they sent back home were carefully planned to show the worst side of the American character, and these reports were considered as solemnly as if they had been extracts from Holy Writ. A mob of a dozen tavern loungers, potboys and wharf rats, yelling insults and throwing stones, would become in the account of British officials a rising of the entire community, needing troops to put it down when, in truth, only a couple of constables were required.

Through the influence of the British commercial classes the Colonies were kept in economic subjection. The resentment caused by this policy ran far deeper than that arising from the imposition of petty taxes or the quartering of troops in Colonial towns.

The Dutch were, for instance, large consumers of American tobacco. But the Navigation Act—imposed by the British on the Colonies—forbade the shipping of the tobacco leaf direct from Virginia to Holland. It had to be sold first to an English merchant, shipped to England, unloaded, and then resold to a Dutch distributor, put on board ship again and sent to Holland. This method of handling the tobacco trade with all countries except England was maintained for no other purpose than to give a profit to the English middleman. In this particular instance—that of tobacco—these restrictions were slowly but surely destroying the sale of the American product abroad. For some time before the American Revolution Turkish tobacco had been sold throughout Europe at a lower price.

Beaver hats, made of the fur of beavers, were popular all over Europe and America during the latter half of the eighteenth century. The Americans caught the beavers and shipped the skins to England, where they were made into hats. In the course of time hat-making became an American industry; instead of shipping the raw furs abroad the Colonials made the hats and sent them. This aroused a protest from the English hatters. They appealed to Parliament and that august body forbade the Colonials to make hats in the future except for their own home use.

The Colonials were permitted to operate iron mines, to smelt the ore, and to produce bars and pigs of the metal, but after 1750 it was illegal to produce any secondary iron products. The owners of the smelting furnaces were required to send the raw iron to England where it might be worked up and shipped back in its finished form to the American Colonies. A young and growing metal-working industry was completely destroyed.

The purpose of the Navigation Act was not to encourage Colonial manufactures, but to discourage them. In the general plan of economic imperialism the American Colonies were expected to function as producers of raw materials which the mother country was to convert into finished products and sell. When the Colonials purchased articles that came originally from any European country—from France, or Prussia, Italy or Spain—they had to buy them from English merchants. This roundabout method of trading greatly increased the prices of foreign imports. Well-informed Americans of the time thought—and could prove—that Colonial purchasers were paying from 25 to 40 per cent more for manufactured articles than they would have had to pay if the goods could have been bought in a free market.

Many of the British laws and regulations were so impractical, or downright stupid, that they could not be carried into effect at all and for ten years preceding the Revolution the entire land was in a turmoil. The Stamp Act could not be enforced; the ports were full of smugglers; the British troops, sent as garrisons to various places, had quarrels and fights with the people; contraband goods were sold openly in the shops; the courts were flouted by the populace. In short, when the Colonies sent their representatives to the first Continental Congress in 1774, the situation was so bad that it called for immediate attention, for cool heads on both sides, and for a generous feeling of magnanimity.

But the British leaders were so tightly set in their resolution to force obedience from the Colonials that no other idea could reach their understanding. King George III said that, let the consequences be what they may, it was his unalterable determination to compel the Colonists to absolute obedience. He would have made a much better record as a monarch if he had called a conference to consider the whole matter at which both sides would have been adequately represented. It is possible that at such a meeting of minds an understanding satisfactory to all would have been reached.

Some of the restrictions against Colonial expansion seem incredible when we read of them today. A proclamation of the British Government in 1763 forbade any settlement of land west of the Alleghenies. This immense tract, stretching from the western border of the sea coast colonies to the Mississippi River, was reserved for the Indians. The territory thus set apart covered part of what is now New York State, all of Ohio, Michigan, Indiana, Illinois, Kentucky, Tennessee and Alabama. Of course it was impossible to enforce such an absurd regulation. Settlers poured into the restricted territory, and they were ready to defend themselves against any attempt to evict them. Lord Dartmouth, Secretary of State for Foreign Affairs, declared in 1774 that all efforts to promote Western settlements were "a gross indignity and dishonor to the Crown and an act of equal inhumanity and injustice to the Indians." In other words, the British Government had decided that the most fertile part of the North American continent was to be turned over in perpetuity to the Indian tribes.

Notwithstanding the bitter objections of the Colonials to these tyrannical and absurd laws, they did not want to secede from the Empire. Even after the fateful day at Lexington—April 19, 1775—John Adams had pronounced against independence and the Massachusetts Provincial Congress declared allegiance to their lawful sovereign.

Paine wrote on November 12, 1778:

I happened to come to America a few months before the breaking out of hostilities. I found the disposition of the people such that they might have been led by a thread and governed by a reed. Their suspicion was quick and penetrating, but their attachment to Britain was obstinate, and it was at that time a kind of treason to speak against it. They disliked the Ministry, but they esteemed the nation. Their idea of grievance operated without resentment, and their single object was reconciliation.

In September of 1775 the North Carolina Provincial Congress disclaimed any thoughts of rebellion. As late as January, 1776, New York, New Jersey, Pennsylvania and Maryland instructed their delegates in Congress to vote against independence if the matter was brought up.

James Truslow Adams says, in *The Epic of America:* "In Boston the upper class, almost without exception, were strongly opposed to it [to independence], and more than half the upper class throughout the whole colony. It was the same in New York, where the bulk of the property owners were Loyalists. In Pennsylvania, a majority of all the people were not only against war and independence in the beginning, but remained so throughout the struggle."

Nevertheless, despite this show of loyalty to Great Britain, half-formed, misty thoughts of a movement toward independence were in the back of the minds of many men. But they were doubtful of such a radical step. When once taken it could not be recalled, and one hesitates naturally at making a decision with such momentous consequences.

The situation may be compared to that of a chemical process

where several diverse elements are brought together to form a single compound. They are all present but they will not unite until a catalyst is added to them.

The catalyst of the situation that has just been described was Thomas Paine. He was the godfather of America. It was he who inspired the Declaration of Independence.

3

Paine himself had undergone a change of heart, for he said in *Common Sense:*

No man was a warmer wisher for a reconciliation than myself, before the fatal nineteenth of April, 1775, but the moment the event of that day was made known, I rejected the hardened, sullen-tempered Pharaoh of England forever; and disdain the wretch, that with the pretended title of Father of his People can unfeelingly hear of their slaughter, and composedly sleep with their blood upon his soul.

A government of our own is our natural right; and when a man seriously reflects on the precariousness of human affairs, he will become convinced that it is infinitely wiser and safer to form a constitution of our own in a cool deliberate manner, while we have it in our power, than to trust such an interesting event to time and chance.

In discussing the confused condition of colonial life he declares that: "The present state of America is truly alarming to every man who is capable of reflection. Without law, without government, without any other mode of power than what is founded on, and granted by courtesy. Held together by an unexampled occurrence of sentiment, which is nevertheless subject to change, and which every secret enemy is endeavoring to dissolve.

"Our present condition is legislation without law, wisdom without a plan; a constitution without a name; and, what is strangely astonishing, perfect independence contending for dependence. The instance is without a precedent, the case never existed before, and who can tell what may be the event? The property of no man is secure in the present unbraced system of

things. The mind of the multitude is left at random, and seeing no fixed object before them, they pursue such as fancy or
opinion presents. Nothing is criminal; there is no such thing as
treason; wherefore, every one thinks himself at liberty to act
as he pleases."

One of the most effective features of *Common Sense* is its
quiet, placid tone. The author never flies into rage; he never
scolds or threatens. Nor does he ever relate the absurd rulings
and pompous pretensions of those in power in order to provoke
a laugh. He says:

I am not induced by motives of pride, party or resentment to espouse
the doctrine of separation and independence; I am clearly, positively,
and conscientiously persuaded that it is the true interest of this Continent
to be so; that everything short of *that* is mere patchwork, that it can
afford no lasting felicity,—that it is leaving the sword to our children,
and shrinking back at a time when a little more, a little further, would
have rendered this Continent the glory of the earth.

As Britain hath not manifested the least inclination towards a compromise, we may be assured that no terms can be obtained worthy the
acceptance of the Continent, or any ways equal to the expence of blood
and treasure we have been already put to.

He argues that everything has been said in the course of the
long dispute which might lead to a reconciliation, that further
talk is useless, and that the olive branch has been worn to a fraz-
zle. This turned out to be one of the most effective points made
in the book. He says along this line:

Volumes have been written on the subject of the struggle between
England and America. Men of all ranks have embarked in the controversy, from different motives, and with various designs; but all have
been ineffectual, and the period of debate is closed. Arms as the last
resource decide the contest; the appeal was the choice of the king, and
the Continent has accepted the challenge. . . .

The sun never shone on a cause of greater worth. 'Tis not the affair
of a city, a county, a province, or a kingdom; but of a Continent—of at
least one eighth part of the habitable globe. 'Tis not the concern of a
day, a year, or an age; posterity are virtually involved in the contest,

and will be more or less affected even to the end of time, by the proceedings now.

Now is the seed-time of continental union, faith and honor. The least fracture now will be like a name engraved with the point of a pin on the tender rind of a young oak; the wound would enlarge with the tree, and posterity read it in full grown characters.

By referring the matter from argument to arms, a new era for politics is struck—a new method of thinking has arisen. All plans, proposals, etc. prior to the nineteenth of April, *i.e.* to the commencement of hostilities, are like the almanacs of the last year; which though proper then, are superseded and useless now. Whatever was advanced by the advocates on either side of the question then, terminated in one and the same point, *viz.* a union with Great Britain; the only difference between the parties was the method of effecting it; the one proposing force, the other friendship; but it has so far happened that the first has failed, and the second has withdrawn her influence.

I have heard it asserted by some that, as America has flourished under her former connection with Great Britain, the same connection is necessary towards her future happiness, and will always have the same effect. Nothing can be more fallacious than this kind of argument. We may as well assert that because a child has thrived upon milk that it is never to have meat, or that the first twenty years of our life is to become a precedent for the next twenty. But even this is admitting more than is true; for I answer roundly that America would have flourished as much, and probably more, had no European power taken any notice of her. The commerce by which she hath enriched herself are the necessaries of life, and will always have a market while eating is the custom of Europe.

Paine's arguments, one may note, are general in character. He avoids the citation of particular incidents; there is no mention of the Stamp Tax, or the Navigation Act, or the squabbling over this and that. That is a mark of the subtlety that runs through most of Paine's polemical writings. A discussion of various grievances in detail in *Common Sense* would have sidetracked the reader's mind away from the main issue.

Below are further extracts:

I challenge the warmest advocate for reconciliation to show a single advantage that this continent can reap by being connected with Great

Britain. I repeat the challenge; not a single advantage is derived. Our corn will fetch its price in any market in Europe, and our imported goods must be paid for, buy them where we will.

As Europe is our market for trade, we ought to form no partial connection with any part of it. It is the true interest of America to steer clear of European contentions, which she never can do, while, by her dependence on Britain, she is made the makeweight in the scale of British politics.

Europe is too thickly planted with kingdoms to be long at peace, and whenever a war breaks out between England and any foreign power, the trade of America goes to ruin, *because of her connection with Britain*.

But Britain is the parent country, say some, then the more shame upon her conduct. Even brutes do not devour their young, nor savages make war upon their families; wherefore, the assertion, if true, turns to her reproach; but it happens not to be true, or only partly so, and the phrase parent or *mother country* hath been Jesuitically adopted by the king and his parasites, with a low papistical design of gaining an unfair bias on the credulous weakness of our minds.

The conciliators, the "middle of the road" fellows, the "peace at any price" people were constantly on Paine's mind. He feared that the whole dispute, despite Bunker Hill and Lexington, might be dropped if the British Government made some paltry concession which would leave the core of the matter untouched. He writes:

Men of passive tempers look somewhat lightly over the offences of Great Britain, and still hoping for the best, are apt to call out, *Come, come, we shall be friends again for all this*. But examine the passions and feelings of mankind; bring the doctrine of reconciliation to the touch-stone of nature, and then tell me whether you can hereafter love, honor and faithfully serve the power that hath carried fire and sword into your land?

If you cannot do all these, then are you only deceiving yourselves, and by your delay bringing ruin upon posterity. Your future connection with Britain, whom you can neither love nor honor, will be forced and unnatural, and being formed only on the plan of present convenience, will in a little time fall into a relapse more wretched than the first. But if you say, you can still pass the violations over, then I ask, hath your house been burnt? Hath your property been destroyed before your face? Are your wife and children destitute of a bed to lie on, or bread to live on? Have you lost a parent or a child by their hands, and are yourself the ruined and wretched survivor? If you have not, then are you not a judge of those who have. But if you have, and can still shake hands with the murderers, then are you unworthy the name of husband, father, friend, or lover, and whatever may be your rank or title in life, you have the heart of a coward, and the spirit of a sycophant.

The pamphlet comes to an end with this paragraph:

Wherefore, instead of gazing at each other with suspicious or doubtful curiosity, let each of us hold out to his neighbor the hearty hand of friendship, and unite in drawing a line, which, like an act of oblivion, shall bury in forgetfulness every former dissension. Let the names of Whig and Tory be extinct; and let none other be heard among us, than those of *a good citizen; an open and resolute friend; and a virtuous supporter of the RIGHTS of MANKIND and of the FREE AND INDEPENDENT STATES OF AMERICA.*

Paine's writing was inspiring, dynamic, sensible—and as simple in style as an ordinary conversation between friends who might unexpectedly run across each other in the street. He had a natural talent for putting plain facts in such a convincing form that his readers wanted to get up right then and there and go into action. He never made scholarly references to Greece or Rome, nor did he ever use words that had to be looked up in the dictionary. His writing was always intensely human.

4

The publication of *Common Sense* was like the breaking of a dam which releases all the pent-up water that stood behind it. The printing presses ran night and day to fill the demand for the thin pamphlet. Men read it in the streets, standing still on the narrow sidewalks, rapt in attention, while people passed to and fro. It was read aloud by schoolteachers and patriotic speakers to audiences of unlettered laborers. In the Continental Army the officers read it while their men stood at attention, listening to every word.

As soon as its authorship was known, within a few weeks after it had first appeared, Thomas Paine became a famous man overnight. A Maryland subscriber to the *Pennsylvania Evening Post* wrote a letter to that newspaper in which he said, "If you know the author of *Common Sense* tell him he has done wonders and worked miracles, made Tories Whigs and washed blackamoors white. He has made a great number of converts here."

On April 1 of that year (1776) George Washington said in a letter to Joseph Reed:

My countrymen, I know, from their form of government and steady attachment heretofore to royalty, will come reluctantly to the idea of independence, but time and persecution bring many wonderful things to pass; and, by private letters which I have lately received from Virginia, I find Paine's *Common Sense* is working a wonderful change there in the minds of men.

Sir George Trevelyan says, in his *History of the American Revolution:*

It would be difficult to name any human composition which has had an effect at once so instant, so extended and so lasting. . . . It was pirated, parodied and imitated, and translated into the language of every country where the new republic had well-wishers. . . . According to contemporary newspapers *Common Sense* turned thousands to independence who before could not endure the thought. It worked nothing short of miracles and turned Tories into Whigs.

In April the North Carolina Provincial Congress, that until then had disclaimed any thought of rebellion, instructed its delegates to vote for independence at the forthcoming meeting of the Continental Congress in Philadelphia. At the September session of the previous year (1776) this body had given explicit instructions to its delegates to vote against independence.

Among the South Carolina delegates to the Continental Congress was Christopher Gadsden, a resolute patriot who stood for independence. Early in February he returned to Charleston, taking with him a copy of *Common Sense*. In the South Carolina Convention he rose and read many passages from Paine's pamphlet, and proposed a resolution to the effect that South Carolina, united with the other Colonies, should declare for independence.

"This declaration," says William Henry Drayton in his *Memoirs*, "came like an explosion of thunder upon the members. There had been no intimation of such a purpose, there was nothing in the resolution of the Continental Congress to suggest such a purpose. That the controversy with the mother country might lead to such a revolutionary attempt had been anticipated and dreaded by many from its very inception, but few at the time were prepared to meet the issue. John Rutledge warmly reproved Colonel Gadsden, pronounced the opinion treasonable, and declared he abhorred the idea." Paine, the author of the pamphlet, was denounced and cursed. Even the few who were ready for independence regretted Gadsden's sudden and inopportune declaration.

Gadsden's resolution was voted down. But less than a month later the South Carolina Convention resolved to establish an independent government for South Carolina, with a president instead of a royal governor. It was further resolved to elect a general assembly, and instead of the royal governor's privy council there was to be a legislative council of thirteen members.

This proceeding inclines one to believe that after the "explosion" at the February meeting others besides Christopher Gadsden had been reading Thomas Paine's *Common Sense*.

When the Declaration of Independence came before the Continental Congress on July 4 of that year the South Carolina delegates voted for it, together with the delegates of all the other Colonies except New York.

New York delegates refrained from voting on July 4, as they had no authority from their Colonial assembly to vote for independence at that time, but such instructions were received later and they cast their votes for the Declaration on July 9.

5

The Tories, or Loyalists, constituted a strong minority in all the Colonies. In some of them, in New York and Pennsylvania, for example, they were sufficiently influential to be a distinct menace to the independence movement. The Tories were conservatives, or reactionaries. They wanted no change, or only minor changes in the relation of the Colonies to Great Britain. They feared that separation from the mother country would lead to disaster, and the vexatious laws and regulations imposed on the Colonies by the king and his government seemed to them a lesser evil than those lying quietly hidden in the background of independence.

Many of the Tories were wealthy; it was, indeed, a party of rich landowners, exporters, merchants and professional men, such as college professors, clergymen and lawyers. The common folk included in the Tory classification were, in most cases, tenants or debtors or servants of well-to-do Loyalists.

The Tories were convinced that the independence of the Colonies, if it ever came about, would lead to mob rule, anarchy and disorganization, with "the illiterate trash," as they called the common people, sitting on top of the heap. And, of course, all private property would be seized or destroyed.

Their fears were wholly groundless, but they could not see far enough in the future to perceive that the ghost lying in wait for them on the dark road was only a flapping white sheet. The social system that followed the Revolution was certainly not governed by a mob. It was not even a democracy but an aristocratic republic. The Tories would have been as safe within it as if they were living in the shadow of St. James Palace.

Yet as late as November 24, 1778, after the French had joined the Colonials and the British were losing the war, the French minister at Philadelphia wrote to his government:

Scarcely one quarter of the ordinary inhabitants of Philadelphia now here favor the cause [of independence]. Commercial and family ties, together with an aversion to popular government, seem to account for this. The same feeling exists in New York and Boston, which is not the case in the rural districts.

To counterattack the revolutionary movement the Loyalists distributed innumerable pamphlets and subsidized newspapers and public speakers. Some of their arguments sound exceedingly strange to a twentieth-century reader. "If I must be enslaved," Samuel Seabury wrote, "let it be by a King at least, and not by a parcel of upstart, lawless Committeemen. If I must be devoured, let me be devoured by the jaws of a lion and not gnawed to death by rats and vermin." Jonathan Boucher declared that "a rebel is worse than the worst prince, and a rebellion worse than the worst government of the worst prince that hath hitherto been."

The anonymous author of *Plain Truth*, a Tory pamphlet, wrote that "Independence and slavery are synonymous terms." A startling idea! If that be true, it would certainly be interesting to have the writer's definition of freedom, which he failed to give.

"God is a God of order and not of confusion," wrote another pamphleteer, "and he commands you to submit to your rulers, and to be obedient to the higher power for conscience sake."

The Reverend John Bullman, a Tory divine, preached a number of sermons against the Whigs and the independence movement. In one of them he put forth this specimen of Tory wisdom:

Every idle projector, who perhaps cannot govern his own household, or pay the debts of his own creating, presumes he is qualified to dictate how the state should be governed, and to point out the means of paying the debts of a nation. Hence, too, it is that every silly clown or illiterate mechanic will take upon him to censure the conduct of his prince or governor and contribute as much as in him lies to create and foment these misunderstandings which, being brooded by discontent and diffused through great multitudes, come at last to end in schism in the church, and sedition and rebellion in the state; so a great matter doth a little fire kindle.

The appearance of *Common Sense* and its wide circulation among people of all classes and conditions was a major disaster to the Tory cause. Their leaders, and the secret agents of Britain, encouraged writers in their pay to answer its arguments. As a result a swarm of pamphlets appeared bearing such titles as *A Friendly Address*; *An Englishman's Answer*; *The Congress Canvassed*; *Patriots of North America*; and *True Interest of America*. All of these effusions are pompous, windy, dull and unconvincing.

CHAPTER V

'A Restless Intellectual

I

THOMAS PAINE accepted nothing on faith. Nothing whatever. He did not possess an atom of respect for tradition or anything that it implies. He was a logician by temperament and daily practice and his mental life was a never-ending search for the why and wherefore of everything. He had no use for any institution, or system of society, that did not fit into the domain of reason.

But the truth is that the logical faculty, so highly praised in schoolbooks and public orations, exhibits a considerable number of disagreeable qualities when actively practiced. Many revered and honored activities, customs and beliefs of the human race —ranging from religion down to a belief in Santa Claus—are not able to stand a critical and logical examination. Those who make such examinations and display the results are likely to find themselves classed as atheists, rebels and scoffers. That was to be the fate of Thomas Paine.

He was not only a logician but also a reformer and an idealist. He endeavored, all his life, to convert the revelations of logic into realities, to get rid of contradictions in human society, and to make common sense the daily guide of both men and nations.

While he was in editorial charge of the *Pennsylvania Magazine* he denounced dueling, slavery, monarchy and hereditary titles, cruelty to animals, the repression of women, and several other practices of people who called themselves civilized.

To put an end to the foolish custom of dueling he suggested that the survivor be hanged immediately after the duel was over and at the same place without any argument or discussion of the rights and wrongs of the affair.

The article against dueling annoyed some people and pleased others. In that era the duel was looked upon as an honorable way of settling quarrels and avenging insults among gentlemen. It was not for common men, but for the aristocracy—for those who wore silver buckles on their shoes, silk stockings, velvet breeches, powdered wigs, and lace cuffs falling over their wrists. To criticize their personal conduct was nothing less than a piece of effrontery, for they did not follow the advice or admonition of the lower orders, and it was presumptuous on the part of anyone to suggest that their conduct could be wrong. "Who is this Paine," said the dueling gentlemen, "this vulgar nobody who takes it upon himself to discredit a gentlemanly custom? What right has he to tell men of substance how they should behave when he is not much more than a printer's errand boy, a penny-a-liner who manages to get his craven notions into print?"

He called slavery a monstrous evil, and wrote:

Certainly one may, with as much reason and decency, plead for murder, robbery, lewdness and barbarity, as for this practice. They are not more contrary to the natural dictates of conscience and feelings of humanity; nay, they are all comprehended in it.

Americans righteously resent, he said, the attempts of the English to enslave the Colonies, but "with what consistency, or decency, do they complain so loudly of attempts to enslave them while they hold so many hundred thousands in slavery; and annually enslave many thousands more without any pretence of authority, or claim upon them?"

Southerners were not alone in disliking Paine's antislavery essay. Among the New Englanders slave-catching was an important and lucrative industry. They sent their ships to Africa and loaded them with Negroes whom they sold as slaves in Carolina and Georgia. Slaves were private property, the same as houses and farms, clothes and furniture. A proposal, such as Paine made, that they be freed without compensation to their owners, sounded to a great many eighteenth-century Americans like the talk of a madman.

But some agreed with him heartily. There was Thomas Jefferson, a slave-owner himself, who wrote in the Declaration of

Independence an antislavery paragraph which was eventually omitted despite Jefferson's efforts to keep it in. The leaders of the movement for independence thought it might antagonize some of the Southern members and prevent them from signing the Declaration.

And in 1775, shortly after Paine's article appeared, the opponents of slavery in Philadelphia—inspired by what Paine had written—got together and formed the American Antislavery Society, which was the first association ever organized on this continent for the abolition of slavery.

Paine's outer life was as simple as that of a plowhand or a furnace tender, while his inner life was so intricate, complicated and intense that he sometimes felt as if he were living in a different world from that of the people around him. He must be judged by his writings, for they alone give him a place in the great world of thought and action. Without them he is just Tom Paine, a commonplace staymaker. It took him thirty-eight years to find his way through his inner maze and discover that he was something more than a staymaker and excise officer.

2

Paine entered the military service of the Colonies in July, 1776, as a volunteer secretary to General Roberdeau, who commanded an organization called the Flying Camp.[1] This force was not attached to the regular service, but was sent here and there as an auxiliary command. It moved quickly and was not long in any one place. Paine did not enlist in regular fashion, but seems to

[1] Before the Revolution Daniel Roberdeau was a prosperous merchant in Philadelphia. He was a native of the West Indies and had received his education at a school in England. A man of much public spirit, he was a member of the provincial assembly, and the chairman of many mass meetings held to build up revolutionary sentiment. To provide lead for bullets for Washington's army he developed a lead mine in western Pennsylvania. He was elected a brigadier-general by the Pennsylvania Associates on July 4, 1776. Roberdeau was a consistent advocate of Paine's ideas.

have been taken on by General Roberdeau, by whom he was well known, with the understanding that he could leave at any time.

When he joined the Flying Camp it was stationed at Amboy, in New Jersey, about twenty miles below New York City. A narrow strait separates Amboy from Staten Island, where the British Army, under General Sir William Howe, was encamped at that time. Roberdeau's command seems to have occupied a post of observation with the duty of reporting the movements of the British. The main force of the Americans, under General George Washington, was on Manhattan, with a few regiments across the East River on Long Island.

It seemed obvious, in view of the disposition of the two armies, that Howe would soon attack the Americans for the purpose of driving them out of New York. The British Army consisted of 20,000 men, all well-trained, well-fed and well-armed. Washington's force numbered about 8,000—a rabble of half-trained, shabby, poorly armed volunteers. On August 27 Howe attacked the American forces on Long Island and drove them back across the East River to Manhattan. A few weeks later Washington had to abandon New York and take his greatly reduced army over the Hudson.

The Flying Camp at Amboy withdrew to Pennsylvania, but Paine left that command and joined General Nathanael Greene at Fort Lee, as a volunteer aide-de-camp. It may be explained, for the benefit of those not familiar with the minor geography of the region, that Fort Lee is on the western bank of the Hudson, and is directly opposite the northern end of Manhattan Island.

General Greene and Paine became good friends, both on political and personal grounds. It was Greene who introduced Paine to George Washington, already an admirer of *Common Sense*. It would be interesting to learn, if we could, what they thought of each other at their first meeting, but we shall never know with certainty. Washington, though gracious and polite in all his human contacts, was a man of cold reserve. He never had an intimate personal friend, for he did not unbend sufficiently to make his companions feel easy in his company. A possible exception was Lafayette, toward whom Washington's manner was that of a kindly father. The penetrating gaze of his chilly gray eyes flustered people whom he met, for he seemed to be weighing them in a balance. We may imagine him sitting at Greene's table, saying little himself but listening to eager Thomas Paine who was, without doubt, anxious to impress his ideas on the Commander in Chief of the American Army.

On November 20, 1776, the British crossed the Hudson and Greene was forced to abandon Fort Lee and retreat across New Jersey. Although Paine was an active member of General Greene's staff he began to write, in the latter part of that month, the first of a series of pamphlets which are known collectively as the *Crisis*. These writings were undertaken to buoy the courage of the Revolutionary soldiers, to inspire them to hold firm in the face of defeat and to look to a future of victory and independence. In accomplishing this the series of *Crisis* papers was extraordinarily successful. They were all written at night, or at odd times, for Paine was busy all day, and every day, with his military duties.

During this sad month of November, 1776, the American cause was declining by the hour, and many observers—some of them staunch patriots—thought the war would be over, with Britain the winner, before the next spring. Washington wrote to his brother:

I am wearied almost to death with the retrograde motion of things, and I solemnly protest that a pecuniary reward of twenty thousand pounds a year would not induce me to undergo what I do; and after all, perhaps to lose my character, as it is impossible, under such a variety of distressing circumstances, to conduct matters agreeably to public expectation.

On December 17 he wrote to Lund Washington:

Your imagination can scarce extend to a situation more distressing than mine. Our only dependence now is upon the speedy enlistment of a new army. If this fails, I think the game will be pretty well up, as from disaffection and want of spirit and fortitude, the inhabitants, instead of resistance, are offering submission and taking protection from Gen. Howe in Jersey.

The land was deep in winter. The ground was covered with snow and swept by icy winds. Washington's army was half-naked; many of the soldiers even lacked shoes and their feet were wrapped in rags. Some were so thinly clad that they could perform no service at all, as they would have been frozen to death while doing their sentry duty.

Nevertheless, the war went on. The American Army had been forced across the Delaware and the British and Hessians held all its eastern bank, including the town of Trenton. Washington conceived the bold plan of taking his men across the icy river and making a surprise attack on Christmas Eve. This was done. The men crossed in rowboats and, with Washington leading them, they surprised the Hessian garrison at Trenton, defeated it and pushed on to Princeton, where they were again victorious. It was a resounding victory, and an unexpected one. Today it lives in history. There is probably not an American of our time who has not seen a picture of Washington crossing the wintry Delaware in a rowboat, with his soldiers pulling at the oars.

Paine's first *Crisis* was published a few days before the attack on Trenton. It was written to inspire the troops and to put heart in the dejected patriots.

Its first paragraph runs like martial music with its soaring quality:

These are the times that try men's souls. The summer soldier and the sunshine patriot will, in this crisis, shrink from the service of their country; but he that stands it *now* deserves the love and thanks of man and woman. Tyranny, like hell, is not easily conquered; yet we have this consolation with us, that the harder the conflict, the more glorious the triumph.

It marches on:

What we obtain too cheap, we esteem too lightly; it is dearness only that gives everything its value. Heaven knows how to put a proper price upon its goods; and it would be strange indeed if so celestial an article as FREEDOM should not be highly rated. Britain, with an army to enforce her tyranny, has declared that she has a right (not only to Tax) but to bind us "in All CASES WHATSOEVER," and if being *bound in that manner* is not slavery, then is there not such a thing as slavery upon earth. Even the expression is impious; for so unlimited a power can belong only to God.

It is interesting to observe that Paine, with a false reputation as an atheist which runs on through the years, makes frequent references in his writings to the wisdom and power of God, as in the following extract from the first *Crisis:*

I have as little superstition in me as any man living but my secret opinion has ever been, and still is, that God Almighty will not give up a people to military destruction, or leave them unsupportedly to perish, who have so earnestly and so repeatedly sought to avoid the calamities of war by every decent method which wisdom could invent.

In the next few pages he narrates the events that have taken place during the past month—November–December, 1776—in the New York and New Jersey military area. Then he puts forth this inspiring thought:

I love the man that can smile in trouble, that can gather strength from distress, and grow brave by reflection. 'Tis the business of little minds to shrink; but he whose heart is firm, and whose conscience approves his conduct, will pursue his principles unto death. My own line of reasoning is to myself as straight and clear as a ray of light.

Not all the treasures of the world, so far as I believe, could have induced me to support an offensive war, for I think it murder; but if a thief breaks into my house, burns and destroys my property, and kills or threatens to kill me, or those that are in it, and to *"bind me in all cases whatsoever"* to his absolute will, am I to suffer it?

What signifies it to me, whether he who does it is a king or a common man; my countryman or not my countryman; whether it be done by an individual villain, or an army of them? If we reason to the root of things we shall find no difference; neither can any just cause be assigned why we should punish in the one case and pardon in the other.

Though Paine wrote nothing until he was nearly forty he had acquired the skill of an experienced writer. He was what is now known in the literary world as a "natural," meaning an author who writes well instinctively, without training or practice. Many writers, even some of those who have much experience, have not acquired the knack of a strong ending; they let their essays or articles peter out in a weak fashion. But Paine knew, or felt, that a strong and eloquent conclusion is one of the necessary features of an argumentative essay. He concluded the first *Crisis* in this manner:

I thank God that I fear not. I see no real cause for fear. I know our situation well, and can see the way out of it. . . .

By perseverance and fortitude we have the prospect of a glorious issue; by cowardice and submission, the sad choice of a variety of evils—a ravaged country—a depopulated city—habitations without safety, and slavery without hope—our homes turned into barracks and bawdy-houses for Hessians, and a future race to provide for, whose fathers we shall doubt of. Look on this picture and weep over it! and if there yet remains one thoughtless wretch who believes it not, let him suffer it unlamented.

The second issue of the *Crisis* came out in the middle of January, 1777, or about three weeks after the first one was published. It was addressed to Admiral Lord Richard Howe, who commanded the British Fleet in American waters. He had recently issued a proclamation in which he commanded all inhabitants of the Colonies to lay down their arms and resume their allegiance to King George.[2] He threatened to make a terrifying example of those who continued to defy the royal authority. Every one of the thirteen Colonies, conquered and helpless, would feel the heavy weight of Britain's displeasure.

The Tories everywhere were hoping that the proclamation would cause serious defections among the adherents of the independence movement and were doing all in their power to make

[2] Admiral Lord Howe was a brother of General Sir William Howe, Commander of His Majesty's land forces in the Colonies. He was the ranking British officer in America; therefore the proclamation was issued by him.

it effective. *Crisis No. II* was circulated to help counteract the influence of the proclamation.

The following extracts are set forth here to show the general tone of the second *Crisis*. Paine is addressing Lord Howe:

> By what means, may I ask, do you expect to conquer America? If you could not effect it in the summer, when our army was less than yours, nor in the winter, when we had none, how are you to do it?
>
> In point of generalship you have been outwitted, and in point of fortitude outdone; your advantages turn out to your loss, and show us that it is in our power to ruin you by gifts: like a game of drafts, we can move out of *one* square to let you come in, in order that we may afterwards take two or three for one; and as we can always keep a double corner for ourselves, we can always prevent a total defeat. You cannot be so insensible as not to see that we have two to one the advantage of you, because we conquer by a drawn game, and you lose by it.

The Tories, in their effort to throw contempt on the author, inspired and fabricated many of the lies that followed him to the end, and still bedevil his memory to this day. One of them described him as a hireling, without principle or conscience, who would write in favor of any cause that would give him a few pounds to buy brandy and pay the rent of a hovel in which he could sleep off his drunken stupors. The truth is that Paine always refused pay for his political writings, such as *Common Sense*, and the various numbers of the *Crisis*. He would not take pay for them even when it was generously offered by friends, nor would he accept any profits from publishers, but instructed them to turn over the proceeds to the treasury of the Continental Congress; yet at times he badly needed the money that his political writings might have brought. He said, "In great affairs where the happiness of man is concerned I love to work for nothing."

In *Crisis No. II* he made this clear.

> I consider INDEPENDENCE as *America's natural right and interest*, and never could see any real disservice it would be to Britain. If an English merchant receives an order, and is paid for it, it signifies nothing to him who governs the country. This is my creed of politics.

If I have anywhere expressed myself over-warmly, 'tis from a fixed, immovable hatred I have, and ever had to cruel men and cruel measures. I have likewise an aversion to monarchy, as being too debasing to the dignity of man; but I never troubled others with my notions till very lately, nor ever published a syllable in England in my life.

What I write is pure nature, and my pen and my soul have ever gone together. . . .

My writings I have always given away, reserving only the expense of printing and paper, and sometimes not even that.

I never courted either fame or interest, and my manner of life, to those who know it, will justify what I say. My study is to be useful, and if your lordship loves mankind as well as I do, you would, seeing you cannot conquer us, cast about and lend your hand towards accomplishing a peace.

In this second number of the *Crisis* Paine says to Lord Howe: "The United States of America will sound as pompously in the world or in history as 'The Kingdom of Great Britain.'" Paine created the expression *United States of America*, and in the sentence quoted above it was used for the first time.

A third *Crisis* appeared on April 19 of that same year—1777 —and thereafter they came out at irregular intervals. There were thirteen in all. Printed in book form they make three hundred and sixty pages, or about ninety thousand words.

The purport of the third *Crisis* was to prove that America was not a child any longer, that it was a full-grown nation and proposed to be treated as such. No. IV came out on September 12, 1777, the day following the Battle of the Brandywine, when the British Army was advancing on Philadelphia.

No. V was issued at Lancaster, Pennsylvania, on March 21, 1778; No. VI from Philadelphia on October 20, 1778; and No. VII addressed "To the People of England" on November 21, 1778. After the seventh *Crisis* there were longer intervals between them; the thirteenth and last was brought out on December 9, 1783, when the war was over.

In this last of the *Crisis* pamphlets Paine advocated a *union of the states* instead of a long string of small independent republics.

The affairs of each state are local. They can go no further than to itself. And were the whole worth of even the richest of them expended in revenue it would not be sufficient to support sovereignty against a foreign attack. In short we have no other national sovereignty than as united states. . . . Sovereignty must have power to protect all the parts that compose and constitute it; and as *UNITED STATES* we are equal to the importance of the title, but otherwise we are not.

Our union, well and wisely regulated and cemented, is the cheapest way of being great—the easiest way of being powerful, and the happiest invention in government which the circumstances of America can admit of.

3

As we have seen, Paine was a propagandist of the most convincing character. He knew just what to say to arouse the indifferent and lukewarm, and to add fire to the enthusiasm of those who were already supporting actively the cause of independence.

When *Common Sense* appeared, early in 1776, he was known to few of the leaders of American life. Benjamin Franklin knew him and was a powerful friend, and he was acquainted distantly with four or five members of the Continental Congress. But he was classed as only an insignificant Englishman—as he certainly was—who had come to our shores to pick up a living. As the author of *Common Sense* he rose at once to a higher place in the estimation of such patriots as Jefferson, Madison, Hancock, Monroe, Richard Henry Lee and Nathanael Greene. Even the cold and stately Washington looked upon him and his work with approval. At the same time, however, he sank to the bottom of the mire of disrepute in the minds of all Tories. They considered him an unspeakable renegade, a traitor and a worthless rascal. If the Americans had lost the war, Paine would have been in the first batch of so-called traitors to swing from the gallows.

As time went on there were increasing indications that Congress intended to take care of him financially by providing him with employment. It was high time, for he had no certain income and looked shabbier and shabbier as the weeks went by. In the latter part of January (1777) he was appointed secretary of a commission to treat with the Indians at a council held at Easton, Pennsylvania. He attended all the sessions, and, for the first time in his life, saw a group of Indian chiefs, their braves and squaws. For his services he was paid three hundred pounds.

Then, on April 17, when Congress turned the Committee of Secret Correspondence into the Committee of Foreign Affairs, and widened the scope of its activities, Paine was elected its secretary.

There was some opposition within the committee. John Adams nominated him, and the motion was seconded by General Roberdeau, but President Witherspoon of Princeton objected. He declared that Paine was known to be a former Tory, that he was a heavy drinker, and a disreputable person in his private life. These remarks caused some discussion, but Witherspoon finally admitted that his criticisms were based entirely on hearsay. It is evident that the Tories had begun their work of defamation, some of which lingers on to this day. John Adams wrote in his autobiography that "no one confirmed Witherspoon's account."

Paine was made secretary of the committee at a salary of seventy dollars a month. He held this official position for two years, and was forced to resign on January 8, 1779, as the outcome of a controversy which was as full of mystery as an orange is full of juice. Some of the facts of this curious squabble are still unknown, but all that has ever been revealed and proved —as well as some of the conjectures—will be set forth in the next chapter.

CHAPTER VI

The Silas Deane Controversy

I

THE prolonged and acrimonious dispute over Silas Deane and his doings was not Thomas Paine's quarrel. He could have stayed out of it and remained an innocent bystander without being dragged in by anybody. But as a patriot, and as Secretary of the Foreign Affairs Committee, he felt that he ought to do something to clear up the situation. He did not succeed in clearing it up, but he dug deep enough to unearth a nest of hornets, and they stung him out of his job.

It grew out of Deane's mission to France in 1776. The evidence is so cluttered with side issues and secret compacts and lost documents and whispered aspersions that it is difficult to follow the thread of the story, unless it is stripped of all uncertain assumptions and limited to the bare facts. But even so, many of the admitted facts lack clarity and cast misty shadows through which strange figures move and mutter.

2

France was still smarting from the blows which England's heavy hand had given her in the Seven Years' War. Besides the loss of Canada, which was the largest of her colonial possessions, France had lost much of her prestige as a great European power. Revenge against the English had become one of the cardinal principles of French policy, but it was carefully concealed by a pleasant manner, for France and England were at peace with each other and the spokesmen of both countries took pains to express publicly, on proper occasions, a hope that these peaceful relations might continue.

To French statesmen the revolt of the American Colonies seemed to be a gift of Providence, and plans to encourage and

sustain the rebels were soon simmering quietly under the powdered wigs at Versailles. Their secret agents in America—in
Boston, New York, Philadelphia, Charleston—reported that
the rebellion was serious but not likely to succeed, principally
because the Colonials lacked arms, ammunition, shoes, clothing
and everything but food. These observations were correct. After
the Battle of Bunker Hill there was not enough gunpowder in
all the thirteen Colonies to furnish Washington's small army
with ammunition for even a month of actual warfare, and if the
British had been so minded they could have marched from Massachusetts to Georgia without encountering much resistance. The
guns in use had been made by village blacksmiths; they were of
all calibers and weights; and there were not enough of them.
A large number were not military muskets but light shotguns,
used for shooting birds, and therefore of little value as weapons of warfare.

The advisers to the French throne, sitting in quiet conferences and sworn to secrecy, decided to do something about the
situation months before the Americans had proclaimed their
formal Declaration of Independence. These aristocratic Frenchmen cared nothing for American ideals, such as freedom, liberty
and human rights, and when they advised their king to furnish
aid to the Colonies it was not for the purpose of furthering
progress, or to help create a new and brighter world, or any
such nonsense. They simply wanted to make trouble for the
British.

But the problem was how to give aid to the rebels with such
secrecy that the British would not be able to prove that it had
come from the French Government. Any help that was worth
while would have to be so large that concealment would
be difficult. Thousands of muskets and hundreds of cannon, tons
of gunpowder, and shiploads of clothing are not readily hidden.
Of course, there were British spies in France, and London would
soon hear of what was going on.

The French Government wanted to be in a position to deny
even the least connection with such a traffic when the English
ambassador called attention to it, as they expected he would

eventually do. Then, acting in the role of a friendly neighbor, they intended to put on a show of trying to stop the shipments of arms, but they would manage to conceive these efforts so badly and carry them out so inefficiently that they would be ineffective.

With such thoughts in mind the Comte de Vergennes, French Minister of Foreign Affairs, or some of his aides, worked out a plan for setting up a commercial establishment, wholly outside the government and ostensibly owned by private individuals, that would engage in the business of exporting goods of French origin and importing foreign merchandise in return. Under cover of this enterprise gifts of arms and other needed supplies might be sent overseas to the armies of the insurgent Colonies.

At the head of the shipping concern they placed Caron de Beaumarchais, an incredible character who seems, to a modern observer, to have stepped out of a romantic novel. He was a spectacular business man as well as a brilliant playwright. His career was a curious pattern of shrewdness, mystery, tricks and dishonesty, dramatic situations, poetry, song, music and laughter.

His father was a watchmaker who had a shop in Paris with an excellent clientele. He was also the official watch-and-clock mender of the royal palace. The son, Pierre Caron, learned his father's trade and did most of the work around the palace. In the course of time he made the acquaintance of some of the nobles. He was a clever youth and his cleverness was untroubled by such middle-class sentiments as honor and honesty.

Without any training at all he became a writer of plays, among them the *Mariage de Figaro* and the *Barbier de Séville*, which are considered classic but lively examples of stage comedy, even today. Figaro is a comic servant—impudent, unscrupulous, plausible. He is, in fact, Beaumarchais himself. Pierre Caron married the widow of the auditor of the royal household, who was well-to-do. She died of typhoid within a year. From her he inherited a small country estate called Beaumarchais. He adopted the name and was thereafter known as Caron de Beaumarchais.

The watchmaking business was abandoned and Beaumarchais

became a courtier with a small niche of authority in the royal household. The King was amused by his humor, his riddles and his laughable verses. By nature he was given to intrigue, and there was plenty of it at the court. In a letter to his father he wrote:

I laugh when I think how nicely the things of this world fit into each other; how odd and diverse are the ways of fortune; and how, above all, in the whirl of affairs, the mind superior to events rejoices at the clash of interests, pleasures, sorrows, which dash and break against it.

We do not know why Vergennes selected this adventurer to handle the French advances of arms and goods to the American rebels, or to set up the false front of a commercial house for that purpose, but one may guess. A plausible conjecture is that Vergennes knew he could force Beaumarchais to keep the matter secret and, furthermore, in case the British should learn that he was shipping arms to the rebels and insist that something be done about it, that Beaumarchais might be thrown in prison as a gesture of appeasement without any great outcry from his friends or relatives, as he was not a noble by birth and had no high and mighty connections.

At that time (it was in 1775) the American Colonies had no agent in Paris, but were represented in London by Arthur Lee, one of the Lee family of Virginia. He was a brother of Richard Henry Lee, then a member of the Continental Congress, and of William Lee, a permanent resident of London and an alderman of that city. All the brothers had been educated in England and had many friends there.

While Louis XVI and his advisers were considering the plan to give aid to the rebellious Colonies Vergennes sent Beaumarchais to London to make the acquaintance of Arthur Lee and sound him out on the project they had in mind. Lee and Beaumarchais met at a dinner given by John Wilkes, Lord Mayor of London, and thereafter they had many conferences. After Beaumarchais returned to Paris Lee wrote to the Secret Committee in Philadelphia that the King of France had decided to send five million livres in arms and munitions to the struggling Colonies and that he had been so informed by Beaumarchais. Neither assertion was strictly true. At that time Louis XVI had not approved the plan to aid the Colonies, but was considering the matter; and the sum of five million livres came from the fertile imagination of Beaumarchais. The largest amount discussed by the secret councils in Paris had been two million livres, half of which was to be furnished by the French treasury, and half by the King of Spain.

In June, 1776, Louis XVI approved the scheme and his treasury turned over a million livres to Beaumarchais. Not long afterward he got another million from Spain. With these funds he established a concern known as Roderique Hortalez and Company. This imitation of a commercial house soon began to ship guns, munitions and supplies across the Atlantic. Their ostensible destination was San Domingo, but their real destination was Boston, or Baltimore or Philadelphia. (New York was at that time in the hands of the British.)

Now let us pause a moment and ask some questions.

First, was the money advanced by the royal treasuries as a gift to the American rebels or a loan to be repaid when they had won their independence?

There is no definite, clear-cut answer to that question. The available evidence indicates that the supplies sent to America were intended as a gift, but there is no document in existence to that effect, nor has there ever been one. The French Government would hardly have made the Colonies a loan without some negotiations concerning it, such as rate of interest, length of time it was to run and other details. But there were no negotiations.

The goods were simply sent here, consigned to the Colonial authorities by Roderique Hortalez and Company. Arthur Lee wrote to the Secret Committee of the Continental Congress that the King of France, and his ally the King of Spain, had furnished the money to purchase the arms and supplies. So he had been assured by Beaumarchais, he informed the committee. He wrote also that Beaumarchais, or his commercial house, would ask payment as a matter of form, but such request might be disregarded.

When the whole affair became a matter of fierce dispute Beaumarchais declared that the royal treasury had never turned over any funds to him, that Arthur Lee was not telling the truth, and that Hortalez and Company was a private commercial venture financed by Beaumarchais himself and some of his wealthy friends. A representative of the French Government confirmed this statement.

Unfortunately for the truth of their assertion a receipt for one million livres paid out to Beaumarchais by the royal treasurer was found in the treasury files in 1794, after the French Revolution. There can be no doubt that Beaumarchais and his commercial house were financed wholly or in part by the French treasury, either as a gift or as a loan.

On August 18, 1776, Beaumarchais himself wrote to the Secret Committee:

An extensive commercial house has been formed solely for the purpose of serving you in Europe, to supply you with necessaries of every sort, clothes, linen, powder, ammunition, muskets, cannon, or even gold for the payment of your troops, and in general everything that can be useful for the honorable war in which you are engaged.

He says also in this letter that payment for the supplies must be made, and asks the committee to send him ten or twelve thousand hogsheads of tobacco from Virginia. This request was politely and smilingly laid aside by the committee, who thought Beaumarchais very clever to play his part so well.

The King, in his effort to preserve the appearance of friendliness with Great Britain, used Beaumarchais as his intermediary or disbursing agent. Color is given to this supposition by a letter of Beaumarchais, written several years later, to Silas Deane in which he mentions casually that "my commission was ten per cent."

3

In July, 1776, Silas Deane arrived in Paris as a commercial agent of the Colonies. He had been appointed to this post by the Secret Committee without the knowledge of Congress. A policy of not letting the right hand know what the left hand was doing ran through all these proceedings, both here and abroad, and it served mightily to complicate matters.

Congress was not informed of the action of Louis XVI in setting aside a large sum of money to give secret aid to the Colonies, nor of the part played by Beaumarchais. Arthur Lee's letter was not read before Congress, but was kept in the committee's secret files. The reason for this concealment was that some of the members of Congress were thought to be Tories in disguise and in communication with the British.

At the time of Deane's appointment as commercial agent in Paris (March, 1776) Beaumarchais had not yet received the fund of two million livres from the French and Spanish treasuries, and the setup with Rodrique Hortalez and Company as a figurehead was still in the future. The mission of Deane was to establish credit among French concerns, and to buy supplies to be paid for later. He was instructed to appear in the character of a merchant "which we wish you to retain among the French in general," the committee wrote, "it being probable that the Court of France may not like it should it be known publicly that any agent of the colonies is in that country."

For his service Deane was to be paid his expenses and a commission of 5 per cent on all supplies purchased by him on the credit of the Colonies. From his instructions it seems that the Secret Committee did not take much stock in the rumor of a gift from the royal treasury, for Deane was definitely expected to get credit from French merchants, who were to be paid eventually in Colonial products, such as tobacco, indigo, rice or furs. He was also instructed to negotiate with the French Government to the end that France would become a favored nation in the overseas trade of the Colonies—a place held until then by

Great Britain. Deane had a reputation for shrewdness and ability in business affairs.[1]

When he presented his credentials to Vergennes, a few days after his arrival in Paris, he was advised to get in contact with Beaumarchais. He met the clever dramatist, playing his role of business man, and was so favorably impressed by him that he wrote to Benjamin Franklin and Robert Morris, both in Philadelphia:

I find M. Beaumarchais, as I before hinted, possesses the entire confidence of the ministry; he is a man of wit and genius, and a considerable writer on comic and political subjects; all my supplies are to come through his hands.

In the meantime Arthur Lee had written to Deane that Beaumarchais had no right to demand payment for the supplies sent by his house to America, as the French administration intended them as gratuities, and that Beaumarchais was only a dispenser of these gifts without any personal financial interest in them. Lee added that this information had been given him by Beaumarchais himself. But the gay French playwright, when told of Lee's statement, denied it utterly and said he had never told Lee any such thing.

Deane preferred to believe Beaumarchais rather than Lee, and thereby made the error that eventually ruined him. Perhaps he was influenced by the matter of his own compensation. His 5 per cent commission was to be paid only on purchases made by him, but if Beaumarchais was a giver and not a seller

[1] Silas Deane, then about forty years of age, was the son of a Connecticut blacksmith. He graduated at Yale, taught school, studied law and married a well-to-do widow. Soon afterward he became a merchant, and a successful one. His wife died in 1767, and his second marriage was to Elizabeth Saltonstall, daughter of the Governor of Connecticut. That marriage gave him a high social standing, for the Saltonstalls were one of the influential families of New England. Deane took part in the movement that led up to the Revolution, was elected a member of the Continental Congress and served two terms, but lost the election for a third term. Then the Secret Committee sent him to France as agent for the Colonies.

Deane was not entitled to any pay at all. So he and Beaumarchais worked together as seller and buyer, Beaumarchais acting as merchant and Deane as customer. Besides the purchases from Roderique Hortalez and Company, Deane bought supplies from other French concerns which were not financed by the royal treasury. To some of these he gave his notes as Colonial agent; to others he promised shipments of tobacco.

Beaumarchais sent his bills along with the guns and supplies, and followed them with urgent appeals for payment. When forwarding his own reports to the committee Deane begged that body to arrange in some way—and quickly—to meet the bills of the Hortalez concern.

There was a British spy in Deane's office, and he reported every move of both Deane and Beaumarchais to Lord Stormont, the British ambassador. Spies also reported that for the gunpowder sold to the Americans at twenty sols a pound Beaumarchais paid only four sols a pound; and that the muskets sent to the Colonies had been discarded by the French Army and turned over to Beaumarchais free of cost while he billed them to the Americans at about half the price of new muskets. The British took it upon themselves to see that this information reached the members of the Continental Congress.

In September, 1776, Congress took up the matter of cultivating closer ties with France, with the hope of inducing the French to enter the war openly against the British. Or, at any rate, to put through a commercial treaty with France beneficial to both the French and the Americans.

To carry out this policy Congress appointed a commission of three members to reside in Paris with authority to represent the Colonies in all matters, diplomatic as well as economic. The commissioners were Benjamin Franklin, Arthur Lee and Silas Deane.

It was a three-man body afflicted by internal discords. Arthur Lee and Silas Deane became implacable enemies, and Lee—who had an unusually suspicious temperament—even suspected Franklin of corrupt financial practices. Deane, on his part, was certain that Lee had a secret connection with the British. Vergennes and the French Foreign Office also had doubts of Lee's integrity.

The three-man commission learned that the French Government did not expect repayment of the two million livres. How and where they acquired this knowledge is not stated in the records, but we know that they wrote to the Secret Committee in October, 1777, saying that "no repayment will ever be required from us for what has already been given us either in money or military stores." This letter was intercepted, or lost in some way, in its voyage across the Atlantic. A duplicate, sent by another vessel, did not reach America until March, 1778.

In the meanwhile Deane had been urging the Secret Committee to pay the bills of Roderique Hortalez and Company. It seems as though Deane, a member of the commission, should have known of the letter referred to above (that of October, 1777). By the end of 1777 it was useless to pretend any longer that arms and supplies were not coming from France, and the matter was openly discussed in Congress. Then there arrived from France (in December, 1777) a Monsieur De Francey, employed by Beaumarchais to persuade Congress to recognize its obligation and begin making payments. De Francey bore a letter of introduction from Deane, which had been written without the knowledge of Lee or Franklin. This agent of Beaumarchais submitted documents, vouchers, bills of lading, and so on, purporting to show that the Americans owed Hortalez and Company the sum of four million five hundred thousand livres.

Congress ordered Deane to return to America to "report on the state of affairs," which was only a polite way of saying that they wanted him to explain his actions. He arrived in May, 1778, without his vouchers or records, which he had unaccountably left in Paris.

By this time France and the insurgent Colonies had entered into a formal military and commercial alliance. The treaty was signed by Franklin, Lee and Deane on behalf of America. M. Gerard de Rayneval, a secretary of Comte de Vergennes in the Office for Foreign Affairs, was given the post of minister to the

Continental Congress. He came over on the same ship that bore Silas Deane.

Upon his arrival in Philadelphia Deane found that Arthur Lee had written a number of letters to members of Congress in which he declared that Deane was a clever and unscrupulous rascal who did not hesitate to use underhand methods. Deane refused to reply to these accusations. Lee, he said, was insane, and he did not mean that statement as a mere figure of speech; he meant that Lee was really demented. In respect to the charges against him he said, "To honor them with the emotions of anger would be degrading to that character which I hope always to maintain."

This pretentious, high and lofty attitude was an essential element of Deane's character, and it contributed toward his undoing. He had an excellent opinion of himself, and always felt offended when his motives and actions were questioned, even in the mildest manner. He appeared before Congress twice in August, 1778, about a month after his return from France, and his demeanor was so haughty that he lost many well-wishers among the members. On these two occasions he contributed nothing worthwhile in respect to the Beaumarchais squabble or anything else. His excuse was that his papers and accounts had been left in Europe. He could not answer most of the questions and he made no effort to refresh his memory.

He expected to be called before Congress again and waited in Philadelphia for several months. His complaints of inattention were many and grievous; he looked upon himself as a martyr. Eventually Congress was moved by his comments, and he was invited to appear again before that body in December, but he ignored the invitation. Instead, he published in the Philadelphia newspapers on December 5 a piece of invective entitled *The Address of Silas Deane to the Free and Virtuous Citizens of America.*

In writing this newspaper article he lowered his screen of haughtiness and honored the Lees with "the emotions of anger." He wrote that he would treat Arthur and William Lee with tenderness as they had two brothers in Congress, but he

had to say, no matter whom it hurt, that Arthur Lee was detested by the French nation, whose aid we were soliciting. Why?
Because he could not help showing a contempt and hatred for
the French people, our gallant allies. Also, it was generally believed by those close to the center of authority in France that
Arthur Lee communicated secretly with the English and gave
them valuable information.

In his blast of criticism he did not spare Congress. Declaring
that no attempt had been made to examine his own case fairly,
he charged the members of Congress with ignorance and lack of
interest. He thought, also, that he had not been treated with the
respect that he deserved, considering his success in obtaining
arms and goods in Europe.

4

Now Thomas Paine stepped into the arena. It was not his
fight; he was Secretary of the Foreign Affairs Committee and,
as such, was supposed to be as close-mouthed as the fabulous
Sphinx. That was not an easy role for Paine.

On the fourteenth of December of that year (1778) he published a *Letter to Silas Deane* in the *Pennsylvania Packet*. He
criticized Deane for assailing Arthur Lee and his brother William when they were thousands of miles away and unable to reply. This was done by Deane, he asserted, for the purpose of
turning public attention away from his own shortcomings, for
he himself had charges to face.

Paine followed up this letter with other statements bearing
on the matter. These comments were printed in the newspapers
and contributed much to the sensational interest that surrounded
Deane and the commission in Paris, and Beaumarchais' claim
for reimbursement. On January 2, 1779, Paine wrote:

If Mr. Deane or any other gentleman will procure an order from
Congress to inspect an account in my office, or any of Mr. Deane's
friends in Congress will take the trouble of coming themselves, I will
give him or them my attendance, and shew them in handwriting which
Mr. Deane is well acquainted with, that the supplies he so pompously

plumes himself upon were promised and engaged, and that as a present, before he ever arrived in France; and the part that fell to Mr. Deane was only to see it done, and how he has performed that service the public are acquainted with.

The inference to be drawn from this statement is that the French Government gave its aid to the Colonies while it was still at peace with England. Such assertions had been made many times before, but Thomas Paine occupied an official position that gave weight to what he had to say. M. Gerard was furious. On January 4 he declared to Congress, "That all the supplies furnished by M. de Beaumarchais to the States, whether merchandise or cannons and military goods, were furnished in the way of commerce, and that the articles which came from the king's magazine and arsenals were sold to M. de Beaumarchais by the department of artillery, and that he has furnished obligations for the price of these articles."

This statement made it quite clear that M. Gerard had identified himself with the interests of Beaumarchais, but it did not end the controversy. The next day—January 5—Paine published an article in which he denied Deane's complaint that he had "suffered" for the American cause. The emissary to France, he said, had lived well and enjoyed himself while American soldiers were half-starving and almost naked. He asserted also that, "Those who are now her [America's] allies prefaced that alliance by an early and generous friendship," meaning that France gave us arms before the alliance. On that same day Gerard sent a protest to Congress against "indiscreet assertions" by an American public official. He asked Congress "to take measures suitable to the circumstances."

That brought a quick response from Congress. Paine was summoned to appear before that august body sitting in secret session with closed doors. John Jay, its president, asked him if he had written the articles that had appeared during the past month over the signature, *Common Sense*. Paine replied that he was their author; thereupon he was ordered to withdraw at once.

Next day, after pondering overnight on the state of affairs, he addressed a memorial to Congress in which he asked for a hearing. It contained this passage:

I cannot in duty to my character as a freeman submit to be censured unheard. I have evidence which I presume will justify me. And I entreat this House to consider how great their reproach will be should it be told that they passed a sentence upon me without hearing me, and that a copy of the charge against me was refused to me; and likewise how much that reproach will be aggravated should I afterwards prove the censure of this House to be a libel, grounded upon a mistake which they refused fully to inquire into.

Congress paid no attention to this communication, but Paine was advised privately by members who were on his side of the argument that action would soon be taken and that it would be unfavorable to him; probably he would be discharged from his office. His dereliction, they said, was in publishing the purport of secret documents concerning the aid given by France before the alliance. The facts presented by him to the public would not be challenged, but only his action in revealing them.

Next day—January 9, 1779—he sent in his resignation as Secretary of the Committee for Foreign Affairs, and it was accepted. In his letter of resignation he said, in part:

My wish and my intentions in all my late publications were to preserve the public from error and imposition, to support as far as laid in my power the just authority of the representatives of the people, and to cordiallize and cement the union that has so happily taken place between this country and France.

I have betrayed no trust because I have constantly employed that trust to the public good. I have revealed no secrets because I have told nothing that was, or I conceive ought to be, a secret. I have convicted Mr. Deane of error, and in so doing I hope I have done my duty.

This letter of resignation was followed by several other communications to Congress, all of them about the French alliance, Silas Deane, and claims of Beaumarchais. In one of them he said:

I have repeatedly written to Congress respecting Mr. Deane's dark, incendiary conduct and offered every information in my power. The opportunities I have had of knowing the state of foreign affairs is greater than that of many gentlemen of this House, and I want no other knowledge to declare that I look on Mr. Deane to be, what Mr. Carmichael calls him, a rascal.

5

Within a week after Paine had lost his job with the Committee for Foreign Affairs he was offered a more lucrative post. Astonishing as it may seem, the offer came from M. Gerard de Rayneval, Minister of France at Philadelphia. On January 17 he wrote a long letter to the Comte de Vergennes, of which the following paragraphs are extracts:

When I had denounced to Congress the assertions of M. Paine I did not conceal from myself the bad effects that might result to a head puffed up by the success of his political writings and the importance he affected. I foresaw the loss of his office, and feared that, separated from the support which has restrained him, he would seek only to avenge himself with his characteristic impetuosity and impudence.

All means of restraining him would be impossible, considering the enthusiasm here for the license of the press, and in the absence of any laws to repress audacity even against foreign powers.

Gerard goes on to say that he offered Paine one thousand dollars a year to "employ his pen mainly in impressing on the people favorable sentiments towards France and the alliance, of the kind fittest to foster hatred and defiance of England . . . you know too well the prodigious effects produced by the writings of this famous personage among the people of the States to cause me any fear of your disapproval of my resolution."

Paine did not accept Gerard's offer. In reference to the matter he wrote several months later: "My answer to the offer was precisely in these words: 'Any service I can render to either of the countries in alliance, or to both, I ever have done and shall readily do, and Mr. Gerard's *esteem* will be the only compensation I shall desire.' "

Beaumarchais kept on nagging at Congress for a settlement of his accounts, and the United States did finally remit to him, through Dr. Franklin, bills—meaning promissory notes—amounting to one hundred thousand pounds sterling, which were to fall due at the end of three years from their date of issue. But the total amount demanded, which Beaumarchais insisted on being paid, was much in excess of one hundred thousand pounds sterling. Beaumarchais wrote at once to the American Commission that the three-year bills were of no value to him. Their maturity was too far away to have them discounted, and the reputation of the Americans for dishonoring their bills made their obligations difficult to handle even if they had a short maturity.

In 1793 Beaumarchais' claims were examined by Alexander Hamilton. He reported that the amount still owed by the United States was two million two hundred and eighty thousand livres at least, but the accounts were such a tangled mess that the full total might run to more than three million livres. Figuring the livre at twenty cents, the amount still due in 1793, if Hamilton's accounting is correct, was about six hundred thousand dollars.

But what had become of the contention that the gift from the French treasury covered the whole of the Beaumarchais claim, and that the United States owed him nothing?

The answer, made by the believers in the probity and fair dealing of Beaumarchais, was that even if he had received the King's gift for disbursement the total amount expended by him on behalf of the Americans far exceeded the two million livres granted by royal favor.

The doubters meet that explanation with sneering disbelief. He did not spend more than the two million livres, they say, if that much; but he doubled or trebled the price of everything he bought when he made out his bills.

Notwithstanding his losses in America—if any—Beaumarchais grew richer as the years went by. In the late 1780's he built a palatial mansion in Paris opposite the Bastille. It cost 1,663,000 francs, and was an enormous structure, surrounded by a formal garden of the English pattern, with grottoes, statues and fountains. The house was equally gorgeous inside, with its high carved ceilings, its gilt chandeliers, its great winding staircase. In Beaumarchais' study the desk that he used for his literary work cost thirty thousand francs.[2]

When the French Revolution began Beaumarchais got on the winning side. The Mayor of Paris appointed him to supervise the destruction of the Bastille. Soon thereafter he was suspected of being a secret agent of the Royalists. He was sent to prison and was in imminent danger of being condemned to death when, at the last moment, he was set free. His release was accomplished by his mistress, Amelie Houret, who used the ancient method of sexual seduction to win the favor of his accuser. At liberty again, he went to Holland to purchase sixty thousand muskets which he endeavored to sell to the Revolutionists.

For some reason which is not clear the Convention decided not to buy the arms. Instead he was denounced before that body —this was in 1792—as "an out-and-out vicious man, who has reduced immorality into a principle and rascality into a system." He was formally accused of conspiracy, correspondence with the Royalists, and embezzlement. He was then in Holland, but he fled at once to England, where he sold secretly his store of arms to the English.

Then he learned that the French Convention had sequestered his property and sent his wife and daughter to prison. He made up his mind to return at once to France, face his accusers in the Convention and vindicate himself. His friends in London tried to persuade him not to go; they pointed out that he would be sent at once to the guillotine. This was during the Reign of Terror in 1793.

Their pleas were unavailing and as a last resort one of them, to whom Beaumarchais owed money, had him sent to the debtors' prison in order to keep him out of France. Somehow he raised the funds to pay off this debt, was released from prison and did go to Paris. He went before the Convention and made

---

[2] This ornate palace was torn down many years ago. The Boulevard Beaumarchais now covers its site.

a speech which was so well received that it was applauded by the members. They suspended the decree against him, returned his property and released his wife and daughter.

The Convention sent him to Holland again to purchase arms, but the Committee of Public Safety found his conduct suspicious and brought fresh charges against him. He evaded capture and wandered about Germany in poverty for two years. In 1796 he was allowed to return to France and his property was given back to him. He died in his sleep in 1799. There was a general belief, at the time, that his death was the result of poison, self-administered.

After his death it was learned that he had given away secretly in the early days of the French Revolution more than 900,000 francs to relieve the distress of artists, men of letters and impoverished gentlefolk. In his will he mentioned his claim against the United States and bequeathed it to his daughter. The American Congress, in a generous mood in the year 1835, paid that lady (Madame Delarue) 800,000 francs, or $160,-000, to settle the claim in full, but there was not then, and is not now, any definite proof that the claim was justified.

In June of the year 1780 Silas Deane returned to France for the purpose of putting his accounts in order and getting his records in such shape that they might be submitted to Congress. Also he intended to settle some private business affairs of his own before returning to the United States. His wife had died, his home in Connecticut was broken up, and his official position was lost, so he might as well take his time about returning to America.

While he was in Europe he wrote, in the early summer of 1781, nine letters to intimate friends in America which were sent in one batch on a vessel that was captured by the British. In these letters he deplored the war, said the Americans were led by unprincipled and vicious men, and expressed his opinion that the Colonies should have remained in the British Empire. In his letter to Robert Morris, he wrote:

Will sovereignty, in the hands of a democracy, be a government under which our persons and property will be better secured than before the contest began? Will the country flourish more under independency than while connected with Great Britain?

In another of the letters he said it was the interest of Great Britain to promote our commerce in fish, lumber and shipbuilding. But if we become independent she will shut her West India ports; sugar, coffee and spices will be high; England will drive us out of our fisheries and Sweden and Russia will undersell us in timber and ships. Without England behind us, we shall be a target for insult on every side.

His letter to another friend laid emphasis on England's restraint in dealing with the misdeeds of the Colonials; there had been no promiscuous hangings, dungeons, or cruelties of any kind.

Each of the nine letters was written in a similar vein. It was plainly evident that his purpose was to create dissensions and doubts among the Americans for the purpose of bringing them back to English sovereignty.

The British, having captured the letters and read them, realized how destructive they could be to the morale of the Americans. In New York there was, at that time, a Tory newspaper, *The Royal Gazette*, and in that periodical Deane's letters were printed in full. Soon afterward they appeared in a book. These publications settled the fate of Silas Deane. If he had returned to America he would have been in danger of lynching. He went to England where he became friendly with Benedict Arnold. His condition was pathetic. He had no business, was in ill health, and lived precariously on loans.

In 1789 he went aboard a ship at Deal with the intention of going to Canada. He died suddenly on board the vessel when it was only a few miles from shore. It put back to port and his body was laid to rest in the cemetery at Deal.

Congress, in 1842, voted $37,000 to his heirs in recognition of his services in his early days in France.

6

The class distinctions that existed in the American Colonies and in the early decades of the republic have been so ignored by historians in general that most of the present generation is unaware of them. The United States, during and after the Revolution until the era of Jackson's administration in the 1830's, was not a democracy but a nation in which all the power was vested in the upper class. Workmen and farmers and laboring people generally had no votes and nothing to say about public affairs. Among the signers of the Declaration of Independence there was no individual who represented the common people.

On the other hand there was an ever-present fear among the higher classes—meaning the wealthy, the learned and the fashionable—that the common people would get out of hand and attempt to take control of the government. Those without fortune or aristocratic connections were known as "the common herd," "the mobility" or "the mobocracy." These distinctions were not only political; they pervaded every department of life. The achievements of those belonging to the common herd were often praised and encouraged but they themselves were expected to keep their places on the lower levels.

When Paine's fate was being discussed in Congress this attitude was exhibited by some of the members. Gouverneur Morris, a confirmed snob who led the New York delegation, rose in the secret session and delivered these sentiments:

"What would be the idea of a gentleman of Europe of this Mr. Paine? Would he not suppose him to be a man of the most affluent fortune, born in this country of a respectable family, with wide and great connections, and endowed with the nicest sense of honor? Certainly he would suppose that all these pledges of fidelity were necessary to a people in our critical circumstances. But, alas, what would he think, should he accidentally be informed, that this, our Secretary of Foreign Affairs, was a mere adventurer *from England*, without fortune, without family or connections, ignorant even of grammar? . . . And yet, Sir, this is the man whom we would remove from office, and this is the man who has been just now puffed as of great importance."

Paine's resignation came in time to stop the discussion of his case. If the matter had come to a vote it is likely that the resolution to put him out of his official position would have been carried. Nevertheless, and despite the class snobbery expressed by Gouverneur Morris, the author of *Common Sense* had some powerful friends. Among them were Thomas Jefferson, James Madison, Henry Laurens, General Nathanael Greene, James Monroe, General Roberdeau and, of course, the venerable Benjamin Franklin.

CHAPTER VII

The Revolution's Financial Crisis

I

THE fact that he was the best known author in America was small comfort to Thomas Paine when measured against the pressing hardships of no work and no money. The Secretaryship of the Foreign Affairs Committee had been too poorly paid to permit him to save money; and his quixotic streak had kept him from accepting any pay for his patriotic writings on American affairs.

In a letter to Henry Laurens he wrote on September 14, 1779:

I find myself so curiously circumstanced that I have both too many friends and too few, the generality of them thinking that from the public part I have so long acted I cannot have less than a mine to draw from. What they have had from me they have got for nothing, and they consequently suppose I must be able to afford it.

He had to borrow money to live on—to buy meals, to pay his laundress, to provide candles, to cover the rent of his room. To a man with his sense of pride such an existence was unspeakably humiliating, and he was relieved when Owen Biddle offered him a petty clerkship.

His duties appear, from this distance in time, to have been the taking care of part of Biddle's correspondence and the filing of documents. The amount of his salary is not known, but it must have been small, for the job was an insignificant one. It brought in enough to keep him alive and, as the work took only a little of his time, he had plenty of leisure for writing.

At that time—in the middle period of the American Revolution—there was a strong and popular movement in Pennsylvania against profiteering. Prices of all commodities had gone up enormously since the beginning of the war and were still rising.

The greater part of the rise was the result of economic conditions, such as the scarcity of goods and the confusion in the matter of currency, but there was also much scandalous profit-grabbing by the principal merchants.

Paine took a prominent part in the campaign against these abuses. The leaders of the movement tried to set what we call today a "price ceiling" on all goods in general use. Paine's activities in this direction made many new friends for himself, and also a number of enemies.

The runaway currency inflation, which ran unchecked for five years—from 1775 to 1780—led to a general economic madness which made it impossible to plan expenses ahead, or to forecast the purchasing power of incomes.

The amount of currency, both coin and paper, in circulation as of May, 1775, in all the thirteen Colonies, was carefully estimated at $12,000,000 (meaning Spanish silver dollars) and the population of the Colonies was about 3,000,000. The standard currency was British, of course, and its values were expressed in pounds and shillings. But a large proportion of the coin actually in use consisted of Spanish silver dollars which the American Colonists obtained through trade with the West Indies. The Spanish dollar was worth four British or American shillings and each quarter of a dollar was divisible further into two "bits." This Spanish currency was in general use, and values were usually stated in its terms.

The Continental Congress had no power of taxation, nor did it possess funds of any kind except those furnished voluntarily by the states. When in need of money to pay its troops, or to buy supplies, or to meet its own current expenses the Congress at first called upon the states, apportioning the amount to be contributed by each state according to its population and wealth. Some of the states paid up promptly, but most of them paid their assessments only in part or not at all. That the war could not be financed in this manner was soon evident; and, as a result, the Congress decided to issue a currency of its own.

This Continental paper money had no actual funds behind it,

and its value rested on the act of Congress which made it full legal tender. Depreciation began almost at once. The situation might have been manageable if the Continental Congress had alone possessed the authority to issue money, but such was not the case. It must be kept in mind, if one hopes to understand these financial complications, that the states had not surrendered their own sovereign powers. Each of them, until they were all united by the Constitution in 1789, was free and independent. The Continental Congress had very little more actual power than that of any advisory council. Every state, from New Hampshire to Georgia, issued paper money of its own which was also legal tender within the state. Then, besides these various issues, British money was still in circulation; and, to make bad matters even worse, the British began to counterfeit the paper money of Congress. The counterfeits, which could not be distinguished from genuine bills, were sent to America in huge quantities and distributed by British sympathizers and secret agents.

2

As the volume of currency increased the prices of all commodities rose in proportion. Congress appealed to the states to fix wages of labor, the charges of innkeepers, and the prices of all necessary commodities, such as food and clothing. At the close of the year 1777 the volume of Continental currency in circulation was $55,500,000 and prices, in spite of all restrictive legislation, were about four times higher than those of 1775.

The paper money kept on pouring from the presses and prices rose to fantastic heights. Paine solemnly records that he paid $300 in Continental money for a pair of woolen stockings. The movement in Philadelphia to prevent profiteering and exorbitant prices had its counterpart in many other parts of the country. Strange as it seems to a modern observer of these events, the agitators against excessive profits seldom considered the rise in the cost of living to be the result of the tremendous increase in the volume of currency; they usually laid it at the door of merchants and shopkeepers, who were accused of extortionate greed. The shops had three or four prices for everything on sale. If the customer paid in Spanish silver dollars he got the benefit of the lowest price; the next higher price was paid in British money; then came the price in Continental currency; and the highest price of all was to the unfortunate holder of the money issued by a state.

All the Continental money issued up to 1781 was called "old tenor" currency to distinguish it from the "new tenor" issues that began to appear in May of that year. The old tenor currency amounted to the huge total of $357,000,000, or about $119 per capita for the three million inhabitants of the country. Congress took the matter in hand and passed an act which deprived the old tenor currency of its legal tender quality. Holders of this disqualified paper could exchange it for new tenor bills at the ratio of forty to one. One hundred dollars of the old money was equal in value to two dollars and a half of the new issue.

It put an end to the inflation, but it must have been hard on the frugal citizens who had been saving their cash. All of a sudden their money became worthless.

About $120,000,000 of the old tenor currency was turned in for exchange within a year or two, and after 1790 the treasury redeemed $6,000,000 more at the ratio of one hundred to one. The remainder of the old tenor—$2,300,000 in all—was never presented for redemption. For many years the Continental currency was the subject of innumerable jokes. A comedian, for instance, had a complete suit made of worthless bills and wore it on the stage amid gales of laughter. In Virginia the owner of a hunting lodge had the walls of its rooms papered with Continental money, and dashing young bloods often lighted their cigars with this blighted currency. In describing anything that was completely worthless one said, "It's not worth a Continental."

On May 27, 1779, there was a mass meeting in Philadelphia at which a Committee of Inspection was formed for the purpose of calling on merchants, innkeepers and all others who dealt with the public. Thomas Paine was made a member of this important committee. Among his fellow members were Colonel J. B. Smith; Timothy Matlack, the "Fighting Quaker"; and Charles Willson Peale, the portrait painter. The committee had no legal standing, but it proposed to accomplish its ends by popular pressure; or by force, if necessary.

Among those who came under the critical stare of the Committee of Inspection was Robert Morris, one of the wealthiest men in Philadelphia. In combination with a Mr. Solikoff, of Baltimore, he had bought up the entire supply of flour in the Philadelphia area and was keeping it off the market in order to raise the price. The families of mechanics and laborers had already given up bread as beyond their means and were using potatoes in its place.

The resolution which the committee adopted in this case was surprisingly mild in tone. It appealed to Morris' patriotism and sense of fair play. He was asked to consider the needs of the people, "for though as a merchant," the resolution read, "he may be strictly within rules, yet when he considers the many public and honorary stations he has filled, and the times he lives in, he must feel himself somewhat out of character."

In this instance the action of the committee was effective. Robert Morris, appealed to as a gentleman and a patriot, was moved to put his large holdings of flour within reach of the public at fair prices, and thereafter he kept out of all speculations which made profit by raising the cost of human necessities. But on the whole, the efforts of the Committee of Inspection were a failure, even though its campaign against profiteering was strongly supported by the community. The currency situation was in such frantic disorder that it threw everything in the economic world out of balance.

In his letter to Henry Laurens in September, 1779, Paine outlined a plan for the publication of *Common Sense* and his other writings in a two-volume edition. He said the paper for these volumes would have to come from abroad, and suggested that Arthur Lee might buy it in France if furnished with the necessary funds. He intended to sell this literary work by subscription, and said he had no doubt the sale would be large. Then, when that was done, he proposed to write a history of the Revolution in three volumes, "and to publish one each year from the time of beginning, and to make an abridgement afterwards in an easy, agreeable language for a schoolbook." [1]

In the last paragraph of his letter he asks Laurens in a shy and timid manner for a loan until he can get the work under way, and he concludes by saying, "I have hitherto kept all my private matters a secret, but as I know your friendship and you a great deal of my situation, I can with more ease communicate them to you than to another."

He wrote also in the same letter:

I know but one kind of life I am fit for, and that is a thinking one, and, of course, a writing one—but I have confined myself so much of late, taken so little exercise, and lived so very sparingly, that unless I alter my way of life it will alter me. I think I have a right to ride a horse of my own, but I cannot even afford to hire one, which is a situation I never was in before, and I begin to know that a sedentary life cannot be supported without jolting exercise.

Henry Laurens probably made him a loan, though there is no record of it, and it is also fairly certain that he was aided financially at that time, and at other periods in his life, by well-to-do and highly placed people who admired his work and desired to encourage it.

3

Paine considered himself the leading propagandist of the American Revolution—as he certainly was—and he did not hesitate

---

[1] Neither of those projects was carried out. No collected edition of Paine's works appeared until 1925, when a ten-volume edition was published under the auspices of the Thomas Paine National Historical Association, which has its headquarters in New Rochelle, New York. The ten volumes contain everything that Paine had written. The history of the American Revolution that he had in mind was never finished.

to say so. On September 26, 1779, he wrote to Joseph Reed, President of the Supreme Executive Council of Pennsylvania, a letter of complaint about the indifference of the state to his welfare. He said in the letter:

I cannot but observe that the course of four years have produced no other signature universally known and read here and abroad except that under which I have constantly published, and should my situation be rendered such as shall oblige me to discontinue the part I have hitherto acted, it will not be easy to establish a new signature that shall collect and keep the sentiments of the country together, should any future emergency arise, which to me appears very probable.

This letter was written near the close of a political campaign in Pennsylvania between the constitutionalists and the reactionaries. In 1776 the State of Pennsylvania had adopted a liberal constitution, with what amounted to practically universal suffrage as its basis. There were also other democratic features. For the campaign of 1779 the conservatives or reactionaries, meaning the big merchants, the wealthy landowners and the aristocrats got together and made a strong effort to win the election and clear the ground for a new and less liberal constitution.

Paine was not a candidate for office, but he was a conspicuous symbol for the reactionaries to attack, and he was discussed violently, pro and con, during the campaign. The election took place on October 12, and the liberals won.

As soon as the newly elected Pennsylvania Assembly met, on November 2, 1779, it elected Thomas Paine its clerk. It was a godsend for him, just at that time. He wrote to Henry Laurens: "The clerkship is not much, but it is something like business and has released me from that burden of idleness, uneasiness and hopeless thinking that got so much the upper hand of me for three or four months past."

On the first day of the new session of the Assembly a bill to abolish slavery in the state was introduced. It became a law on March 1, 1780, and the six thousand slaves owned by Pennsylvanians were freed. This was gratifying to Paine, who was one of the first agitators in the antislavery cause.

It was not a cheerful period for the American Revolutionists. Washington's troops passed a miserable winter at Morristown, in New Jersey, where at times it seemed as if the army would have to disband, not because of unwillingness to carry on, but because of their destitution.

In a letter written by Washington on January 5, he said:

The troops, both officers and men, have borne their distress with a patience scarcely to be conceived. Many of the latter have been four or five days without meat entirely and short of bread, and none but very scanty supplies. Some, for their preservation, have been compelled to maraud and rob from the inhabitants, and I have it not in my power to punish or reprove the practice. If our condition should not undergo a very speedy and considerable change for the better, it will be difficult to point out all the consequences that may ensue.

Washington was, without a doubt, the gloomiest letter writer among all the great names in American history, but it must be said that his depressing communications during the Revolution were fully justified by the state of affairs.

The alliance with France, from which so much was expected, had produced nothing except some inconsequential naval co-operation until July, 1780, when Rochambeau and his army arrived. The British were winning in the South; they had over-run Georgia and had taken Charleston after a siege. Moreover, the ragged, poorly fed and half-trained American forces were no match for them and were put to rout when they met the British in battle.

The monetary inflation hung over the land like a vast black cloud and defeated the half-hearted attempts to provide for the armed forces. The price of a soldier's overcoat was anywhere from $200 to $500 in Continental money, and if the quarter-master's department waited until the next week to buy it the price would probably be still higher.

On May 28 Washington wrote to Joseph Reed that "every idea you can form of our distresses will fall short of the reality. There is such a combination of circumstances to exhaust the patience of the soldiery that it begins at length to be worn out, and we see in every line of the army the most serious features of mutiny and sedition."

Paine, as Clerk of the Assembly, read this letter to the legislative body. Nothing was done at that session to meet the impending disaster to the army, for no one knew exactly what to do. Next day Paine went to the state treasurer and drew his salary of $1,699. With $500 of this money he headed a subscription list for relief of the army. He turned over the money and the subscription paper that he had prepared to Mr. McClenaghan (one of the members of the Assembly) for the purpose of getting more contributions. Robert Morris and McClenaghan each subscribed two hundred pounds in "hard money," which meant that it was either in British or Spanish silver dollars.

This particular effort to raise a fund for the army became extremely popular. Everybody, rich and poor, was expected to contribute according to his means. The ladies took up the idea and organized "The American Daughters of Liberty" as a collection force. They went all over the city and a householder who could not spare any money might make a contribution of clothing or food. When the campaign was over it was found that 300,000 pounds had been raised. These funds were used to establish a bank which looked after the army's needs during the campaign of 1780, and was incorporated as the Bank of Pennsylvania in December.

During the year Paine wrote and published three issues of the *Crisis*. In March he brought out No. VIII, addressed *To the People of England*. On June 9 there was another issue which dealt with the reverses suffered by the Americans during that spring. Paine pointed out that these defeats, as grievous as they were, struck at no vital spot but were only ineffectual nibbles. He wrote:

They [the British] have deserted their capital design, prudently contenting themselves with what they can get, and thus give a flourish of honor to conceal disgrace.

But this piecemeal work is not conquering the continent. It is a discredit in them to attempt it, and in us to suffer it. It is now full time to put an end to a war of aggravations which, on one side, has no possible object, and on the other has every inducement which honor, interest, and safety and happiness can inspire.

In October he produced *Crisis Extraordinary: On the Subject of Taxation*. Paine realized that the Americans of that era hated taxes of any kind and were inclined to fight even a suggestion that the expenses of the government and the support of the army be raised by taxation when the printing presses were ready and waiting to print paper money in vast quantities.

He attempted in the *Crisis Extraordinary* to convince his readers that taxation is preferable to debt and financial chaos, and that all necessary outlays for the war and the expenses of government could be met by a tax program which would be much lighter than that imposed on the inhabitants of England.

The pamphlet is full of statistics and Paine's explanation of them. "The average tax per head in England is forty shillings," he wrote; and he went on to say that "a tax of thirteen shillings four pence a head in America should be quite sufficient to support the army and carry on the government of all the states and the expenses of the Continental Congress."

It contains sound ideas—this pamphlet of twenty-five pages —and was, no doubt, widely read, like everything else that he wrote, but there is no evidence that it had any pronounced effect on taxation measures.

On July 4, 1780, Thomas Paine was given an honorary degree of Master of Arts by the University of Pennsylvania. Among the trustees who voted for him in awarding the degree were Joseph Reed, President of the State; and a bishop and four ministers.

4

A French fleet, convoying a swarm of troopships with 5500 soldiers aboard, arrived at Newport in July of the memorable year of 1780. This small French army sat down in Rhode Island and did absolutely nothing for a year except entertain the inhabitants. They went in for sports, receptions, balls, brass band music and amateur theatricals. Even Washington, meeting Rochambeau in a solemn conference speckled with maps and figures, was unable to persuade him to move out of Newport and lend his aid to an attack on New York, then held by the British.

Nevertheless, the presence of the French army in Rhode Island was indirectly effective. As long as they were within striking distance of New York Sir Henry Clinton, the British Commander in Chief, refrained from moving troops to reinforce Cornwallis in the South. Moreover, the mere presence of the French army inspired the American soldiers to take on renewed courage and determination.

Paine had still kept alive his intention of writing a history of the American Revolution, and was eager to begin the actual work on it. He had saved enough from his salary as Clerk of the Pennsylvania Assembly to give him means to live a few months without earning money. Early in November, 1780, he wrote to the Speaker of the Assembly that he intended to give up his position when his year of service had expired, which meant that he would not continue as Clerk after the middle of that month. His resignation was accepted, and as soon as he found himself at liberty he began to assemble his notes for the history that he had planned to write.

But Fate, in her familiar role of interfering with the affairs of men, had other plans for Thomas Paine. He was to go to France as the unofficial secretary of a special envoy whose mission was to explain the military situation to the King and his ministers and to plead with them for money and supplies.

In the secret sessions of the Continental Congress during the winter of 1780–81 the good faith of France as an ally of the revolting Colonies had been called in question. The French fleet, after escorting Rochambeau's troops from France, had sailed away to the West Indies on business of its own. The French army in America dawdled away its time in Newport while the southern Colonies were being devastated by Lord Cornwallis. The American army was on the point of mutiny because of destitution and lack of pay. Besides there were rumors that the French did not want to bring the war to a close but were devising means to have it continue for years, to exhaust the British.

After much debate Congress decided to send to France Colonel John Laurens, of Washington's staff, for the purpose of giving the French High Command full information concerning the military problem in America. He was expected also to supply fresh arguments to induce the French to furnish money, clothing and munitions. In making this move it was not the intention of Congress to supersede the American Commission then in Paris, which consisted of Benjamin Franklin, Arthur Lee and John Adams. The latter had taken the place formerly held by Silas Deane on the three-man commission. Laurens' place was that of an aide, or military expert.

John Laurens, a son of Henry Laurens, was a young South Carolina gentleman. Like many Americans of that time, he had received his education in Europe. He was intensely patriotic, chivalrous and courteous, but his courtesy was of the aristocratic kind; it ran swiftly from a polite demeanor into an insulting churlishness. Like most people who are quick to take offense, he was also prompt in being offensive to others. He was only twenty-six years old and, if character and disposition mean anything, he was distinctly unfitted for a diplomatic mission. That it was a success, in spite of his maladroitness, is convincing proof that the French were determined to aid the Americans to the full extent of their means, and to bring the war to a close with the defeat of the British.

Laurens said he would accept the mission if Thomas Paine could accompany him. He liked Paine, who was seventeen years his senior and of a wholly different station in life. They were bound together in their detestation of the British, and both young Laurens and his father were great admirers of Paine's writings. At that very time his father was a prisoner in the Tower of London. He had been sent by Congress to Holland to arrange a loan in that country, and on the way his vessel was captured by a British frigate.

Paine accepted the offer of young Laurens, who wanted him

as his official secretary. But it became apparent that the proposal to give Paine an official standing would meet determined opposition in Congress, so it was arranged that he would accompany Laurens in a private capacity. There was probably some agreement under which Laurens would pay his expenses and, perhaps, a small salary—but, if so, no record of it exists. At any rate, Paine was penniless on his return from France and had to borrow money to go from Boston to Philadelphia.

Before they left America Laurens received a letter from Washington to be given to Benjamin Franklin in Paris. In it the General wrote: "What I have said to him [Colonel Laurens] I beg leave to repeat to you that, to me, nothing appears more evident than that the period of our opposition will very shortly arrive if our allies can not afford us that effectual aid, particularly in money and naval superiority, which are now solicited." Washington told Laurens that Franklin had his consent to show the letter to the French ministry.

Paine and Laurens sailed from Boston on the frigate *Alliance* February 11, 1781. They arrived at L'Orient, France, March 9. Laurens went at once to Paris, but for some unexplained reason Paine proceeded more slowly in company with Jonathan Williams, a nephew of Franklin.

There were no official duties for him on this mission; he appears to have been merely an onlooker and a counselor, in private, to John Laurens. As in some other periods of his life, there is an exasperating lack of information about his stay in Paris. He had never before been in France, and what he saw on his first trip must have seemed strange and interesting and vivid. But not a word of it appears in his writings. He might have been making a trip to Newark, New Jersey, if one judges of the place by Paine's lack of excitement. He could not speak French, but that did not prevent him from looking at the sights. We do not even know where he lived, whether with friends or in a *pension*. On his return to America he wrote a long letter to Jonathan Williams, who was still in France (he became the Consul of the United States at Nantes) and thanked that gentleman for his courtesies, but nearly all the letter was taken up with impersonal matters. At its conclusion he says: "Remember me to Mr. and Mrs. Johnstone, Dr. Pierce, Mr. Watson & Ceasey and Mr. Wilt. Make my best wishes to Mrs. Williams, Mrs. Alexander, and all the good girls at St. Germain." Evidently he met some people socially, and all of them were Americans.

Young Mr. Laurens was so brusque in addressing Vergennes that the dignified minister sent for Franklin and told him that unless Laurens mended his manners he would not be received again. It seems, from reports of his conduct, that he threatened Vergennes, telling him that unless the French took a more active part in the war America would make peace with the British and then join them in their war against France. He asked not only for more military and naval assistance, but also for an outright gift of twenty-five million livres.

Franklin called in the hotheaded young man and counseled him in a fatherly way to approach Vergennes in a more respectful manner. Laurens may have followed this advice in part, or as far as his nature would allow him, but at any rate the French Ministry made the Americans a gift of 2,500,000 livres and two shiploads of supplies.

On their return from France Paine and Laurens reached Boston on the French frigate *La Resolute* on August 25, 1781. In the hold of the ship the 2,500,000 livres lay in casks, and there were two accompanying ships freighted with goods for the American army.

This generous contribution to the American cause just at that time was of immense help. The silver money was carried in sixteen ox-carts from Boston to Philadelphia. Robert Morris, then Superintendent of Finance, had the whole sum deposited in the bank where it was not sent immediately to the vaults, but piled high on the bank's counters as an exhibit. The public got an impression that the bank had more coin than it could find room for in its vault. Business began to get better, and people grew more cheerful. Washington's soldiers got all their back pay, and fresh outfits. Rochambeau's French army, in obedience to orders from

Paris, moved out of Newport and marched across New England and down through New Jersey to join Washington. Lafayette, in Virginia, was slowly driving Cornwallis into the little pen of Yorktown. With drums beating and flags flying the combined American and French armies marched through Philadelphia on their way to Virginia.

The Revolutionary War was drawing swiftly to a close.

5

On his return from France, by way of Boston, Paine had to borrow a dollar to pay his passage on the ferry across the Delaware River. Laurens had hurried on ahead to announce the news of the French gift to Congress. Evidently Paine arrived in Philadelphia without a penny or any means of support. But he could always borrow from his friends.

He wrote on October 4, 1781, to John Laurens, who was then with Washington's army in Virginia, about a lost trunk, a mislaid letter and a pair of boots which Laurens had ordered before he left Philadelphia.

I went for your boots the next day after you left town, but they were not done, and I directed the man to bring them to me as soon as finished, but have since seen nothing of him, neither do wish him to bring them just now, as I must be obliged to borrow the money to pay for them; but I imagine somebody else has taken them off his hands. I expect Col. Morgan in town on Saturday who has some money of mine in his hands, and then I shall renew my application to the bootmaker.

I wish you had thought of me a little before you went away, and at least endeavored to put matters in a train that I might not have to re-experience what has already past.

CHAPTER VIII

Paine as a Propagandist

I

IF YOU want to know how Paine looked at this period of his life just conceive a mental picture of a slender man, five feet nine inches in height, with a large head and rather narrow shoulders. He stood perfectly erect, straight as a ramrod. His hands and feet were rather small for his size and height. His eyes were large, dark blue in color, and were usually remembered by those who met him after the rest of his appearance had faded from memory. They had a piercing, blazing quality.

His voice was strong and sharp, and when he spoke there was no slurring of words, but every syllable and tone cut into the air distinctly. This was in keeping with his mental character, which was clear-cut and entirely devoid of shadowy convictions and misty ideas. He was always impatient with those who spoke or wrote in doubt and hesitation.

His disparagement of the opinions of others when they did not coincide with his own views caused many of his listeners and readers to look upon him with disfavor. Sir Leslie Stephen, writing of Paine in the *Dictionary of National Biography,* says: "Paine's bigotry was of the logical kind which can see only one side of a question, and imagines that all political and religious problems are as simple as the first propositions of Euclid."

Although he did not wear costly or showy clothes he was usually well-dressed. In his composition there were, no doubt, some reminiscent Quaker traits, for his garments were plain, sober in color and staid in appearance. He never sported the lace and frills and foppish ornaments which were fashionable among men of that period. Now and then he appeared in a soiled shirt or a frowsy neckpiece because of forgetfulness, and not as an evidence of a love of dirt, as some of his enemies have claimed. His occasional slovenliness meant that he had become so completely immersed in his projects and the labor of writing that he had forgotten to change his linen. There were days when he forgot to eat his meals.

He liked horseback riding, walking and skating. He rode well, could walk long distances over country roads and he was a graceful skater. In the evenings he seldom played cards, preferring such games as chess or checkers. But he never became absorbed in any form of amusement.

Paine's enemies, in their eager search for anything that might conceivably cast discredit upon him, have asserted frequently that he disliked women, treated them discourteously, and looked upon them as mere drudges and servants. He has been so often depicted as an unmannerly boor that the slander has taken root in the mind of the public, and is believed today by a countless number of people.

There is not a word of truth in it. Paine was courteous and pleasant in his relations with women, and some of them were among his cherished friends. He did not like off-color stories and would not listen to those who told them if he could leave the company without giving offence. He had a pronounced aversion to profanity, a dislike that probably grew out of his Quaker upbringing. No one ever heard him utter even a mild oath.

He was highly esteemed by most of the leaders of the American people during the Revolution. They were conscious of his ability and of his wholehearted devotion to their cause. But he was seldom invited to their houses, for by the social standards of that time he belonged to a lower class of society despite his intellectual attainments. He was, after all, they said among themselves, a common workman. The prevailing social rules were not wholly rigid, however, and there were exceptions. General Nathanael Greene and his family received Tom Paine in their home, and so did General Roberdeau—his wife and daughters—and these were not all. In New York, after the British had evacuated the city, Paine was received and entertained by a number of families of wealth and social position.

In this connection it should be said here that his social status did not cause him much—if any—distress, for he preferred the argumentative comradeship that is found in the taprooms of cheerful inns. The elegant life, with its luxuries and etiquette, held no attraction for him. He was a natural inhabitant of the typical furnished room that had a bed in one corner, a writing desk and bookcase near the window, and a washbowl and pitcher over by the closet.

If he had possessed only a small amount of diplomacy his talents would have lifted him to a high place among the statesmen of the period. But he was so candid that his frankness now and then ran into a contemptuous attitude toward those who did not agree with his ideas. He was far too outspoken for a civilization where courtesy was honored above ideas and where a duelist would bow gracefully to his opponent before sending a bullet through his heart.

Paine's confidence in the correctness of his own opinions, and of their importance, sometimes led him into exhibitions of intellectual vanity. In his manner of living, in his personal appearance, in his daily habits, he was commonplace and conventional; but in the mental arena he was no shrinking violet. In the *Rights of Man* he wrote this about himself:

With all the inconveniences of early life against me, I am proud to say, that with a perseverance undismayed by difficulties, a disinterestedness that compels respect, I have not only contributed to raise a new empire in the world, founded on a new system of government, but I have arrived at an eminence in political literature, the most difficult of all lines to succeed and excel in, which aristocracy, with all its aids, has not been able to reach or to rival.

Almost wholly lacking in modesty of the intellect, Paine was ready and willing to confront any adversary—no matter how distinguished—and, it must be said, in sober truth, that his arguments were usually sounder and more vital than those of his opponents. That is what made his career so disturbing in an age that was dominated largely by tradition, false assumptions and honored pretenses.

2

Cornwallis and his army of seven thousand men surrendered at Yorktown, Virginia, on October 19, 1781, to Washington and Rochambeau. Although the British still held the ports of New York, Charleston and Savannah, and a few other places of minor importance, everyone felt that the war was really over, and that there would be no more fighting.

The American people celebrated in their large-handed, joyous manner. Feasting and fireworks, music and dancing were the order of the day. Washington came to Philadelphia, was welcomed by Congress, and was received by the people with the acclaim that grateful nations give to their heroes.

In the midst of this jubilation one patriot who had done much to strengthen the courage of the people walked the streets with a heart full of gloom. Paine had given all he possessed in ability and energy to the American cause and now, in its day of triumph, it seemed to him that he was neglected and forgotten like a worn-out tool that had served its purpose and is finally thrown away.

Under date of November 30, 1781, he wrote to General Washington. His letter is too long to quote in its entirety, but here are some of its significant passages:

It is seven years *this day*, since I arrived in America and tho' I consider them as the most honorary time of my life, they have nevertheless been the most inconvenient and even distressing. From an anxiety to support, as far as laid in my power, the reputation of the Cause of America, as well as the Cause itself, I declined the customary profits which authors are entitled to, and I have always continued to do so; yet I never thought (if I thought at all on the matter) but that as I dealt generously and honorably by America, she would deal the same by me. But I have experienced the contrary—and it gives me much concern, not only on account of the inconvenience it has occasioned to me, but because it unpleasantly lessens my opinion of the character of a country which once appeared so fair, and it hurts my mind to see her so cold and inattentive to matters which affect her reputation.

Almost everybody knows, not only in this country but in Europe, that

I have been of service to her, and as far as the interest of the heart could carry a man I have shared with her in the worst of her fortunes, yet so confined have been my private circumstances that for one summer I was obliged to hire myself as a common clerk to Owen Biddle of this city, for my support; but this and many others of the like nature I have always endeavored to conceal, because to expose them would only serve to entail on her the reproach of being ungrateful, and might start an ill opinion of her honor and generosity in other countries, especially as there are pens enough abroad to spread and aggravate it.

Further on he says that he feels himself left in a very unpleasant situation and is at a loss as to why it should be so—

... for wherever I go I find respect, and everybody I meet treats me with friendship; all join in censuring the neglect and throwing the blame on each other, so that their civility disarms me as much as their conduct distresses me. But in this situation I cannot go on, and as I have no inclination to differ with the Country or to tell the story of her neglect, it is my design to get to Europe, either to France or Holland. I have literary fame, and I am sure I cannot experience worse fortune than I have here. . . .

In thus speaking to your Excellency I know I disclose myself to one who can sympathize with me, for I have often cast a thought at your difficult situation to smooth over the unpleasantness of my own.

They moved slowly in those days. Paine's letter to General Washington was written on the last day of November, but the Father of Our Country did nothing about it for some time.

On January 26 of the next year (1782) Robert Morris, who was at that time the Superintendent of Finance, records in his diary that Washington had spoken to him twice about Paine's financial difficulties and had suggested that something be done to assist him. Two weeks later there was a meeting at which Robert Morris, Robert Livingston (the Secretary of Foreign Affairs) and General Washington were present. These gentlemen agreed to give Paine, from the Secret Service fund, a salary of $800 per annum. As the Superintendent of Finance was not required to make any report on the disposal of Secret Service moneys the entire affair could be kept under cover, and that was thought to be the best policy at the time.

This payment of $800 annually was really not a salary within the ordinary meaning of the word. It was in the nature of a retainer fee. Paine had no fixed duties, no office nor office hours. He was expected to comment, from time to time, on public affairs but he was not subject to restraint or direction, although he might be called upon occasionally for some special duty.

He was really a public relations official, or press agent, of the flimsy central government, subject to restriction in expressing his own personal opinion concerning events.

The tenth *Crisis* appeared in print on March 5, 1782, about three weeks after the financial arrangement had been made. The last previous *Crisis* (No. IX) had been published in October 4, 1780. For more than a year Paine had been occupied with other matters. His trip to France with John Laurens had taken nearly six months of that period.

The theme of the tenth *Crisis* is the speech made by George III, King of England, before Parliament on November 27, 1781. The King urged a continuance of the war and, after some debate, his position was sustained by a vote of Parliament. Nevertheless, the war was over despite George III and his political henchmen. The British had lost two armies through surrender and they held only three ports—New York, Charleston and Savannah—on the Atlantic seaboard. The burden of the war on the English taxpayers had become almost unbearable. Moreover, the English people were unmistakably in favor of making peace and resuming trade relations with the Americans.

The chief purport of this latest number of the *Crisis* was to caution Americans not to take too much for granted, nor to assume hastily that the British would not undertake another campaign. Paine wrote: "Perhaps one of the greatest dangers which any country can be exposed to, arises from a kind of trifling which sometimes steals upon the mind when it supposes the danger past; and this unsafe situation marks at this time the peculiar crisis of America."

The next *Crisis* (No. XI) was published on May 31 of that year, which was 1782. Its incentive was the well-founded supposition that Britain would endeavor to break up the French-American alliance and make a separate peace with France. That would remove a powerful ally of the Americans and leave Britain in a position to continue the war. Paine wrote:

The policy of Britain has ever been to divide America in some way or other. In the beginning of the dispute she practiced every art to prevent or destroy the union of the states, well knowing that could she once get them to stand singly she could conquer them unconditionally. Failing in this project in America, she renewed it in Europe; and, after the alliance had taken place, she made secret offers to France to induce her to give up America; and what is still more extraordinary, she at the same time made propositions to Dr. Franklin, then in Paris, the very court to which she was secretly applying, to draw off America from France.

During the year 1782 Paine was as busy as a desk man on a modern daily paper. He turned out another *Crisis*—the twelfth —on October 29. It was addressed, on its title page, to the Earl of Shelburne, who was one of the well-known members of the war party in Parliament. Here is one passage from the pamphlet which indicates the spirit and style of the whole:

But is it possible that Lord Shelburne can be serious in supposing that the least advantage can be obtained by arms, or that any advantage can be equal to the expense or the danger of attempting it? Will not the capture of one army after another satisfy him, or must they all become prisoners? Must England ever be the sport of hope and the victim of delusion? Sometimes our currency was to fail; another time our army was to disband; then whole provinces were to revolt. Such a general said this and that; another wrote so and so; Lord Chatham was of this opinion; and lord somebody else of another. Today twenty thousand Russians and twenty Russian ships of the line were to come; tomorrow the Empress was abused without mercy or decency.

Then the Emperor of Germany was to be bribed with a million of money, and the King of Prussia was to do wonderful things. At one time it was Lo here! and then it was Lo there! Sometimes this power, and sometimes that power, was to engage in the war, just as if the whole world was mad and foolish like Britain. And thus, from year to year, has every straw been catched at, and every Will-with-a-wisp led them a new dance.

Observe the simplicity of Paine's style; it was one of his most outstanding literary characteristics. In that era it stood out like a white wall on a brown hillside, for the writers of the time took pride in presenting their ideas in tortuous, involved sentences.

In September appeared Paine's *Letter to the Abbé Raynal*, a pamphlet on which he had worked off and on for months, writing and revising. The Abbé was a distinguished French philosopher who was in exile on account of his pronounced liberalism. He was the author of a recent historical work entitled *Observations on the Revolution in America* that had been widely read in America and in Europe and had made a deep impression. The Abbé discussed the Revolution in a broad and scholarly manner and asserted that it was a mistake for America to insist on her independence. Everything that she gained thereby, he wrote, could have been obtained by remaining in the British Empire. The Americans had succeeded only in weakening themselves and the mother country by their separation. The whole controversy arose, he declared, because England laid a light, really insignificant stamp tax on the Colonies.

Paine, in his reply, points out that the Stamp Tax was only one of a series of stupid and autocratic efforts to control the whole course of American economy and industry by a government that existed three thousand miles from American shores— a government in which the Colonies had no representative and which they had no hand in shaping. He also defends, in this tract, the American alliance with France which Abbé Raynal (himself a Frenchman) characterized as an absurd union of a republic and a monarchy that could bring no happiness to mankind.

Reduced to its simplest form, Paine's reply is that the alliance with France accomplished its purpose; it won the war. But it went further than that, according to Paine, for he wrote:

Perhaps no two events ever united so intimately and forcibly to combat and expel prejudice, as the revolution of America and the alliance with France. . . . Our style and manner of thinking have undergone a revolution, more extraordinary than the political revolution of the country. We see with other eyes; we hear with other ears; and think with other thoughts, than those we formerly used. . . . It was not all the argument, however powerful, nor all the reasoning, however eloquent, that could have produced this change, so necessary to the extension of the mind, and the cordiality of the world, without the two circumstances of the revolution and the alliance.

The *Letter to the Abbé Raynal* is more than a reply to the Abbé's critical comments on the French-American alliance. Its chief quality, and its most convincing one, is its argument for internationalism, for a federation of all the nations of the world. Paine had ceased to think in national terms; he had begun to think in terms of humanity.

We can read in these pages, as in other writings of his later years, a growing conception of universal philanthropy; of the belief that the decent human spirit could be made an inalienable and ever-present element of the policy of all nations. He believed that collective *interest* and collective *good* are one and the same, but neither individual nor collective interest can be sound if it infringes on the rights of others. The idea that all nations, and all men, can attain peace, content and happiness, became a cardinal principle of Paine's way of thinking. "Nations, like individuals," he wrote, "who have long been enemies, without knowing each other, or knowing why, become the better friends when they discover the errors and impositions under which they had acted."

The reply to Abbé Raynal is called a "letter," but the term is misleading. It is not a letter but a book; it occupies one hundred printed pages. It will interest any student of American history, although it is more than a hundred and fifty years old, for Paine wrote in it his account of the beginning of the war and of the American methods of carrying it on.

Paine's genius—and it was distinctly a type of genius—lay in his ability to perceive truth and to present it to its readers so simply, so deftly and yet so forcibly that it carried a blaze of conviction to all except the addle-heads whose minds had hardened into a granite-like structure of error. He could take an abstruse and tiresome philosophic speculation, comprehensible in the original to only a few scholars, and set it forth in such a manner that anyone who had enough intelligence to read could grasp its import.

He was a propagandist of astonishing ability but, during his first thirty-seven years in England, neither he nor anyone else suspected that he possessed this hidden talent. America gave him a new life; here he was born again. In this second manhood abilities that had been latent within him came into dynamic movement.

Paine had managed to save enough money from his stipend and the small sums he received from articles and casual literary work to buy a house at Bordentown in New Jersey, about thirty-five miles above Philadelphia on the Delaware River. There is no existing record of what the house cost nor any adequate description of it. We know, however, that it stood on a tenth of an acre—a plot of forty by one hundred feet—and that it was a small, plain cottage.

He bought this house because his devoted friend, Colonel Joseph Kirkbride, lived in Bordentown and Paine wanted to live near him. The two houses were close together; side by side, in fact. Whenever he was in Bordentown Paine took his meals at the Kirkbrides'. He lived there, off and on, for years; but he was often away for weeks and months at a time. Now and then he rented his cottage to casual tenants. The size and quality of this residence in the country may be judged from the fact that he leased it to others for twenty-five dollars a year.

The folks in Bordentown looked upon Paine as the most distinguished and beloved citizen of their village. His work for American freedom was well-known, and he was honored for it. He rode daily in the neighborhood on Button, his cherished horse, and exchanged kindly greetings with the men and women he met, all of whom knew him. In the little Jersey town he was remote from the centers of snobbery and malice.

3

When Robert Morris resigned from his place as Superintendent of Finance in January, 1783, the payments made to Paine from the Secret Service Fund came to an end, and he was soon involved again in the difficulties that arise from lack of money. On June 7, 1783, he wrote from Bordentown to Elias Boudinot, President of Congress, and asked him for employment of some kind. If there was any reply to this letter it has been lost, and for months Paine continued to exist on whatever tiny income he could earn from casual writings and on loans made by friends.

On September 10 Washington wrote him from Princeton, where Congress was then in session. The General had a residence for the time being at Rocky Hill (near Princeton), in order to be closely in touch with Congress, and he invited Paine to visit him. He wrote also that: "Your presence may remind Congress of your past services to this country; and if it is in my power to impress them, command my best services with freedom, as they will be rendered cheerfully by one who entertains a lively sense of the importance of your works and who, with much pleasure, subscribes himself your sincere friend."

Paine replied on September 21. He wrote a rather long letter in which he accepted the General's kind invitation to visit him and gave his distinguished friend some indication of his impoverished condition. In the final paragraph of his letter he said:

I am hurt by the neglect of the collective ostensible body of America, in a way which it is probable they do not perceive my feelings. It has an effect in putting either my reputation or their generosity at stake; for it cannot fail of suggesting that either I (notwithstanding the appearance of service) have been undeserving in their regard or that they are remiss towards me. Their silence is to me something like condemnation, and their neglect must be justified by my loss of reputation, or my reputation supported at their injury; either of which is alike painful to me. But as I have ever been dumb on everything which might touch national honor so I mean ever to continue so.

At this period of his life Paine was flatly destitute. There were days when he did not have enough to eat, and his wardrobe was so shabby that he had to borrow clothes from friendly neighbors—chiefly from Colonel Kirkbride—before he went to Washington's headquarters as a guest.

That visit, with its pleasant dinners and anecdotes and good-natured discussions, helped greatly to restore Paine's self-esteem. He met there many of those who had been his friends during the war, and renewed a pleasant acquaintance with them.

But he encountered others whose outward courtesy concealed a deep, underlying dislike of Paine and all his works. Why? What reason was there for anyone in Washington's circle to dislike a patriot who had accomplished so much in aid of the American cause?

The answer to that question involves so many half-understood feelings and wordless antagonisms that it is hard to express in the clear-cut precision of nouns and verbs. Nevertheless, I shall outline the skeleton of this unfriendly attitude, and the reader must call on his imagination to supply the flesh and the features.

In the first place, American society as it then existed was an aristocracy. It was not a democracy in any true sense and the founders of the nation hoped it would never become one, for they constituted a caste of well-bred, well-to-do gentlemen who proposed silently to retain the governing power in their own hands. Their distrust of the common people was profound, and they intended to keep the members of the so-called "mob" down and under, as a permanent lower class. Even Thomas Jefferson was socially ostracized in Philadelphia in the 1790's, despite the fact that he was Vice-President of the United States. Yet Jefferson was an aristocrat himself and far superior in intellect and achievement to his critics. His social offense was that he had faith in democracy and in the common people.

To men of this pattern Tom Paine was just a plain, low-caste bounder who had some effective literary tricks. His proper place was among the mechanics, hostlers, cordwainers, tailors and innkeepers. They were his class, and there he belonged. Instead he was to be found at General Washington's table, invited by the

General himself as a house guest. The General was far too high and mighty to be criticized at all, but like all great men, he might make mistakes now and then, and such high recognition of Paine was considered one of them by those who did not like the author of *Common Sense* or the ideas which he represented.

Furthermore, Paine was English, and his powerful influence as a writer on political subjects was resented by certain people even when they agreed with his arguments. That a common English workingman had become the leader of American revolutionary propaganda was a situation that seemed to conceal some hidden menace to American institutions. What could this English staymaker know of the inner life, the hearts and souls, of American folk? Nothing at all; he was an outsider who had, without invitation, taken a part in American affairs. Was there an ulterior motive in his conduct? That was a hard question to answer, but certainly Mr. Thomas Paine should be closely watched.

Much of the secret, underground opposition to Paine was inspired by Tories in disguise. A campaign against Tories openly known as such had run along throughout the Revolutionary War. Their lands were confiscated, they were subjected to violence at the hands of unruly mobs, and large numbers of them fled to Canada. But thousands of them concealed their sentiments and posed as patriotic Americans. They exercised their ingenuity in creating discord among the patriots, in sowing the seeds of distrust around all the leaders of the Revolution, and in doing whatever they could to make every military campaign a failure.

Toward Paine the animosity of these fifth columnists was pronounced and vicious, and it was kept alive to the day of his death. Many of the lies created and spread by them are still current. Paine's mild drinking in the taprooms of taverns, or in the evenings at the homes of his friends, was depicted as drunken carousals, and this was in an era when heavy drinking was so common and so respectable that some of the signers of the Declaration of Independence, as well as many of the distinguished men of the time, fell now and then into a state of senseless inebriety and had to be carried home bodily by their servants and put to bed. People in general gave such matters little attention, but the enemies of Paine made a special point of hammering fantastic notions of his drunkenness into the American mind.

During this long campaign of vilification the reactionaries who were behind it financed two lying biographies of Paine. One was published in England in 1791, and the other in America a few months after his death in 1809. They were written by a couple of mercenary rascals who overshot the mark in both cases and depicted Paine as such a filthy, dissolute wretch that he appears incredible, and the reader wonders why he was allowed to live in a civilized community.[1]

Congress took no action in respect to Paine's affairs that fall, as it had more important matters on hand. But good news came from another direction. In the spring of 1784 the State of New York gave Paine a farm of two hundred and seventy-seven acres, with a handsome house on it, near the town of New Rochelle. The gift was an unexpected piece of generosity. The farm had been the property of Franklin DeVoe, a confessed and convicted Tory whose possessions had been confiscated.

As soon as Washington got the news he wrote to some leading members of the Virginia Legislature and proposed that his native state do something similar for Paine's benefit. In his letter to James Madison he said, in part:

His writings certainly have had a powerful effect on the public mind —ought they not then to meet an adequate return? He is poor! He is chagrined! And almost if not altogether in despair of relief.

New York, it is true, not the least distressed nor best able state in the Union, had done something for him. . . . His views are moderate—a decent independency is, I believe, all he aims at. Should he not obtain

---

[1] *The Life of Thomas Pain, Author of The Rights of Man, with a Defence of his Writings.* By Francis Oldys, A.M., of the University of Pennsylvania. London, 1791.
Life of Thomas Paine. By James Cheetham. New York, 1809. It is full of libels.

this? If you think so I am sure you will not only move the matter but give it your support.

But, despite this plea of her most distinguished son, Virginia would have nothing to do with any plan to benefit the author of *Common Sense*, because Paine had also written a pamphlet called *Public Good*, which was brought out on December 30, 1780. When the average Virginian heard *Public Good* mentioned he frothed at the mouth—in a figurative sense, of course.

In *Public Good* Paine called on Virginia to give up her claim to a vast stretch of territory in the Northwest. He suggested that these lands claimed by Virginia, as well as the western territory claimed by Connecticut, Massachusetts, North Carolina and Georgia, be turned over to the Union or Confederacy of States, so that the Continental Congress would possess something and cease being a pauper dependent on thirteen independent small republics for its sustenance. He pointed out that, in the natural course of events, new states would be formed in the West. Would Virginia then claim such states as subsidiary provinces? [2]

His argument was absolutely unanswerable, but students of human nature have learned that unanswerable arguments are the kind that make people furious, and Virginia was mad clear through. What made it even worse was that her title to the western territory was more than doubtful; it rested on some misty titles granted by an English king long before the geography of the continent was known.

A bill was offered in the Virginia Legislature by James Madison on June 28, 1784, in which it was proposed to sell a tract of public land in Northampton County and apply two thousand pounds of the money to the purchase of a farm for Thomas Paine. This measure was lost by only a very few votes, a fact which surprised many observers who knew the feelings of the

[2] The land claimed by Virginia stretched back to the Mississippi River and then ran northwest. The states of Michigan, Illinois and Wisconsin are in this territory. With the adoption of the Constitution these lands became national territory under the control of Congress.

legislators in regard to Paine and who thought the bill would be defeated by an almost unanimous vote. It is entirely probable that the large vote in favor of the bill was merely a complimentary gesture directed to George Washington, who was known to be Paine's sponsor.

Though the action of the Virginia Legislature was depressing, Paine's fortunes were on the mend. In December of that year (1784) the State of Pennsylvania voted him a gratuity of five hundred pounds (hard money), and on October 3, 1785, Congress instructed its treasurer to pay him three thousand dollars as compensation for his services during the Revolution. The resolution adopted by Congress says, "The early, unsolicited, and continued labors of Mr. Thomas Paine, in explaining and enforcing the principles of the late revolution by ingenious and timely publications upon the nature of liberty and civil government, have been well received by the citizens of these states, and merit the approbation of Congress; and that in consideration of these services, and the benefits produced thereby, Mr. Paine is entitled to a liberal gratification from the United States."

In 1785 Paine was forty-eight years old, and for the first time in his life was free from immediate money worries. He had the Pennsylvania gift of five hundred pounds, the Congressional award of three thousand dollars, the farm and house at New Rochelle and the house at Bordentown.

In the fall of that year he went to New York and remained there about a month. No doubt he visited his New Rochelle place and looked it over but he says nothing about it in any existing letter or memorandum. The farm was rented to a tenant who cultivated the land. Apparently he did nothing on his New York visit except enjoy himself with his friends, of whom he had many in that lively town, as well as a considerable number of influential enemies.

4

Meanwhile a controversy over the Bank of North America developed in Pennsylvania—a controversy in which much illtemper was displayed by both parties to the dispute.

This was the bank that was organized in 1780, and—it will be remembered—the first contribution toward its funds was five hundred dollars which came from Paine's salary. At the beginning its title was the Bank of Pennsylvania, but this was later changed to Bank of North America when it was given a charter by Congress. It had the distinction of being the first bank ever incorporated in America.

The war was followed by a number of lean years. Britain and its colonies had closed their doors to American exports, but English merchants sold their manufactured products in America, not for paper money but for hard cash which was sent to England. The country was being depleted of gold and silver currency. The banks did not want to take depreciated paper money in settlement of their debtors' obligations, such as mortgages and the interest and principal of notes.

The Bank of North America, in its attempt to keep solvent and put its house in order, adopted a policy of demanding complete and immediate payment on notes and mortgages whenever these obligations fell due. In the past the bank had let the debts run, sometimes for months. Its insistence on prompt payment was bitterly opposed by the farmers and small merchants, many of whom were borrowers from the bank. They also constituted the majority of the Constitutionalist Party, to which Paine belonged. The bank's affairs grew into a political issue, and the Constitutionalist Party managed to get the bank's state charter revoked by the Pennsylvania Assembly in September, 1785. But it continued to do business, in a limited way, under a charter granted by Congress.

In this controversy Paine did not agree with his party but took the bank's side of the dispute. To set forth his views he wrote, in December, 1785, and January, 1786, a lengthy essay, or pamphlet, entitled *Dissertations on Government, the Affairs of the Bank, and Paper Money*, which was published on February 18, 1786. These *Dissertations* are ably written. Though the issues discussed in the pamphlet have been settled long ago it is still a pleasure to read what Paine wrote, for the reason that his arguments are so logical and so clearly set forth.

Needless to say, Paine was looked upon by many of his former supporters as a deserter from their cause. But they were wrong. In his crusade for democracy, freedom and equal rights he had never argued that men should evade their responsibilities or use underhand methods in their dealings with other men. The Assembly, he insisted, had no authority to cancel a legitimate contract, and the bank's charter was a perfectly valid and useful contract, made by the Assembly (or state) on the one hand and the bank's stockholders on the other. The bank had not failed in carrying out its duties and functions under the charter. Not even its most persistent opponents were able to point out any dereliction or to show that it had misused the powers granted it by the representatives of the people. The cancellation of its charter was therefore a brazen attempt to prevent the bank from collecting the moneys due from its debtors. So Paine argued for the restoration of the charter.

Some of his enemies asserted that the bank had purchased Paine's support, but those of his friends who knew him well declared that such an accusation was a slander without a word of truth in it. As a matter of fact, no evidence of any kind has been found to sustain the charge that Paine had sold his services to the bank, though strenuous searching has been done by various interested parties who have had access to the bank's records and to the papers left by Robert Morris, its president.

After the publication of Paine's pamphlet there came about a gradual, slow-moving change in public opinion. The bank's side of the case gained favor, and in March, 1786, the Assembly restored its charter.

SILHOUETTE OF THOMAS PAINE

BY JOHN WESLEY JARVIS

This likeness by the famous American portrait painter was probably the last made during Paine's lifetime.

CHAPTER IX

Iron Bridges and Tallow Candles

I

LIKE many other people of his time and of our time, Tom Paine had a hobby. He did not collect rare stamps, or grow flowers, or paint furniture, or devise fancy drinks. His hobby was mechanics. All his life, even in his early youth, he had been deeply interested in mechanical devices of all kinds. His hands had an unusual deftness and as a lad in Thetford he did odd jobs around the house now and then that would ordinarily require the attention of a skilled workman, such as repairing cabinets and kitchen utensils and regulating clocks. But those accomplishments belong to the category of the commonplace. The distinct strain of inventiveness that was a part of his personality did not show itself until he came to America. Here again, America was the catalytic agent that brought about a miracle in his transformation.

He invented an iron bridge.

The bridge was to be supported by iron girders, without piers, just a single span, reaching clear across the stream or river. A bridge made wholly of iron was thought of, in those days, as a startling and probably impossible contrivance, for iron had always had very limited uses. Nobody had really thought of doing anything big with it, and it was used chiefly in household utensils and for making cannon and muskets.

The proposal to do away with piers (except at each end of the bridge) was even more astonishing to the eighteenth century mind. What could hold up such a bridge built across a wide river? Why, Paine answered, the iron girders, arranged crisscross in spider web fashion, would distribute the weight and carry the burden to the piers at each end of the bridge.

His invention of the iron bridge, supported by crisscross girders, probably grew out of his fondness for geometry. He liked to lay out geometrical designs—in circles and triangles—and to calculate imaginary stresses. This way of passing the time had no particular objective; it was a habit like that of playing solitaire. When bridging the Schuylkill became a subject of daily discussion among the people of Philadelphia ingenious Paine thought of his designs and wondered if they could be adapted practically to the construction of a bridge without piers set in mid-stream.

The Schuylkill River was just west of the town, and in that era the only way to cross it was by a ferry which was frequently inoperative in winter when the river was full of floating ice. As the city grew the facilities of the ferry became more and more inadequate to handle the traffic, especially the transportation of carriages and wagons. As soon as the war was over the matter of the proposed Schuylkill bridge was taken up in earnest, and various designs were submitted. All of them except Paine's were of the conventional type—a wooden bridge resting on a number of stone piers laid in the bed of the river.

In those days the modern caisson method of uncovering a solid bed beneath the mud of a river was unknown, and the only way of setting up a mid-river pier was to sink loads of stone in the river until an island was made; on that the piers were built. There were a number of serious objections to this method. In the first place, there could be no certainty that the base of the pier was solid and firm and would not shift; in the second place, the foundations of the piers were so wide, necessarily, that they frequently diverted the course of the stream and sent it flowing over its banks.

To assist him in building a large size model of his bridge Paine hired John Hall, a middle-aged English mechanic who had emigrated to Philadelphia in 1785. Hall came to Bordentown and lived, as a boarder, in the home of Colonel Kirkbride. Paine also took his meals with the Colonel's family, although he had a young servant around his place. This boy, whose name was Joe, assisted Hall in building the bridge model.

Hall kept a diary, a dry, matter-of-fact record from which the following extracts are taken:

1785

Nov. 17th. At dinner Mr. Pain told us a tale of the Indians, he being at a meeting of them with others to settle some affairs in 1776. The Doctor visited Mr. Pain.

Nov. 22nd. A remark of Mr. Pain's—not to give a deciding opinion between two persons you are in friendship with, lest you lose one by it; whilst doing that between two persons, your supposed enemies, may make one your friend.

Nov. 24th. This evening pulled Mr. Pain's boy a tooth out.

In those days dentists were few and far between. The pulling of teeth was usually done by mechanics, or barbers, and the instruments employed in the operation were tweezers or pliers.

Dec. 12th. With much pain drawd the Board in at Hanna's chamber window to work Mr. Pain's bridge on. I pinned six more arches together, which makes the whole nine. I sweat at it; Mr. Pain gives me some wine and water as I was very dry. Past nine o'clock Dr. Hutchinson called in on Mr. Paine.

The December journal is chiefly occupied with mention of Paine's visitors. Among them were Benjamin Franklin, Gouverneur Morris, Dr. Rush, Tench Francis, Robert Morris, Rittenhouse, Redman. A rubber of whist in which Paine won is mentioned. In the entries for the latter part of December Hall begins to spell properly the name of his employer.

He remained in Paine's service in connection with the bridge model during the whole of the next year, which was 1786. On Nov. 21 he wrote: "I put on Mr. Paine's hose yesterday. Last night he brought me in my room a pair of warm cloth overshoes as feel very comfortable this morning. Had a wooden pot stove stand betwixt my feet by Mr. Paine's desire and found it kept my feet warm."

The entry for Dec. 14, 1786, is not so cordial. It reads in this fashion:

Dec. 14th. This day employed in raising and putting on the abutments again and fitting them. The smith made the nuts of screws to go easier. Then set the ribs at proper distance, and after dinner I and Jackaway [?] put on some temporary pieces on the frame of wood to hold it straight, and when Mr. Paine came they then tied it on its wooden frame with strong cords. I then saw that it had bulged full on one side and hollow on the other. I told him of it, and he said it was done by me —I denied that and words rose high. I at length swore by God that it was straight when I left it, he replied as positively the contrary, and I think myself ill-used in this affair.

Three days before Christmas the thirteen-foot model was packed, tied on a sled and carried into Philadelphia, where it was set up in the garden of Franklin's house on Market Street. There it was a nine-days' wonder. Visitors were invited to walk on it and stamp hard, but it held up their weight without cracking.[1] On New Year's Day the model was moved to the large committee room of the Assembly where it remained for weeks and was stared at by virtually all the inhabitants of the town who could walk.

The Assembly appointed a committee to inspect the model and test it. Within a week the committee made its report in which it weakly endorsed Paine's bridge but spoke highly of bridges in general. The plain fact is that the idea was so novel that most people—including the members of the committee— were afraid of it, and rightly so. The bridge should have been promoted by a different method, by building one over a smaller stream than the Schuylkill and trying it out that way. In respect to the Schuylkill project no one, not even Paine, had any idea of the cost, and there was some doubt if the iron could be procured. The plans for the structure, as drawn by Paine, called for five hundred and twenty tons of metal. That was a very large order for the infant iron-smelting industry to fill.

[1] I have not been able to find a model of Paine's bridge, or even a picture of it. Moncure D. Conway, in his *Life of Thomas Paine*, which was written about 1890, says that he searched Philadelphia in vain for a model, or "a relic."
But I have a mental picture of the structure which is correct, I think, except possibly in some small detail. The iron girders were under the structure (not above as in a suspension bridge) and were fastened to the piers, from which they reached out across the river. Their crisscrossing gave them a spider-web appearance. The bridge was arched, and its highest point was the center.

So the matter remained, without decision or action, month after month.

2

Paine's iron bridge was an achievement of practical value; it was indeed a forerunner of the many iron and steel bridges of the present day. But it was not his sole invention. He devised a planing machine; also a newfangled crane for lifting heavy weights with a minimum of exertion; also an improved carriage wheel; and a smokeless candle. None of these inventions—except the iron bridge—has ever amounted to a great deal. They were, indeed, Paine's playthings which he contrived in following his impulse toward mechanical creation.

He had a high opinion of his smokeless candle—much higher, as a matter of fact, than the contrivance deserved. He wrote many letters in which he described it at length, and he exhibited it publicly here and there so effectively that several candlemakers were inspired to produce and sell it. The candle, according to Paine's design, had three straight holes, running parallel to the wick, from the top to the bottom of the candle.

In the following letter to Benjamin Franklin, written on December 31, 1785, Paine set forth the supposed merits of the candle:

Dear Sir,—I send you the Candles I have been making;—In a little time after they are lighted the smoke and flame separate, the one issuing from one end of the Candle, and the other from the other end. I supposed this to be because a quantity of air enters into the Candle between the Tallow and the flame, and in its passage downwards takes the smoke with it; for if you allow a quantity of air up the Candle, the current will be changed, and the smoke reascends, and in passing this the flame makes a small flash and a little noise.

But to express the Idea I mean, of the smoke descending more clearly it is this,—that the air enters the Candle in the very place where the melted tallow is getting into the state of flame, and takes it down before the change is completed—for there appears to me to be two kinds of smoke, humid matter which never can be flame, and enflameable matter which would be flame if some accident did not prevent the change being completed—and this I suppose to be the case with the descending smoke of the Candle.

．　　．　　．　　．　　．

I do not, my Dear Sir, offer these reasons to you but to myself, for I have often observed that by lending words for my thoughts I understand my thoughts the better. Thoughts are a kind of mental smoke, which require words to illuminate them.

My own thoughts continued to be a mental smoke after reading this letter to Franklin and other descriptions of the candle. It seemed to me that the smoke (mixed with air) would not go down but upward, even if the candle had holes running from top to bottom. It is the nature of flame to rise and to carry smoke and air up, and not down. But I had never seen a Paine candle, so I could not be sure that I understood its possibilities.

Eventually I got in touch with the Candle Manufacturers Association, which has its headquarters in New York City, and asked them if they had any information concerning the candle. In reply the secretary of the association wrote: "A candle having two or three holes parallel to its length was manufactured many years ago by members of this industry. Experience showed that the item was largely a novelty type and had no advantage over the solid candle of standard manufacture."

I obtained a sample of the candle and spent an hour lighting and blowing it out, and setting it in various receptacles. If it had any merits over an ordinary candle I was unable to perceive them. It gave out smoke, and its flame was no brighter than that of other candles made of the same material.

The most interesting thing about this contrivance of Paine's is that, in his day, so many people really thought it a distinct improvement over the ordinary candle. Paine surely did, and so did Benjamin Franklin, and many others—so many, indeed, that candles of this type were manufactured and sold for years.

3

Everything concerning the iron bridge dragged along at a snail's pace. The idea of building a bridge entirely of iron was startling and even more disturbing was the proposal to do away with piers. The Schuylkill was four hundred feet wide; could a single span of that width support even its own weight, to say nothing of the moving load that it would have to carry?

The model of the bridge, which everyone had seen, appeared to be perfect in all respects. But after all, it was only a thirteen-foot model, and there was a lot of difference between a span of that length and one of four hundred feet.

In the midst of these perplexities, further mystified by the wholly unsolved problem of what the newfangled bridge would cost, the committee of the Assembly did nothing at all. In the meantime, Paine was building, at Bordentown, a new model made of wrought iron, as some of the engineering critics had pointed out that cast iron was too brittle and too stiff for such a structure.

In March, 1787, it became certain that a decision about the bridge would not be reached for many months. Paine decided, perhaps on Franklin's advice or maybe on his own initiative, to take his bridge model to France and have it examined by the Academy of Sciences. With the approval of that learned body he thought there would be little difficulty in having it adopted into the standard bridge-building technique of America and England. He wrote to Franklin on March 31 and said he intended to depart in April. Further on he wrote:

My stay in Paris, when with Col. Laurens, was so short that I do not feel myself introduced there, for I was in no house but at Passy, and the hotel Col. Laurens was at. As I have taken a part in the Revolution and politics of this country, and am not an unknown character in the political world, I conceive it would be proper on my going to Paris, that I should pay my respects to Count Vergennes, to whom I am personally unknown; and I shall be very glad of a letter from you to him affording me that opportunity, or rendering my waiting on him easy for me; for it so often happens that men live to forfeit the reputation at one time they gained at another, that it is prudent not to presume too much on one's self.

The Marquis Lafayette I am the most known to of any gentleman in France. Should he be absent from Paris there are none I am much acquainted with. I am on exceeding good terms with Mr. Jefferson which will necessarily be the first place I go to. As I had the honor of your introduction to America it will add to my happiness to have the same friendship to me on the present occasion.

Further on in this letter he mentions the committee that had been appointed to confer with him on the subject of the iron bridge and says, "The matter will remain suspended until my return next winter. It is worth waiting this event, because if a single arch to that extent will answer, all difficulties in that river, or others of the same condition, are overcome at once."

Evidently he expected to return to his home in America in a few months, but it was fifteen years before he set foot again on our soil.

With his thirteen-foot bridge model stowed away in the hold of the French packet Paine sailed from New York on April 26, 1787, and was at sea just a month before he arrived at Havre on the twenty-sixth of May. He went straight on to Paris at once, but the model of his bridge was held at Havre for examination by the customs authorities and was not delivered to him in Paris until the last week in June.

We know nothing whatever about this voyage across the Atlantic except that one of the passengers on the vessel was Thomas Paine, and that he arrived safely in France. In his letters and notes he says nothing about the people he must have met on the ship, or about the weather, or the food. Nor does he record any incidents of the trip overland from Havre to Paris.

All this is in perfect accord with his character. We know so little about his daily life in Philadelphia, Bordentown or elsewhere, that the lack of knowledge is exasperating. The fact of personal, day-by-day existence made only a fleeting impression on him. He was not really interested in people but in ideas. He was a logician, a philosopher, an argumentative writer on economics and social problems. Accustomed to a hard life, he cared very little for comfortable living—so little, indeed, that he seldom thought of making any comments on his deprivations.

He brought with him to Paris a dozen or more letters from Benjamin Franklin to Frenchmen of distinction. These were helpful to him in getting the Academy of Sciences to consider his bridge. Soon after his arrival in the French capital he called on Thomas Jefferson, who was at that time the American minister at the court of Louis XVI. Paine and Jefferson had been friends for ten years or more and in the way of political ideas they had much in common. Jefferson was also mechanical-minded and an inventor himself, so he found the iron bridge an interesting topic.

The Academy soon took up the matter of the bridge, and a committee of three—Leroy, Borda and Bosson—was appointed to consider its merits and demerits and give their opinion as to its practicality.

The report which the committee made on August 29 was favorable. They pointed out that the erection of a single span four hundred feet long had never been accomplished, or even attempted, in actual engineering practice, but they thought that Mr. Paine's plan of an iron bridge "is ingeniously imagined, that the construction of it is simple, solid, and proper to give it the necessary strength for resisting the effects resulting from its burden, and that it is deserving of a trial. In short, it may furnish a new example of the application of a metal which has not hitherto been used in any works on an extensive scale, although on many occasions it is employed with the greatest success."

Reading between the lines, one may perceive that the committee approved the idea and the design, but was not at all sure that it could be done successfully in a big way. The great era of iron and steel was still in the dim future, and would not astonish the world until the nineteenth century had reached middle age. In Paine's time iron was used chiefly for horseshoes, pots and pans, nails and the rims of wagon wheels. A bridge built wholly of iron and without piers would be a startling innovation, and that is what the French engineers meant to say in their courteous way.

Paine was impatiently awaiting the report of the committee, as he wanted to go to England and see his mother. She was then in her ninetieth year.[2] The day after the committee made its report he started on his journey. The model was sent to Sir Joseph Banks, president of the Royal Society in London, with whom Paine had had some correspondence about the bridge. England was at that time the chief iron-producing country of the world and Paine had reason to believe that British ironmasters and bridge-builders would not be frightened out of their wits at the thought of building an iron bridge with a four-hundred-foot span.

4

He saw his native Thetford again after having been away for thirteen years. Nothing much had changed; it was the same sleepy village. There were the drab, narrow streets with the houses close together, standing shoulder to shoulder. No doubt he thought, by way of contrast, of the American villages with which he had become familiar—of his own Bordentown, with its spacious lawns and gardens, and its brightly painted houses.

His mother, a bent and decrepit old lady, still lived in her ancient cottage. Paine arranged for her to receive nine shillings a week from his own meager funds for the rest of her life. A weekly income of nine shillings seems to us today to be too small to do much good but in an English village in the 1780's it was sufficient to provide food, clothing and firewood for an aged widow.[3]

Paine was well remembered in Thetford by the older people and they told the younger ones of the staymaker's son who ran away to sea, and then went to London, where he was something or other in a school; and afterward got into the King's service as an excise officer, and he married a girl who died—no, he married twice, or so we've heard. First wife died, and the second one left him. Then he lost his place as an excise officer—guilty of some kind of crooked doings, maybe, or perhaps it was just because he was no-account and lazy. We who know him

[2] His father, Joseph Pain, had died of smallpox on November 14, 1786, about six months before Thomas Paine arrived in France.

[3] She died in 1791 at the age of ninety-four.

wouldn't hire him to watch a flock of sheep, much less a lot of
liquor sellers and shopkeepers. His head would be buried in a
book in no time, and everything else could go to the devil, so
far as he cared. And he could tell you all about Charles I and
human rights but not much about keeping a little shop, and buying and selling.

The excise people threw him out and we heard he'd gone to
America, but what he worked at over there we don't know—
except that it had something to do with writing. The big trouble
with Tom Paine is that he wants to make the world over; he's
not satisfied with God's work. A new world where there'll be
no poor folks, and everybody'll be happy. It's a foolish notion.

That is about what his native village thought of him in 1787.
His famous pamphlets, *Common Sense,* and the *Crisis,* were
unknown in Thetford, for the King's government would not
permit their sale or circulation.

He did not remain long in England; in December of that year
(1787) he was back in Paris. The model of his bridge had been
left in London, and he had applied for a patent on it before
returning to France.

5

During the time when Paine was building his bridge model
at Bordentown, and taking it to France and England, momentous events were taking place in America.

In the fall and winter of 1786 the thirteen small republics,
or states, loosely united in a Confederation called the United
States, were selecting delegates to meet in a convention which
would either weld them all together firmly or give up the Confederation entirely and let each state go its own way. The convention was to meet in Philadelphia on May 14, 1787.

The flimsy Confederation had become unworkable as a governing power. Each state, regardless of its population or wealth,
had only one vote in Congress. Whenever a vote on any proposition was called the delegates from each state retired into their
separate rooms or cubbyholes to decide among themselves how

that particular state would cast its vote. Delaware, with its 50,000 people, had the same voting strength in Congress as Virginia, which was inhabited by 650,000 persons. To carry any measure the affirmative votes of nine states were required. That being the rule, the five states that stood at the bottom of the list in respect to population and property—New Hampshire, Rhode Island, New Jersey, Delaware and Georgia, with an aggregate population of 470,000—could defeat the will of the 2,600,000 people in the eight other states.

The bickerings among the states never ceased. New York imposed a customs duty on firewood and vegetables brought across the Hudson from New Jersey for sale in the markets of New York City. The Jerseymen retaliated by levying a tax of thirty pounds per month on the lighthouse at Sandy Hook, which stood on Jersey soil though it was the property of the State of New York. Connecticut and Pennsylvania were on the verge of warfare against each other because Connecticut claimed that a part of Pennsylvania settled by Connecticut Yankees was really part of Connecticut and its inhabitants should pay their taxes to collectors from Hartford.

The funds needed by Congress for carrying on the national government could not be raised by direct taxation, for Congress, under the Articles of Confederation, had no power to levy taxes. Instead, the total amount required was apportioned among the states in direct ratio to the value of their surveyed lands and the houses standing on them; a real estate tax, in other words. But if a state refused to pay, or failed to pay because of negligence, Congress had no way of enforcing payment. In the late 1780's New Jersey declined to pay on the ground that the assessment was too high. Some of the other states made unwarranted deductions, and still others delayed their payments for a year or more.

Each state imposed its own tariff on imported goods, and the confusion that resulted from this situation sounds almost incredible. There was no tribunal corresponding to our Supreme Court and, consequently, no method of settling controversies that were country-wide.

The delegates to the Convention of 1787 were elected before Paine left for Europe in April of that year, but no one, as far as we know, nominated him for membership in the Convention, nor does he appear to have aspired for membership. The Convention created the Constitution and made the United States a nation. It was a body composed of distinguished patriots, and men of substance and understanding, of military and intellectual leaders. Offhand, any observer of intelligence would naturally suppose that the author of *Common Sense* and a dozen other patriotic works would have been chosen unanimously for membership in the Convention.

What is the explanation?

In the first place, the organizers of the Convention knew that Paine was too uncompromising to be at home in a deliberative assembly that would be saturated with the spirit of compromise. Under its surface many smoldering quarrels would lie concealed; also many latent and undeveloped antagonisms. It was no place, they thought, for a delegate who thought only in terms of true or false and detested milky phrases.

That was one reason why Paine was not a member of the Convention, but it was not the only one. Since the close of the Revolution American opinion had undergone a change. The Americans were no longer a swarm of ragged Colonials fighting desperately for their liberty and begging the aid of foreign powers. The Colonies had become a nation with a strong element of conservatism in its outlook. Paine was certainly not a conservative, nor was he a radical in the sense implied today by that term. There was nothing resembling Communism in his store of ideas. He believed that every man ought to stand on his own feet, and win or lose by his own exertions. He was a pronounced individualist. Government ought to be reduced to a minimum, he said in words to that effect, but no man, be he prince or magistrate, should inherit power.

He thought, also, that pauperism should be abolished, for there was work and food for everybody. But, strange as it may seem to us today, there was in that era a body of conservative opinion strongly in favor of pauperism. Those who held such views expressed the conviction that prosperity would destroy the economic value of the laborer, the craftsman and the mechanic. They argued that the well-paid workingman would soon grow lazy, would take to drink and other vices, and would neglect his work. The way to make workers do their best work, according to this school of economists, was to keep them always close to the raw edge of starvation.

These views were so hateful to Tom Paine that they always sent him into a fuming rage whenever he encountered them.

Paine's opinions do not seem to us to be alarming, but the leading minds of 1787 were uneasy over them, and did not want them brought out on the floor of the Convention. Paine argued that every man, whatever his condition in life, should have the right to vote; that there should be free schools for all children; that there should be old-age pensions for working people; that slavery ought to be abolished. To the aristocratic conception of civilization these ideas were like deadly rattlesnakes slithering about under foot, so it was quietly resolved that Mr. Thomas Paine be given no part in the deliberations of the Convention.

Moncure D. Conway, commenting on the deliberate omission of Paine from the delegates to the Constitutional Convention, wrote in his *Life of Thomas Paine* (vol. 1, page 224):

Paine was altogether too inventive for the kind of work contemplated by the colonial politicians. He had shown in all his writings, especially his *Dissertations on Government*, that he would build a constitution as he built his bridge: it must be mathematical, founded and shaped in impregnable principles, means adopted and adapted strictly for an ideal national purpose. His iron span did not consider whether there might be large interests invested in piers, or superstitions in favor of oak; as little did his antislavery essays consider the investments in slavery, or his *Public Good* the jealous sovereignty of States.

6

Much of his time in Paris during the first six months of 1788 was spent in trying to sell his bridge to the French Government, which had under consideration various plans for a new bridge across the Seine. But nothing came from his efforts in that direction; the matter hung fire for months, and in the end the Paine project was rejected on the grounds that his proposed bridge was an untried novelty, also that nobody could estimate its cost in advance of its construction.

Thomas Jefferson, the American minister in Paris, was thoroughly in touch with the undercurrents of French political affairs and it was he who first pointed out to Paine that an upheaval was maturing beneath the surface. Under his guidance and that of Lafayette, who had known Paine in America, he became a student of the situation in France.

Also he tackled the French language with assiduity. He hoped to become proficient in its use, but he was disappointed, for he never acquired a fluent speaking acquaintance with the language, although he learned to read it and could write a fairly grammatical letter in French if he gave himself plenty of time and a good dictionary.

When all matters concerning the bridge had come to a standstill in France Paine set out for England to see what could be done there. This was in August, 1788. For months his model of the bridge had been in the keeping of Sir Joseph Banks and the Royal Society and it had been inspected by many men of mechanical ability and experience. Most of their comments had been favorable. Soon after his arrival in London he made a financial arrangement of some kind with Peter Whiteside, an American merchant then living in England. It may have been a limited partnership, but if so the details and scope of the contract are unknown, as all the documents have disappeared. Whiteside advised him to apply for a patent to cover the design of the bridge. Paine took steps accordingly, and the patent was granted in September of that year.

A bridge resting on iron girders, arranged in spider-web fashion, was a curious novelty at that time—as much so as automobiles were a hundred years later, in the 1890's. Though engineers and scientific authorities were impressed favorably it must be said that the general public was convinced that such a bridge was an impracticable, harebrained device conceived by a visionary and that, when once erected, it would fall of its own weight.

To overcome this prejudice against the bridge Paine and Whiteside decided to have a bridge built according to Paine's designs and have it set up in London—not across a stream but in some public place on dry land where it might be seen and tested by anyone.

After months of dickering, Paine made a contract with the Walker iron-works at Rotherham, in Yorkshire, to construct a bridge with a span of one hundred and ten feet. Paine went to Rotherham, where the Walkers had set aside a shed for the work on his bridge, and he remained there for weeks, until the bridge was half completed and he felt that he could leave the rest of the work in the hands of the Walkers' capable mechanics.

On July 13 of the next year—1789—Paine wrote from Rotherham to Thomas Jefferson in Paris:

The Walkers are to find all the materials, and fit and frame them ready for erecting, put them on board a vessel and send them to London. I am to undertake all expense from that time and to compleat the erecting. We intend first to exhibit it and afterwards put it up to sale, or dispose of it by private contract, and after paying the expences of each party the remainder to be equally divided—one half theirs, the other mine. My principal object in this plan is to open the way for a Bridge over the Thames. . . . I shall now have occasion to draw upon some funds I have in America.

I have one thousand Dollars stock in the Bank at Philadelphia, and two years interest due upon it last April, £180 in the hands of General Morris; £40 with Mr. Constable of New York; a house at Borden Town, and a farm at New Rochelle.

The stock and interest in the Bank, which Mr. Willing manages for me, is the easiest negotiated, and full sufficient for what I shall want. On this fund I have drawn fifteen guineas payable to Mr. Trumbull, tho' I shall not want the money longer than till the Exhibition and sale of the Bridge. I had rather draw than ask to borrow of any body here.

If you go to America this year I shall be very glad if you can manage this matter for me, by giving me credit for two hundred pounds, on London, and receiving that amount of Mr. Willing. I am not acquainted with the method of negotiating money matters, but if you can accommodate me in this, and will direct me how the transfer is to be made, I shall be much obliged to you.

As there is no mention in this letter of Peter Whiteside, it is possible that Whiteside was not a partner in any real sense, but merely a lender of money to Paine. At any rate, when Whiteside failed in business and was declared bankrupt Paine was on his books as a debtor to the extent of six hundred and twenty pounds.

It seems, judging from the context of this letter to Jefferson, that Paine was the sole owner of the bridge patent, and that he had a profit-sharing arrangement with the Walker iron concern. On September 15, 1789, he wrote again to Jefferson, and said that: "I am looking out for a place to erect my bridge . . . I had thought of Soho Square, where Sir Joseph Banks lives, but he is now in Lincolnshire. I expect it will be ready for erecting and in London by the latter end of October. Whether I shall then sell it in England or bring it over to Paris, and re-erect it there, I have not determined in my mind."

In the same letter he refers, rather pathetically, to Jefferson's coming departure for America. "Absent from America," he wrote, "I feel a craving desire to return and I can scarcely forbear weeping at the thoughts of your going and my staying behind."

The bridge was eventually set up on Paddington Green, in London, and opened to the public in June, 1790. Anyone who paid a shilling might see it, walk across it, and test it by stamping on it or dragging weights across it. The shilling fees ran into a considerable income, for the bridge was talked about by everybody and was looked upon as one of the current wonders of London. Paine's financial interest in the bridge was small, and he did not receive much of its income.

During the three years of 1787, 1788, and 1789 Paine's attention appears to have been almost wholly taken up by the bridge; then he dropped the subject abruptly and devoted himself to French and English public affairs. If he had any more than a remote interest in the matter after he went back to Paris in 1789 it is not shown in his letters or other writings, nor in reported conversations with his friends.

After he had left England a bridge with a span of 236 feet was built across the River Wear at Sunderland. It was built according to Paine's patented design, and the builders used the materials of the Paddington Green bridge, which was torn down for the purpose. That was in the year 1796. Paine never saw the bridge over the Wear.

7

To Paine's surprise he was invited to be a guest during this stay in England at the homes of various leaders of public opinion. He spent a week as a house guest of Edmund Burke at Beaconsfield, his country estate. He dined with the Duke of Portland—then the head of the Whig party—and he was on familiar terms with Charles James Fox, the Marquis of Lansdowne, Sir George Staunton and other Parliamentary leaders. In a spirit of friendly humor they called him the "unofficial American ambassador."

One wonders, naturally enough, why the author of *Common Sense* and the *Crisis* pamphlets, an inveterate enemy of kings and nobles, an instigator of the American Revolution, should be taken up in a friendly social way by the aristocratic leaders of the English Whigs.

To answer that question one does not need to be much of a psychologist. The English Whigs were trying at that time to build up closer relations with the American states. They had watched the doings of the Constitutional Convention and had studied the result of its labors—the Constitution of the United States. They had seen the thirteen colonies free themselves from Britain, and now the colonies had turned themselves into a nation with a vast territory. The Whigs wanted to build up closer commercial relations with the newly formed nation, to contrive in some way to put Great Britain on a favored nation basis.

The Whig leaders believed Thomas Paine could be of immense help to them in bringing about this desirable result. They knew, to their sorrow, how immensely influential his writings had been during the late war, and they wanted him to be on their side in any possible future disagreement.

That was sensible enough in theory, but not in practice. They did not know Paine; if they had known him well they would not have wasted their time. He was not the kind of man who can be moved by social attentions, or flattery, or official recognition or monetary bribes.

After these gracious but artful and designing folks had cultivated Paine's acquaintance for several months they began to realize that their work was wasted, that the author of *Common Sense* could not be governed by another mentality, and that he made up his mind to suit himself. In March, 1789, Paine wrote to Jefferson: "I believe I am not so much in the good graces of the Marquis of Lansdowne as I used to be—I do not answer his purpose. He was always talking of a sort of reconnection of England and America, and my coldness and reserve on this subject checked communication."

While he was in England news came to him of the marriage of Kitty Nicholson, daughter of Commodore Nicholson, of New York. Paine was on very friendly terms with the Nicholson family and he had known Miss Kitty since her childhood days. She married Colonel William Few, a wealthy planter of Georgia.

Paine felt that he ought to write young Mrs. Few a letter of congratulation and affection. The letter that he wrote to her from London on January 16, 1789, is quite too long to reproduce here, but a few quotations from it may be interesting.

I very affectionately congratulate Mr. and Mrs. Few on their happy marriage, and every branch of the families allied by that connection; and I request my fair correspondent to present me to her partner, and to say, for me, that he has obtained one of the highest prizes on the wheel. . . .

When I see my female friends drop off by matrimony I am sensible of something that affects me like a loss in spite of all the appearances of joy. I cannot help mixing the sincere compliment of regret with that of congratulation. It appears that I had outlived or lost a friend. It seems to me as if the original was no more, and that which she is changed to forsakes the circle and forgets the scenes of former society.

On the next page, following his doleful view of the matter, as set forth above, he proceeds to describe his own state, in these words:

Though I appear a sort of wanderer, the married state has not a sincerer friend than I am. It is the harbour of human life, and is, with respect to the things of this world, what the next world is to this. It is home; and that one word conveys more than any other word can express. For a few years we may glide along the tide of youthful single life, and be wonderfully delighted; but it is a tide that flows but once, and what is still worse, it ebbs faster than it flows, and leaves many a hapless voyager aground.

I am one, you see, that have experienced the fate, I am describing. I have lost my tide; it passed by while every thought of my heart was on the wing for the salvation of my dear America, and I have now as contentedly as I can, made myself a little bower of willows on the shore that has the solitary resemblance of a home.

Should I always continue the tenant of this home, I hope my female acquaintance will ever remember that it contains not the churlish enemy of their sex, not the inaccessible cold hearted mortal, nor the capricious tempered oddity, but one of the best and most affectionate of their friends.

The letter ends with remembrances of their mutual friends, in this fashion:

Remember me to the family of Morrisania, and all my friends at New York and Bordentown. Desire Gen. Morris to take another guinea of Mr. Constable, who has some money of mine in his hands, and give it to my boy Joe. Tell Sally to take care of "Button." Then direct for me at Mr. Peter Whiteside's London. When you are at Charleston remember me to my dear old friend Mrs. Lawrence, Col. and Mrs. L. Morris, and Col. Washington; and at Georgia, to Col. Walton.

Thomas Jefferson sailed for home in September, 1789. Paine

had hoped to see him before his departure, but he could not get away from England and the affairs of his bridge before Jefferson had left France.

Paine reached Paris in December, 1789, and began at once to interest himself in the French Revolution. In its turmoil he felt at home.

CHAPTER X

The Rights of Man

I

PAINE sought truth not as a duty or self-imposed task but instinctively, as a hungry person searches for food. Facts, so-called, meant little or nothing to him until he had divested them of the ornamental disguises and historic lies in which they were clothed. He was a debunker of the shallow, the pretentious, the base and the tyrannical. This truth-seeking impulse—which, in Paine's hands, had the explosive force of mental dynamite—made for him both friends and enemies. And, as one might expect, there was always a flaming dispute over Paine and his ideas and actions.

He saw clearly the false assumptions and the injustices—hallowed by time—that lie under our civilization, and he dedicated his life and energy to the task of revealing them in their true colors. Why should there be a royal family, Paine asked, inheriting for centuries the vast prerogatives of authority and wealth? Why should there be cruel and destructive wars between nations over controversies that have no real merit and might readily be settled by the use of a little common sense and human charity? And why should the common people, the plowmen, the mechanics, the tradesmen, be forced to fight in these senseless conflicts from which they can receive no benefit whatever? Why should men and women, who are ready and willing to work, starve in the midst of plenty? Why should great estates—thousands of acres and stately homes—belong to lordly proprietors who never earned a shilling in their lives and who make a profession of profligacy and idleness? Why should there be palaces and almshouses in the same county, sometimes standing side by side? Why should greed and money-getting, called commercial enterprise, be highly honored by those whom it swindles?

These questions, and others like them, are not unusual. They occur to many thoughtful persons in every generation, but most of us who are vexed by them finally let them drop and decide to accept the bad with the good as part of the general scheme of things. But now and then, in the course of time, there appears a man, like Thomas Paine, who cannot live in peace with himself unless he attacks injustice and stupidity. Such men give their lives gladly for the benefit of humanity.

Paine was not a mystic; he did not live in the clouds of fancy, or have daydreams of utopias, nor did he play with ideas for the pleasure of exercising his mind. He was a realist and as practical as a carpenter. It was just this rugged soundness of mind that made him feared and hated by those at the top. They would have ignored a dreaming visionary who invented ideal civilizations for future generations of mankind. But Paine talked and wrote of Here and Now. His feet were planted firmly on the ground.

2

When he arrived in Paris late in 1789 the French Revolution was well under way and gathering strength as it moved. Like all great upheavals of society it had arisen without plan or definite intention. In other words, it was a spontaneous revolt against social and economic conditions that had become unbearable. But those who were leading the movement did not know how far it would go, or what the ultimate result would be.

For centuries France had been an absolute monarchy. The King had unlimited power to tax his subjects, to spend the resources of the nation in any manner that appealed to his judgment or fancy, to turn over to his favorites huge gifts of money and power—no matter how little they merited such rewards—and he was not required, by law or custom, to make any report of his doings to the nation or to its representatives. The government was not restricted by a written (or unwritten) constitution or charter of the people's rights. Nevertheless, the monarch's absolute authority was limited in practice, if not in theory, by custom and precedent The lands of the Church—meaning the Catholic Church and its prelates—were not taxable at all. The

Roman Catholic Church and its subsidiaries possessed about one-third of all the land in France.

The King—Louis XVI at the time of the Revolution—was a young monarch, without experience or sound judgment. His ignorance of the world and its people—even of his own subjects—was like a bottomless pit into which one drops a pebble, and listens in vain to hear it strike bottom. He was married to Marie Antoinette, a flighty, pleasure-loving Austrian princess. They lived in the vast, wide-spreading, gorgeous palace of Versailles, where their situation was practically that of prisoners. This does not mean that they were locked in cells, or confined to any particular part of their palatial residence. No, indeed; they were at liberty to travel anywhere—to any part of their kingdom—but they could not go a quarter of a mile to see a flower garden without being accompanied by a swarm of courtiers, princes, counts, toadies, ingratiating rascals and a dozen or more over-dressed, over-perfumed ladies of the court.

Every person who came within speaking distance of the King was planning to wheedle him out of some privilege, or a draft on the treasury for a large sum of money, or a gift of land, or an appointment to an office where the duties were light and the salary large. Louis XVI never knew the real facts concerning any serious problem of the government, nor did he know his own people. The real causes of the Revolution were a mystery to him without rhyme or reason. He never had an honest heart-to-heart talk with any of its leaders.

Although the French Government was a despotism, without a parliament or any kind of legislative assembly, there were rare occasions when a representative body called the States-General was convened as advisers to the King. It consisted of three parts—the Nobles, the Clergy, and the Third Estate (which meant the commoners). In voting for a delegate to the chamber of Nobles the voter had to belong to the nobility; and only priests and church officials might vote for delegates to the clerical body. But all men of twenty-five or over, classed as commoners but not serfs, had the privilege of voting for Third Estate delegates.

The tricky catch in this division into classes is that the three chambers of the States-General met separately and, in passing on any proposed reform, or governmental procedure, the votes of any two chambers constituted a majority. In short, the Nobles and the Clergy—who almost invariably agreed in their conclusions—could vote down any proposal that originated in the Third Estate. But the Third Estate was really the voice of the French people; its constituents were at least a hundred times more numerous than the constituents of the other two chambers.

In the fall of 1788 the French Premier, Loménie de Brienne, called for a convocation of the States-General, which had not met since 1614. It was high time, for the affairs of the government had become almost unmanageable because of the huge public debt, the heavy taxes, the confusion of conflicting laws, the vast expenses of the King and his satellites, and the constant rise in the cost of living.

There were so many persons of one kind or another who were exempt from taxation, and so many thousands of square miles of tax-free land, that the burden of taxes fell mainly on the commercial and laboring classes.

Uniformity of administration was utterly lacking in the royal government, which was a jumble of long-established contradictions. Some of the provinces of the nation were called *Pays d'état,* which meant that they had their own laws and were separate in a certain sense from the rest of the kingdom. Other provinces were *Pays d'administration,* governed directly by the Crown. Then there were certain duchies called *Pays de droit coutumier,* which were feudal states with laws and traditions that dated from the Dark Ages. In southern France there was still another type of provincial government founded on the ancient Roman law. These provinces were called *Pays de droit écrit.*

The States-General met at Versailles on May 5, 1789. Within twenty-four hours the spirit of change, of revolution, stepped to the front of the stage. The deputies of the Third Estate, representing the common people, demanded that the three-chamber system be abolished, and that all three orders—the Nobles, the Clergy and the Third Estate—meet together in one body, to be called the "National Assembly." The Nobles and the Clergy rejected this proposal, and their attitude may be readily understood, for more than half of the eleven hundred delegates belonged to the Third Estate. This controversy lasted six weeks; then the Third Estate took action by meeting separately and declaring itself a National Assembly.

The first resolution passed by the Assembly was that no taxation should be levied without its assent. To the King, as well as to the Nobles and the Clergy, this was a startling move. It showed that a stream of force and fire was running under the Third Estate, which had been patient and subservient for generations. The King, urged on by the privileged orders, thereupon sent his guards and closed the Salle des Menus Plaisirs, at Versailles—the meeting place of the Assembly—so that when the members of that body appeared next day they found the doors locked and could not enter. A childish, petulant move it was, characteristic of much of the opposition to the uprising of the masses that we call the French Revolution.

Of course, the closing of the hall had no real effect; it was merely a minor irritation. Next day, June 20, 1789, the Assembly convened in the Tennis Court near the palace of Versailles. This court was not in the open, but in a lofty building with ample room for all the delegates.

Three days later Louis XVI announced that he accepted financial reform, but would not countenance any change in the social order, or in the character of the existing government. He ordered the estates to meet separately, and when the Assembly declared that there must be only one chamber, with the Nobles and Clergy as part of its membership, the King commanded the army to disperse the Assembly; but his orders were not carried out, for the soldiers stoutly refused to interfere with the delegates' plans.

Soon afterward the lesser nobility and the inferior clergy went over to the Tennis Court and took their seats as members of the Assembly. Then King Louis changed his mind again—

this was on June 27—and commanded the Nobles and the Clergy to meet with the Third Estate.

The floundering, indecisive policy of the King was one of the notable features of the early revolutionary period. He was lacking in ability, in decisiveness, in understanding, but he was not lacking in trickiness and double-dealing. He pretended to make peace with the reformers, the Third Estate, and to declare publicly that he would work with them, but at the same time he was secretly plotting their overthrow. He wore ostentatiously the tri-color cockade—a symbol of the revolutionary spirit—and, to show his good faith, he appointed Lafayette, a republican, commander of the National Guard. Nevertheless, he was quietly surrounding Paris with mercenary troops, many of them Swiss, so that by the end of June of that year (1789), the capital of the French nation lay like a beleaguered city between the camps of an army.

The people of Paris, always quick of temper, rose on July 14, sacked the armories for firearms and ammunition and marched against the Bastille, the grim state prison and emblem of despotism.

At the close of that reverberating day the Bastille was an empty shell, without garrison or prisoners, and Paris was rejoicing.

But the rejoicing soon subsided, and a spirit of gloom spiced with resentment took its place. There was a scarcity of food in Paris: hundreds of grocers and bakers closed their doors, as they had nothing more to sell. Rumors ran around that the King— safe and snug in his lordly palace at Versailles—intended to starve the people of Paris as a punishment for the destruction of the Bastille; and whenever they had been brought through hunger into a state of submission, then he would have his foreign mercenaries seize the city.

These fears were probably without any foundation in fact, but while they were current the misguided monarch foolishly gave a sumptuous banquet at Versailles to his Royal Flanders regiment, a body of troops that were royalist in sentiment. The King and Queen attended the banquet and the occasion turned into a vociferous anti-republican rally. Soldiers who wore the tri-color cockade had it torn from their hats, and all the insignia of the liberal or revolutionary party were taken down from the walls of the banquet room amid the cheers of the participants and spectators. Next day, all this—greatly exaggerated in the telling—was known in Paris.

Boiling with resentment, the women who lived in the slums ceased their search for bread and bakers and started in a long and noisy procession to Versailles. This march of eight thousand bedraggled women nine miles across country to surround a king's palace is one of the strangest events in modern history. Why was it done by a mob of women instead of a mob of men? No one knows precisely; the fact is that women composed the marching column; and after they were well on their way Lafayette summoned his National Guard to accompany them, to save the royal family from mistreatment and also to prevent the palace guards from firing on the women who composed the mob.

When the screaming multitude got to Versailles the women surrounded the royal palace and demanded that the King and his family accompany them back to Paris, and remain there. Lafayette advised the King to go. He told Louis XVI and Marie Antoinette that such a move would help restore their lost popularity. They could live at the Tuileries palace which, though not as gorgeous and bedizened as that at Versailles, was still a regal residence. And there they would be, he explained, in the right place, a king and queen among their people. The royal couple accepted his advice and decided to leave Versailles.

When the riotous, half-crazed procession started back to Paris, Lafayette had his guardsmen keep close to the royal carriage as a protection to its occupants. They reached the Tuileries at ten o'clock that evening, with the King in the smiling humor that characterized his behavior at all times, even in the face of disaster. Whether his cheerfulness was real, or merely assumed for the occasion, still remains a minor mystery, but there is no doubt whatever about the genuine quality of his appetite. He was what might be called today a valiant trencherman, or a gourmand, or a gourmet, or all three combined. His love of food was not disturbed by personal troubles. As soon as he reached the Tuileries he insisted that a sumptuous dinner be cooked and served. He dined placidly while the mob that yelled and banged at the palace gates was restrained from entering by a cordon of Lafayette's national guards.

The National Assembly, after viewing the departure of the King from Versailles, resolved to transfer its place of meeting to Paris. When Paine arrived late in December the rioting had ceased and the people were going quietly about their affairs. The King was still in the Tuileries, and the Assembly's place of meeting was the Salle de Manège, or riding school, which stood then on the Rue de Rivoli, almost directly opposite the palace.

3

On this occasion Paine remained in Paris less than three months; he was back in London around the middle of March of the next year, which was 1790. Why did he go to Paris at all? What did he hope to accomplish? Ostensibly he went there in the interest of his project to build an iron bridge across the Seine, but from that standpoint it must be classed as a foolish excursion, for the French Government was too disorganized just then to think of building bridges. A more probable supposition—and one more in accord with Paine's character—is that he went to France to be close to the revolutionary movement, to get acquainted with its leaders, and to make suggestions to them. He was by nature a crusader, but his long and arduous crusades were not made to recover Holy Grails or to glorify sacred myths. His mission, as he conceived it, was to redeem humanity from tyranny, poverty, cruelty and ignorance.

While he was living in England in 1789 he had followed the course of the revolution in France through correspondence with Thomas Jefferson, Lafayette, and other friends who were actually on the scene. He had seen—from a distance—the abolition of the feudal system by an act of the National Assembly, the confiscation of church property in the interest of the state and the growth of democratic ideas. But these changes in the French political and economic system were not sufficiently sweeping to satisfy the author of *Common Sense*. The King was still recognized as the head of the state, the nobility had lost some of its privileges but it had not been abolished, and many other objectionable features of the old regime remained untouched.

The reform legislation, as enacted, appealed to Jefferson and many other liberals, who thought and said, in the autumn of 1789, that the main purposes of the revolution had been accomplished. On September 13, Jefferson—who was still in Paris —wrote to Paine, then in Yorkshire: "I think there is no possibility now of anything's hindering their final establishment of a good constitution, which will in its principles and merit be about a middle term between that of England and the United States."

Those were the cheerful words of an optimist. The French Revolution was not over; it had hardly begun when Jefferson departed, near the end of September, for his home in America.

On February 4 of the new year—1790—the King and Queen went before the Assembly and declared in a florid, pompous ceremony that they accepted the new order and were ready to become a part of it. Amid the cheers of the members and the spectators the monarch donned the colors of the Revolution. We know now, what was not known then, that both the King and Queen were—at that very time—conspiring with Austria and other foreign powers and plotting an invasion of France.

Paine had a number of friends in the French capital. Among Frenchmen, besides Lafayette—who had been for many years a close friend and admirer of Paine—there were Condorcet, Brissot, Barère and Danton, all of whom spoke English fluently. Brissot had known Paine in America. They had many tastes in common, and both of them were ardent advocates of the emancipation of Negro slaves.

Lafayette had acquired the key of the Bastille when that famous fortress-prison was taken by the Revolutionists on July 14, 1789. His intention was to send it to George Washington as a memento of the historic occasion, and he selected Thomas Paine as his emissary, for Paine planned to go back to America within a few months. The key was turned over to Paine in February, 1790, and he took it to England when he returned to that country in March. After his arrival in London he found that his departure for America would be delayed and he decided to send the key by some American who might be crossing the ocean.

On May 1, 1790, he wrote a letter to President Washington from which the following extracts are taken:

Our very good friend the Marquis de la Fayette has entrusted to my care the Key of the Bastille, and a drawing, handsomely framed, representing the demolition of that detestable prison, as a present to your Excellency, of which his letter will more particularly inform. I feel myself happy in being the person thro' whom the Marquis has conveyed this early trophy of the Spoils of despotism, and the first ripe fruits of American principles transplanted into Europe, to the great master and patron. When he mentioned to me the present he intended you, my heart leaped with joy. It is something so truly in character that no remarks can illustrate it, and is more happily expressive of his remembrance of his American friends than any letters can convey. That the principles of America opened the Bastille is not to be doubted, and therefore the Key comes to the right place.

· · · · ·

I should rejoice to be the direct bearer of the Marquis' present to your Excellency, but I doubt I shall not be able to see my much loved America till next Spring. I shall therefore send it by some American vessel to New York.

I returned from France to London about five weeks ago, and I am engaged to return to Paris when the Constitution shall be proclaimed and to carry the American flag in the procession. I have not the least doubt of the final and compleat success of the French Revolution. Little ebbings and flowings, for and against, the natural companions of revolutions, sometimes appear; but the full current of it is, in my opinion, as fixed as the Gulf stream.

Washington received the Bastille key, in due course, and it may be seen, hanging today, on a wall of a room in the historic Mount Vernon mansion.

In July Paine went again to France. He did not stay there

long; he was back in London in October of that same year, which was 1790.

Peter Whiteside, his partner or financial backer in the venture of the iron bridge, had failed in business and was declared a bankrupt. His assignees, after studying his accounts, declared that Paine owed Whiteside six hundred and twenty pounds, and they demanded that it be paid. Paine may have looked upon Whiteside as a partner, but if so, he was unable to prove that point and he was adjudged a debtor. The court decided that Whiteside had advanced the money as a loan. Two American merchants, Cleggett and Murdoch, who were living then in London, signed Paine's bond and kept him out of the debtors' prison. Then they helped him raise money to pay off the judgment that stood against him.

4

The French Revolution, in its early stages, was not called a revolution but a much needed movement toward reform and the abolition of obsolete remnants of feudalism in the French pattern of government. That is what English liberals thought of it, and they hoped it would succeed. Well-informed observers, in France as well as in England, believed that the movement would die out after a parliament was established, the abuses in taxation corrected, and the people given a share in the enactment of laws. No one foresaw the days of wholesale slaughter, the glittering and busy guillotine, the yelling mobs, the execution of the King and the Queen, the abolition of religion and the redistribution of the property of the nobility.

The prevailing thought in England, at that time, was that France would be a better neighbor in the years to come, after the change in governmental practices had brought her up to the English level.

The English system, as it existed in 1789, was also archaic, tyrannical and unjust if considered by present-day standards. It was full of abuses and lying pretences, though they did not happen to be the same as those prevailing in France. The English had a Parliament while the French had none, and the English Parliament was supposed to represent all the people, though—in reality—it represented only a small section of the population. Most adult males could not vote; they did not possess enough property to qualify as voters.

Englishmen could not be sent to prison, or executed, without jury trial. On the other hand, Frenchmen were often taken from their homes at night by officers of the law and were never heard of again. An Englishman's goods could not be seized without good cause, though that could be done in France.

But English workingmen, like those across the Channel, had virtually no hope of bettering their condition. The common people were overworked, underpaid, poorly clothed, housed and fed. Labor unions were banned in England and wages were fixed arbitrarily on such a low scale that all manual workers expected to end their days in the parish almshouses.

The English Government was really an arbitrary power in the hands of the wealthy and the aristocrats. The position of ordinary folks, common and middle-class people, was clearly defined—not in words but in custom and tradition. They were expected to work hard, to accept their fate cheerfully, to respect their superiors and to say nothing about governmental reform. Bishop Horsley put forth that conception of the matter quite concisely in a speech before the House of Lords, in which he said, "I do not know what the mass of the people in any country have to do with the laws but to obey them."

The English King, a German by descent, was churlish, ignorant and half-crazy. If he had been left to make his own way in the world his feeble talents might have been equal to the management of a tiny sausage shop or beer-cellar. But Parliament, supposed to represent the nation, paid him annually the sum of eight hundred thousand pounds—about four million dollars in modern American currency. In that era a skilled workman who could earn fifty pounds a year was considered well paid.

Despite the tacit repressions that pervaded the political and economic scheme there was much liberal and even revolutionary sentiment in England. It was usually silent and under cover, without means of expression or action, though it came out occasionally as on November 4, 1789, when Dr. Richard Price, a highly esteemed Unitarian clergyman, preached a sermon in London on "Love of Our Country," in which he reviewed the recent events in France and warned "all the oppressors of the world" that "you cannot now hold the world in darkness. Struggle no longer against increasing light and liberality. Restore to mankind their rights; and consent to the correction of abuses, before they and you are destroyed together."

Dr. Price was not by nature, or inclination, a revolutionist, but only a gentle-mannered clergyman of philosophical temperament. His sermon would have been soon forgotten if Edmund Burke had not taken it as a pretext for writing his *Reflections on the Revolution in France*, a book in which he condemned the French Revolution, liberal thought, democracies and political freedom.

One of the most interesting features of the situation is that Burke himself was for years a Whig, a political liberal, and a former friend of Thomas Paine. But in 1790 he was, and had been for some time, a secret agent of the Crown and was being paid fifteen hundred pounds a year from King George's private funds for his services as an orator and author. This was not known to the public, and Paine himself, in his association with Burke, never suspected it.

All the facts concerning Burke's under-cover employment are now known. For a lifelong salary of fifteen hundred pounds a year he had abandoned the political principles which had brought him distinction as a defender of the people's rights, and had gone over to the Tories.

In his *Reflections* Burke upheld the "divine right of kings," termed the delegates of the Third Estate a violent, ignorant rabble "in which was scarcely to be perceived the slightest traces of what we call the natural landed interest of the country."

He argued, with foolish insistence and lack of common sense, that whenever a nation has selected its royal family and has placed a king of that family on its throne no future generation has a right to make a change in the regal succession or to alter the form of the government. The royal family, according to Burke, owns the nation just as a family of landed proprietors owns a forest or a field, and the ownership passes as a matter of right and equity from father to son in perpetuity.

All this must have been inspired by a fear on the part of the English royalists that the French Revolution might be followed by a similar revolution in England.

5

Edmund Burke began the writing of his *Reflections on the Revolution* in February, 1790. Paine, while still in France, heard, in a roundabout way, that his former friend Burke was engaged in the preparation of such a book, or pamphlet, and on his return to England he made some inquiries about it.

On April 16, 1790, he wrote to a correspondent [1] in Paris a long letter from which the following extracts are taken:

My dear Friend:

To begin with our journey, we had a very pleasant one. . . . For three or four days after our arrival I missed the little box for Mr. Macpherson, which gave me exceeding great concern, and it appeared to me that I had rather have lost my portmanteau. Neither Mr. Rutledge nor I could divine what had become of it, when, to our great satisfaction it appeared, as of itself! I know not how for, going one evening into my room, it presented itself to me on the table. "Thou little runaway; where hast thou been, and why hast thou plagued me so?" It had, I suppose, slipped into some corner, and the girl in putting the room to rights, had found it!

The morning after my arrival I went first to Debrets, bookseller, Piccadilly; (he is the opposition bookseller.) He informed me that Mr. Burke's pamphlet was in the press, (he is not the publisher,) that he believed Mr. Burke was much at a loss how to go on; that he had revised some of the sheets, six, seven, and one nine times!

I then made an appointment with Lord Stanhope, and another with

---

[1] The name of Paine's friend to whom the letter was sent does not appear, but the context of the missive indicates that it was addressed to Thomas Christie, a nephew of Priestley, the famous English chemist.

Mr. Charles James Fox. The former received me with saying "have I the pleasure of shaking hands with the author of 'Common Sense'?" I told him of the condition of Mr. Burke's pamphlet, and that I had formed to myself the design of answering it, if it should come out at a time when I could devote myself to it. From Lord Stanhope I went to Mr. Fox, but how was I disappointed to find that he had not received my letter from Paris. That letter, (as you will recollect the contents of it,) laid down all the principal points with respect to the French Revolution, the Test Act, etc., which I intended for subjects for conversation when we met. . . .

I talked to him of Mr. Burke's pamphlet, and said that I believed I should reply to it. I afterwards saw Sir George Staunton, to whom I mentioned the same thing.

. . . . .

But I am now inclined to think that after all this vaporing of Mr. B., he will not publish his pamphlet. I called yesterday at Debrets, who told me that he has stopped the work. (I had not called on Mr. Burke, and shall not, until his pamphlet comes out, or he gives it up.) I met Dr. Lawrence, an intimate friend of Mr. Burke, a few days ago, to whom I said, "I am exceedingly sorry to see a friend of ours so exceedingly wrong." "Time," says he, "will show if he is." He is, said I, already wrong with respect to time past.

. . . . .

I shall in a few days write to my dear friend, the Marquis de Lafayette. In the meantime I wish you to call upon him and tell him my intention. I shall send it in the Marquis de la Lucerne's despatches. Forget not to remember me to him very affectionately, and also to Madame de Lafayette. Shake hands for me with my old friend, Mr. Mazzei. Call upon our friends at No. 36 Palais Royal, and forget me not among the rest of our acquaintances. And if there is anything I can serve you in here, or elsewhere, the greatest favor you can do me is to inform me of it. I am, my Dear Friend,

Yours very affectionately,

THOMAS PAINE.

It may be seen, from this letter, that the general tone and intent of Burke's pamphlet was known to Paine before it appeared, and that he had resolved to write a reply to it.

He returned to France in July after his bridge had been set

up on Paddington Green for public exhibition, and he stayed in Paris during the summer of 1790, taking an unassuming part in the revolution as an adviser to the active liberals who proposed to turn France into a republic. They considered him a man of great distinction, one of the founders of the American nation, and an authority on the vexing question of human welfare. He was greatly hampered in his contact with the French because of his inability to speak their language, or to understand it unless it were spoken slowly, and in the simplest of sentences. This disadvantage was partly overcome by a number of willing and eager interpreters who were always at his service.

In October he returned to England, for Burke's diatribe on the French Revolution was about to appear, and Paine wanted to study its effect at close hand among the people to whom it was addressed. He took lodgings in the quiet old Angel Inn, at Islington, which was then a sedate and sleepy suburb of London. Undoubtedly he wanted to live in solitude for a while in order that he might devote all his time to writing. He had numerous friends in London who were in the habit of calling on him at all hours of the day and night. They were talkative and argumentative people who thought nothing of staying for a whole afternoon or evening. Most of them knew that he was living at the inn at Islington, but in those days there were no buses, streetcars or trains and the Angel Inn was remote and not easy to reach.

Burke's *Reflections* was published on November 1, 1790. As soon as Paine had read it he set to work on his reply which he called *Rights of Man*. He wrote swiftly, for Part I—which was issued separately—appeared in print in March, 1791. The second half of the work—Part II—was brought out a year later. After the second part appeared the book was published as a single volume.

Paine's *Rights of Man* stands today, in historical and literary perspective, as the most important book on human society and the relation of men to one another, that was produced anywhere in the world during the eighteenth century.

But it is hardly worth reading today unless one is interested in Paine's manner of expressing his ideas, or in the evolution of modern governments, for every principle of human rights set forth in the book has been accepted by the people of our time. This treatise on civilization, its origin and its aims, is as modern as the telephone or the automobile, yet when it appeared in the 1790's it was looked upon by the ruling class in England with horror. A bomb it was, or so they thought—a bomb filled with explosive ideas, lying in the road and apt to go off any moment to scatter fire and fury in all directions.

Well, let's see. Here is a characteristic extract from the *Rights of Man*. It is rather hard to be frightened by it, even if it is read slowly and with awe:

In casting our eyes over the world, it is extremely easy to distinguish the governments which have arisen out of society, or out of the social compact, from those which have not: but to place this in a clearer light than a single glance may afford, it will be proper to take a review of the several sources from which governments have arisen, and on which they have been founded.

They may be all comprehended under three heads—1st, superstition: 2d, power; 3d. the common interests of society, and the common rights of man.

The first was a government of priest-craft, the second of conquerors, and the third of reason.

When a set of artful men pretended, through the medium of oracles, to hold intercourse with the deity, as familiarly as they now march up the back stairs in European courts, the world was completely under the government of superstition. The oracles were consulted, and whatever they were made to say became the law; and this sort of government lasted just as long as this sort of superstition lasted.

After these a race of conquerors arose, whose government, like that of William the Conqueror, was founded in power, and the sword assumed the name of a sceptre. Governments thus established, last as long as the power to support them lasts; but that they might avail themselves of every engine in their favor, they united fraud to force, and set up an idol they called *divine right,* and which, in imitation of the pope who affects to be spiritual and temporal, and in contradiction to the founder of the Christian religion, twisted itself afterwards into an idol of another shape, called *church and state*. The key of St. Peter, and the key of the treasury became quartered on one another, and the wondering, cheated multitude worshipped the invention.

In respect to Mr. Burke's assertion that England and the English people are permanently bound to maintain the existing form of government, Paine says:

There never did, nor can exist a parliament, or any description of men, or any generation of men in any country, possessed of the right or the power of binding or controlling posterity to the "end of time," or of commanding forever how the world shall be governed, or who shall govern it; and therefore all such clauses, acts, or declarations, by which the makers of them attempt to do what they have neither the right nor the power to do, nor the power to execute, are in themselves null and void. Every age and generation must be free to act for itself, *in all cases,* as the ages and generations which preceded it. The vanity and presumption of governing beyond the grave, is the most ridiculous and insolent of all tyrannies. Man has no property in man; neither has any generation a property in the generations which are to follow.

And further on he continues in the same strain:

I am not contending for, nor against, any form of government, nor for nor against any party, here or elsewhere. That which a whole nation chooses to do, it has a right to do. Mr. Burke denies it. Where then does the right exist? I am contending for the right of the *living,* and against their being willed away, and controlled and contracted for, by the manuscript-assumed authority of the dead; and Mr. Burke is contending for the authority of the dead over the rights and freedom of the living. There was a time when kings disposed of their crowns by will upon their death-beds, and consigned the people, like beasts of the field, to whatever successor they appointed. This is now so exploded as scarcely to be remembered, and so monstrous as hardly to be believed: but the parliamentary clauses upon which Mr. Burke builds his political church are of the same nature.

This line of reasoning is so sensible that one naturally wonders why anyone objected to it. The matter of a constitution, as discussed below by Mr. Paine, was particularly irritating to the British standpatters:

A constitution is not a thing in name only, but in fact. It has not an ideal, but a real existence; and wherever it cannot be produced in a visible form, there is none. A constitution is a thing antecedent to a government, and a government is only the creature of a constitution. The constitution of a country is not the act of government, but of the people constituting a government. It is the body of elements, to which you can refer, and quote article by article; and contains the principles on which the government shall be established, the form in which it shall be organized, the powers it shall have, the mode of elections, the duration of parliaments, or by whatever name such bodies may be called; the powers which the executive part of the government shall have; and, in fine, every thing that relates to the complete organization of a civil government, and the principle on which it shall act, and by which it shall be bound. A constitution, therefore is to a government, what the laws made afterwards by that government are to a court of judicature. The court of judicature does not make laws, neither can it alter them; it only acts in conformity to the laws made; and the government is in like manner governed by the constitution.

Can then, Mr. Burke produce the English constitution? If he cannot, we may fairly conclude, that though it has been so much talked about, no such thing as a constitution exists, or ever did exist, and consequently the people have yet a constitution to form.

As the reader has no doubt perceived, Paine's *Rights of Man* is much more than a reply to Burke's *Reflections on the Revolution in France*. Paine argues specifically, here and there, against some statement made by Burke, but it is plain that the *Rights of Man* is not a mere rebuttal of Burke's arguments. It is essentially a basic philosophy, written to explain and advocate a democratic form of government in place of a monarchy. Paine wrote:

Reason and ignorance, the opposites of each other, influence the great bulk of mankind. If either of these can be rendered sufficiently extensive in a country, the machinery of government goes easily on. Reason shows itself, and ignorance submits to whatever is dictated to it.

The two modes of government which prevail in the world, are 1st, government by election and representation; 2d, government by hereditary succession. The former is generally known by the name of republic; the latter by that of monarchy and aristocracy.

Those two distinct and opposite forms erect themselves on the two distinct and opposite bases of reason and ignorance. As the exercise of government requires talents and abilities, and as talents and abilities cannot have hereditary descent, it is evident that hereditary succession requires a belief from man, to which his reason cannot subscribe, and which can only be established upon his ignorance; and the more ignorant any country is, the better it is fitted for this species of government.

On the contrary, government in a well-constituted republic, requires no belief from man beyond what his reason authorizes. He sees the *rationale* of the whole system, its origin, and its operation; and as it is best supported when best understood, the human faculties act with boldness, and acquire, under this form of government, a gigantic manliness.

Paine was a staunch believer in internationalism, in the brotherhood of man, at a time in the world's history when such a belief was looked upon as a mild form of lunacy. He advocated what we call today a League of Nations and a World Court. He wrote in *Rights of Man*:

It is attributed to Henry IV. of France, a man of an enlarged and benevolent heart, that he proposed, about the year 1620, a plan for abolishing war in Europe. The plan consisted in constituting an European congress, or, as the French authors style it, a pacific republic; by appointing delegates from the several nations, who were to act, as a court of arbitration, in any disputes that might arise between nation and nation.

Had such a plan been adopted at the time it was proposed, the taxes of England and France, as two of the parties, would have been at least ten millions sterling annually, to each nation, less than they were at the commencement of the French revolution.

To conceive a cause why such a plan has not been adopted, (and that instead of a congress for the purpose of preventing war, it has been called only to *terminate* a war, after a fruitless expense of several years,) it will be necessary to consider the interest of governments as a distinct interest to that of nations.

As soon as Paine had completed the manuscript of Part I of

the *Rights of Man* which makes two hundred and eleven pages in his collected works, he took it to a printer named Johnson, who was also a publisher. Johnson agreed to bring it out, but his courage failed after he had put the book in type and had printed a few copies. It was too outspoken and too critical of the existing order of things. Thereupon Paine showed the book to J. S. Jordan, a Fleet Street printer, who undertook to publish it. Paine wanted to return to Paris, so he left all matters concerning the publication of the book in the hands of three of his friends—William Godwin, Thomas Holcroft and Thomas Brand Hollis—and went on his way. The few dozen copies printed by Johnson were completed in February, 1791, and the large first edition brought out by Jordan appeared a month later, on March 13 of that year.

Part I was dedicated to George Washington, President of the United States, in the following terms: "Sir, I present you a small treatise in defence of those principles of freedom which your exemplary virtue hath so eminently contributed to establish. That the rights of man may become as universal as your benevolence can wish, and that you may enjoy the happiness of seeing the new world regenerate the old, is the prayer of your much obliged and obedient humble servant, Thomas Paine."

6

The book aroused great interest at once throughout Great Britain and had a large sale at three shillings a copy. On March 23 the English Society for Promoting Constitutional Knowledge met and adopted a resolution in which the *Rights of Man* was highly praised.

The reverberating controversy over the book began—strange as this fact may seem—not in England, but in America. The *Rights of Man* was the first powerful exposition of the republicanism of Jefferson, Madison and Edmund Randolph that had appeared in print. At that time these liberal ideas were fighting for their life in our American republic. The party of reaction, which was led by men of distinction, such as John Adams and

Gouverneur Morris, was endeavoring to divide the American people into upper and lower classes, to make the office of President hereditary, and to build up a social and political economy closely resembling that of the Kingdom of Great Britain. These opponents of democracy believed sincerely that universal suffrage would lead to chaos. To them and their followers Thomas Paine was a demon of discord, yet John Adams himself had said "History is to ascribe the Revolution to Thomas Paine." But he uttered that memorable phrase in the early 1780's when the Colonies had just won their freedom and the American people were flushed with a feeling of victory and good will. Times had changed; the self-styled aristocrats of the young republic had decided that Paine was an upstart, a worthless disturber of the peace, a penniless nobody who ought to keep his mouth shut and leave the direction of human affairs to his betters.

Nevertheless he had the effrontery, as they termed it, to dedicate his disturbing book to George Washington. Moreover, he sent fifty copies to the Father of Our Country for distribution among the President's friends. At that time Washington, as our chief executive, was making every effort to effect a commercial treaty with Great Britain and, with that end in view, he had sent Gouverneur Morris to Europe for consultation with the British cabinet. That he was embarrassed by Paine's dedication goes without saying.

Paine, sending the *Rights of Man* to Washington in the early summer of 1791, had also written him a letter to accompany the gift. No acknowledgment came from Washington for nearly a year; then he sent to the author this cautious, evasive letter:

Philadelphia, 6 May, 1792.—Dear Sir.—To my friends, and those who know my occupations, I am sure no apology is necessary for keeping their letters so much longer unanswered, than my inclination would lead me to do. I shall therefore offer no excuse for not having sooner acknowledged the receipt of your letter of the 21st of June (July). My thanks, however, for the token of your remembrance, in the fifty copies of 'The Rights of Man,' are offered with no less cordiality, than they would have been had I answered your letter in the first moment of receiving it.

The duties of my office, which at all times, especially during the session of Congress, require an unremitting attention, naturally become more pressing toward the close of it; and as that body have resolved to rise tomorrow, and as I have determined, in case they should, to set out for Mount Vernon on the next day, you will readily conclude that the present is a busy moment with me; and to that I am persuaded your goodness will impute my not entering into the several points touched upon in your letter. Let it suffice, therefore, at this time, to say, that I rejoice in the information of your personal prosperity, and, as no one can feel a greater interest in the happiness of mankind than I do, that it is the first wish of my heart, that the enlightened policy of the present age may diffuse to all men those blessings, to which they are entitled, and lay the foundation of happiness for future generations.—With great esteem, I am, dear Sir &c.

George Washington.

P.S. Since writing the foregoing, I have received your letter of the 13th of February, with the twelve copies of your work (Part II, of the "Rights of Man") which accompanied it, and for which you must accept my additional thanks.

In the meantime Jefferson, who was the Secretary of State in Washington's cabinet, had received a copy of the *Rights of Man* which he read and liked. Then he sent it to a printer who had agreed to publish it in America, and with the book he sent a letter to Smith, the printer, in which he said:

I am extremely pleased to find it will be reprinted, and that something is at length to be publicly said against the political heresies which have sprung up among us.

I have no doubt our citizens will rally a *second* time round the *standard* of Common Sense.

The term "political heresies" was understood by everybody —and correctly so—to refer to John Adams and his adherents, and Adams was Vice-President at the time. Jefferson's note, as given above, was inserted in the book as a sort of preface.

Thomas Jefferson was a friend of Paine, but he had no intention of going into a rough-and-tumble fight in defense of Paine and his principles, as he had his eye on the presidency and hoped to succeed Washington. He did not want to make an enemy of Adams, and he had to make some explanation. To Washington he wrote on May 8, 1791:

I am afraid the indiscretion of a printer has committed me with my friend Mr. Adams, for whom, as one of the most honest and disinterested men alive, I have a cordial esteem, increased by long habits of concurrence in opinion in the days of his republicanism; and even since his apostasy to hereditary monarchy and nobility, though we differ, we differ as friends should do.

With all deference and respect for Jefferson one must say that his explanation sounds rather shallow, but it was doubtless the best he could do in the circumstances.

Then Major Beckwith, official agent of the British Government, entered the discussion and wanted to know what reason, or animus, inspired the Secretary of State to endorse a book that was insulting to His Majesty's Government. So it came about that Attorney-General Randolph, in an effort to smooth over the matter, visited Jefferson and asked him if he had authorized the publication of his note in the *Rights of Man*. After the visit he told Tobias Lear, who was Washington's secretary, that—

Mr. Jefferson said that, so far from having authorized it, he was exceedingly sorry to see it there; not from a disavowal of the approbation which it gave the work, but because it had been sent to the printer, with the pamphlet for republication, without the most distant idea that he would think of publishing any part of it. And Mr. Jefferson further added that he wished it might be understood, that he did not authorize the publication of any part of his note.

Mr. Lear wrote out this statement, as it was given to him by Randolph, and sent it to General Washington. He added that he had heard Vice-President John Adams say, in reference to the *Rights of Man*, "I detest that book and its tendency from the bottom of my heart."

Jefferson himself then wrote a letter to John Adams in which he said, "I was thunderstruck with seeing it [his note] come out at the head of the pamphlet."

One of the most interesting facts about Tom Paine was his remarkable ability to create controversies around himself and his opinions.

The *Rights of Man* (Part I) was reprinted serially in the *Daily Advertiser* of New York City during the early summer of 1791. That newspaper carried also, alongside Paine's work, a series of letters answering and deriding the views expressed in the *Rights of Man*. These contributions were signed "Publicola," which was a pen name used by John Quincy Adams.

7

Paine was not a radical within the meaning of that term as it is used today. He was an individualist. That every man should be independent was one of the cardinal points in his pattern of things to come. He did not want to put beggars on horseback; neither did he want to put on horseback a flock of overbearing and snobbish nobles. He detested men whose only claim to leadership was the possession of inherited wealth. That every generation should start afresh, should make its own way in the world, and that power in any form should not be inherited—these are conceptions that permeate his philosophy.

Paine did not want to destroy civilization, as his enemies declared. By no means. His ardent desire was to see civilization grow so that it would permeate the entire social fabric. He wanted to do away with slums, illiteracy, dirt, disease and absurd distinctions among human beings.

In the *Rights of Man* he said:

Every history of the creation, and every traditional account, whether from the lettered or unlettered world, however they may vary in their opinion or belief of certain particulars, all agree in establishing one point, the *unity of man*; by which I mean that man is all of *one degree,* and consequently that all men are born equal, and with equal natural rights, in the same manner as if posterity had been continued by *creation* instead of *generation,* the latter being only the mode by which the former is carried forward; and consequently, every child born into the world must be considered as deriving its existence from God. The world is as

new to him as it was to the first man that existed, and his natural right
in it is of the same kind.

Is there any statement in that extract from Paine's writings
that should make any human being furious? You will probably
say No, but you are reading this book in the middle of the
twentieth century, and Paine wrote a hundred and fifty years
ago.

CHAPTER XI

More Books—More Trouble

I

IN THOSE stirring times all of Paine's roads led to France. He could not leave the French Revolution alone; his desire to take part in it was an irresistible impulse. He believed that the upheaval in France was the beginning of a new and better era in the world's civilization, the dawn of an age which would be characterized by a worldwide feeling of kindliness, justice, generosity and equality. It was a forerunner of the brotherhood of man—or so he considered it.

He was to be bitterly disappointed, and the disillusionment endured to the end of his life.

2

Part I of the *Rights of Man* was published in March, 1791. As soon as he saw it off the press he started for Paris, and was there during the months of April, May and June. He brought with him from London a copy of the book and turned it over to his friend Lathenas for translation into French.

In revolutionary Paris he felt more at home than he did in London, despite the fact that he was in a foreign land and among people who spoke a language that he did not understand. But he felt that his own ideas and those of the French radicals were closely related; they belonged to the same family of conceptions—and when he was in France he could express himself freely without being looked upon as a crank or an anarchist.

The commander of the National Guard at this period was Lafayette, whom Paine had known since the French marquis came to America to offer his services to the struggling Colonials. Lafayette had been in sympathy with the reform movement in France from its beginning, but he was not a violent revolutionist, and, consequently, he lost favor with the leaders as their program of reform changed gradually into a reign of terror. He and Paine were intimate friends, and during this sojourn in Paris Paine was his guest.

As the commanding officer of the troops in Paris Lafayette had the custody of the King and Queen and other members of the royal family. Since their departure from Versailles Louis and Marie Antoinette had resided in the Tuileries palace. Lafayette was supposed to keep in daily touch with them, and the palace was surrounded by troops under his command. Notwithstanding this ever-present watchfulness the royal couple succeeded in escaping from the palace—and from Paris—during the night of June 20, and were well on their way to the German border before their departure was known to those whose duty it was to look after them.

An exotic air of the theater pervaded this escapade. King Louis managed to leave the palace disguised as a valet; Marie Antoinette played the part of a governess in charge of her own children, who were given new names for the occasion, while Madame de Tourzel—the real governess—was dressed as a fine and haughty lady and was supposed to own the luxurious carriage in which they left Paris. The royal princess, Madame Elizabeth, was disguised as a lady's maid; three members of the King's bodyguard were dressed as serving men, one of them acting as coachman.

Early next morning Paine was awakened by Lafayette who rushed into his bedroom, white-faced and agitated, and exclaimed, "The birds have flown! The King is gone, the Queen and family with him, and no one knows where!"

To Paine this was good news. To his way of thinking it seemed that, with the royal family out of France by an act of their own free will, there could be no great objection on the part of anybody to the establishment of a French republic on the American model. He advised Lafayette to let them go, and not to pursue them, and declared that their departure was an unexpected bit of good fortune. But this view of the matter did not appeal to Lafayette. He said emphatically that he would be held personally responsible if the King and Queen escaped. Paine knew that to be so; he knew, from his contact with the leaders of the popular front, that many of the more rabid revolutionaries believed Lafayette to be already in secret accord with the royal family and with the underground forces of the country that were plotting the overturn of all that the revolution had accomplished.

In a few hours Lafayette had armed horsemen moving speedily along all the roads leading from Paris to the border in the hope of overtaking the fugitives. But the army failed in the pursuit; the horsemen never caught even a glimpse of the luxurious carriage. The fugitives were stopped and captured by the occurrence of a curious bit of luck—one of those happenings that make one believe in fate, or destiny.

It came about in this fashion. The carriage and its outriders halted at a tiny village inn for a bit of refreshment, and to change the horses. The innkeeper, whose name was Drouet, happened to be reading *L'Ami du Peuple*, Marat's revolutionary journal, and when the carriage stopped at his door he had just read that Louis XVI and the Queen ought to be locked up, as they might attempt to leave the country secretly and quietly. Drouet was a revolutionist himself, without any love for the royal family.

When the horses had been changed the valet (Louis XVI in disguise) handed the innkeeper a fifty-franc note. Drouet glanced at it, and then at the valet's face. His features and the portrait of the King on the fifty-franc bill were identical. He recalled vividly what he had just read in the newspaper, and the thought flashed through his mind that the King might be trying to leave France, just as the paper said, and was there at that moment, disguised as a servant. Before giving change for the bill to the supposed valet he made some excuse to approach the carriage and he saw sitting in its shadows a governess who had the well-known features of Marie Antoinette.

Drouet had no authority to hold the carriage even if he had been able to do so, but after it had gone on its way he took a short cut to the next town on the road and told his story to the municipal authorities. When the royal carriage arrived they held it up until they could communicate with Paris. In a couple of days an order came to send the fugitives back under guard. They arrived on June 25, and thereafter they were treated as prisoners although they continued to live in the palace of the Tuileries.

Before the carriage with its royal occupants had reached the city the news of their forced return had spread far and wide and a vast, tumultuous crowd had gathered in front of the palace. This threatening mob greeted the King and Queen with a roar of insults. If their carriage had not been protected by a cordon of soldiers it is probable that all of its occupants would have been dragged out and massacred right then and there.

Tom Paine was in the midst of the crowd. He said nothing, but stood in bewildered silence, wondering why in the name of all common sense the vociferous, raging people around him wanted to bring the King back to Paris. Why didn't they give him an escort to take him across the border? They had said thousands of times that they wanted to get rid of kings and all royal trappings, yet when there was a chance to accomplish just that they defeated it by using force. So Paine thought, as he stood in the June sunlight before the gray palace.

Then suddenly the maddened crowd turned against Paine himself. He had forgotten to put a tri-color cockade—the symbol of the revolution—in his hat on that particular, exciting morning, and some of the hotheads in the mob noticed the omission and began to yell that there was an ill-wisher, a traitor, a dog, among them. One may readily imagine the scene. Paine could not understand the words that were shouted at him, but he knew they were terms of hatred, for he was pushed this way and that. He did his best to explain who and what he was—all without effect until an English-speaking Frenchman came up and asked him some questions. Tom Paine talked and the Frenchman translated. The mob was told that he was Thomas Paine (or To-mass Pah-een, as the French pronounce the name), a famous man of whom they had all heard, an American sympathizer with the republican movement who had come from

America to join them, and that the absence of a cockade was an unintentional oversight.

So volatile is the mob spirit that before all the words of Paine had been translated into French the men in the crowd were taking off their caps before him as a gesture of respect; and, as he walked away they made an open lane so he could pass through the crowd without being jostled.

In the first week of July of that year (1791) Paine was the prime mover in the organization of the *Societé Républicaine* which had, as its objective, the overthrow of the monarchy and the establishment of a French republic. The society had, at the time of its formation, only four members besides Paine. They were Condorcet, Brissot, Achille Duchatelet and Nicolas Bonneville. Paine and the other founders of the organization hoped and planned for a membership that would run into the thousands, but its growth was slow and it never had much influence in the affairs of the nation. Until the flight of the King and his forced return to Paris the purpose of the reformers—or the revolutionaries, as we call them today—was not to set up a republic but to correct the manifold abuses that had grown up in and around the royal court, and to give the people of France a share in forming the laws and policies of the kingdom.

The proposal of the Republican Society to abolish the monarchy was embodied in a manifesto written by Paine in which he dropped the King's regal title and referred to him as Monsieur Louis Capet. It was the first time Louis XVI had been so designated, and—strange as it seems to us today—it shocked many of those who had actually taken part in the uprising which was changing the structure of French civilization. Those who felt that way about it thought a reference to the King as Monsieur Capet was undignified and vulgar.

It simply goes to show how long and how rigorously custom and tradition can bind mankind. Even the Jacobins, who were destined to create in 1793 a world-resounding Reign of Terror in France, and to send both the King and the Queen to the scaffold—even they were disturbed in 1791 by the Republican

Society's outspoken declaration. They thought it went too far. The royalists were incensed and demanded the prosecution of Paine and his associates.

All social and political revolutions in which force is used go far beyond their initial objectives. The French Revolution was inspired by intelligent, social-minded subjects of Louis XVI. They had no intention of inaugurating an era of chaos, or of carrying on a series of massacres. Their purpose was to modernize the government, to abolish the archaic laws and absurd customs which had been inherited from the Middle Ages, to develop the nation's economic resources, and to reduce governmental expenditures and taxes. These were all worthy objectives, but as time went on the Revolution turned France into a human slaughter house.

The Republican Society placarded the City of Paris on July 1 with the *Manifesto* written by Thomas Paine. It was not signed by him, but bore the signature of the *Societé Républicaine*. It demanded the abdication of the King and the abolition of royalty in France. Here are some of its characteristic paragraphs:

The nation can never give back its confidence to a man who is false to his trust, perjured to his oath, conspires a clandestine flight, obtains a fraudulent passport, conceals a King of France under the disguise of a valet, directs his course towards a frontier covered with traitors and deserters, and evidently meditates a return into our country with a force capable of imposing his own despotic laws.

· · · · · ·

What kind of office must that be in a government which requires neither experience nor ability to execute, that may be abandoned to the desperate chance of birth, that may be filled with an idiot, a madman, a tyrant, with equal effect as by the good, the virtuous, and the wise? An office of this nature is a mere nonentity: it is a place of show, not of use. Let France then, arrived at the age of reason, no longer be deluded by the sound of words, and let her deliberately examine, if a King, however insignificant and contemptible in himself, may not at the same time be extremely dangerous.

Paine and the Republican Society, and a multitude of Frenchmen who were kindly and decent, were of the opinion that Louis XVI should not be tried or imprisoned but simply deprived of his official position as head of the state, and perhaps banished. The last paragraph of the *Manifesto* said:

As to the personal safety of Louis Capet, it is so much the more confirmed, as France will not stoop to degrade herself by a spirit of revenge against a wretch who has dishonored himself. In defending a just and glorious cause, it is not possible to degrade it, and the universal tranquillity which prevails is an undeniable proof, that a free people know how to respect themselves.

One of the handbills was posted on the door of the National Assembly. It was torn down by an indignant royalist who insisted that the author of the *Manifesto*—whoever he might be —should be prosecuted for writing and circulating such a seditious document. Not long afterward he learned that Thomas Paine was the author. Thereupon a group of royalists in the National Assembly brought up the matter in that legislative body in the hope that some drastic action might be taken. But nothing was done; there was a lot of talk and then the subject was dropped.

3

The English liberals who looked with favor on the revolutionary doings in France decided to celebrate the fall of the Bastille on July 14—the second anniversary of that historic event—and they invited Paine to come over to England and be a guest of honor at the celebration. He accepted the invitation, and arrived in London on the thirteenth of July. He went as a guest to the White Bear Inn, in Piccadilly.

The meeting to celebrate the fall of the Bastille was abandoned at the last hour because of the hostility of the British Government. The landlord of the Crown and Anchor, where the meeting was to be held, was intimidated by those who did not look with favor on the liberal movement and, in a wave of fright, he drove out of his inn everybody who looked like a liberal.

Nevertheless, a meeting of those who sympathized with the struggle for liberalism in France did eventually take place on August 20 at the Thatched House Tavern. Paine attended the meeting and read a paper written by himself and entitled *An Address and Declaration of the Friends of Universal Peace and Liberty*. This address was adopted by the unanimous vote of the meeting as an expression of the views of those present, and plans were made to give it a wide circulation in Great Britain.

The address did not attack the King or the English form of government. It was essentially a plea for doing away with abuses of one kind or another, and it urged a more liberal policy in handling problems concerning the welfare of the people.

When Paine arrived in England in mid-July he had already decided to write the second part of the *Rights of Man*. More than fifty thousand copies of Part I had been sold, and the book had earned over a thousand pounds for its author, but he got no financial benefit from its big sale, as he had turned over all the profits to the Society for Constitutional Information, one of his pet projects.

The major portion of Part I, the reader will recall, was a reply to Burke's *Reflections on the Revolution in France*. In Part II it was Paine's intention to widen the scope of the work, to discuss human rights in general with only incidental reference to the struggle in France.

While he was writing the book he lived in London as a welcome guest in the home of Thomas Rickman, whom he had known since they had both lived in Lewes, back in 1774. Rickman, who was often called "Clio," a nickname, was an ardent republican and Paine's devoted friend. One of his sons was named Thomas Paine Rickman. In London he had established himself as a printer and bookseller. He wrote a short biography of Paine in 1819, ten years after the death of his friend. In describing Paine's everyday life at that period Rickman wrote:

Mr. Paine's life in London was a quiet round of philosophical leisure and enjoyment. It was occupied in writing, in a small epistolary correspondence, in walking about with me to visit different friends, occasionally lounging at coffeehouses and public places, or being visited by a select few. . . . At this time he read but little, took his nap after dinner, and played with my family at some games in the evening as chess, dominoes, and drafts, but never at cards; in recitations, singing and music, etc.; or passed it in conversation.

Occasionally we visited enlightened friends, indulged in domestic jaunts and recreations from home, frequently lounging at the White Bear, Picadilly, with his old friend the Walking Stewart [an eccentric Scotchman who traveled all over Europe and the Near East on foot examining the state of the world], and other clever travellers from France and different parts of Europe and America. . . .

Mr. Paine in his person was about five feet ten inches high, and rather athletic; he was broad-shouldered and latterly stooped a little. His eye, of which the painter could not convey the exquisite meaning, was full, brilliant and singularly piercing; it had in it "the muse of fire." In dress and person he was generally very cleanly, and wore his hair cued, with side curls, and powdered, so that he looked altogether like a gentleman of the old French School . . . , In mixt company and among strangers he said little, and was no public speaker.

One gets the impression of a pleasant, leisurely gentleman of gracious manners who liked to meet people, and whose conversation was fascinating. But in reading this pen portrait let us keep in mind the important fact that Rickman was a lifelong friend of Thomas Paine, and an enthusiastic admirer of his literary work and his ideas. Any description of Paine, his habits and methods, would undoubtedly be influenced to some extent by Rickman's friendship for him.

Royall Tyler, who was neither a friend nor a foe, met Paine in England around 1790, and was in his company on many occasions. Here is his description of Paine, as it appears in his book *The Algerine Captive:*

He was dressed in a snuff colored coat, olive velvet vest, drab breeches, coarse hose. His shoe buckles were of the size of a half dollar. A bob-tailed wig covered that head which worked such mickle woe to courts and kings. If I should attempt to describe it would be in the same style and principle with which a veteran soldier bepraiseth an old standard:

the more tattered, the more glorious. It is probable that this is the same, identical wig under the shadow of whose curls he wrote *Common Sense* in America many years before.

He was a spare man, rather undersized,[1] subject to the extreme of low, and highly exhilarating spirits; often sat reserved in company; seldom mingled in common chitchat; But when a man of sense and elocution was present and the company numerous, he delighted in advancing the most unaccountable, and often the most whimsical paradoxes which he defended in his own plausible manner.

If encouraged by success or the applause of the company, his countenance was animated with an expression of feature which, on ordinary occasions, one would look for in vain, in a man so celebrated for acuteness of thought; but if interrupted by an extraneous observation, by the inattention of his auditory, or in an irritable moment, even by the accidental fall of the poker, he would retire into himself, and no persuasion could induce him to proceed on the most favorite subject.

It was during this sojourn in London, in the fall of 1791, that Paine sat for his portrait by George Romney. A reproduction of the painting appears as the frontispiece of this volume. It shows Paine as he looked in his fifty-fourth year. Note the high forehead, the large eyes, the prominent nose and the gentle mouth. The original of this portrait disappeared long ago, without leaving a trace but not before an engraving was made of it.

In November of that year he was the guest of honor at the annual dinner of the Revolution Society, which had been formed to commemorate the English Revolution (so-called) of 1688. Paine made a speech in giving his toast "To the Revolution of the World." His remarks on this occasion were carefully noted by some of his listeners who did not agree with his revolutionary sentiments, and his spoken opinions were turned over quietly to the representatives of the royal government. Trouble was brewing for Thomas Paine during that London autumn, and it reached a boiling point early in 1792.

Paine's reply to Burke's *Reflections*, with its caustic criticism

[1] Rickman says that Paine was five feet ten in height, and another personal acquaintance described him as "five feet eleven, straight and slim." The weight of evidence is that he was just under six feet in height.

of the English social and economic system, was deeply resented by the conservative upper class that ruled England. They looked upon Paine as a dangerous revolutionary who would bring their house crashing down upon their heads if he had the power to do so. If his book—Part I of the *Rights of Man*—had attracted only a little attention the wisest course would have been to say nothing at all about it, to ignore the book and its author, and the whole thing would have been soon forgotten—or so they thought. But the book became immensely popular; it outsold Edmund Burke's two to one, and everybody was talking of Paine.

Burke's friends then thought of bringing out a book about Paine himself, a biography that would show him up as a contemptible person and as an ignorant, illiterate writer unworthy of serious attention.

To carry out this plan they hired George Chalmers, a Tory refugee from Maryland. His employment was kept a secret, and when his life of Paine was published in 1791—under the nom de plume of Francis Oldys—its readers were led to believe that the author had written it of his own free will, and for no other purpose than to tell the truth—the *real, downright* truth, concerning Tom Paine, a notorious rascal who made it his business to fling verbal mud at men of honor and ability in an endeavor to inspire the British people to overthrow their government.[2]

Paine's wealthy and powerful opponents also made a determined effort to prevent Part II of the *Rights of Man* from

---

[2] George Chalmers was a clerk in the office of Lord Hawksbury, a high official in the royal administration. His authorship of the lying biography of Thomas Paine was kept a closely guarded secret for several years, but Chalmers himself eventually admitted that he had been paid five hundred pounds for the job. He confessed also that many of the discreditable actions and sayings of Paine which appeared in the book were pure inventions. The book was entitled *The Life of Thomas Pain, Author of the Rights of Man*, by Francis Oldys, A.M., of the University of Pennsylvania. (Note that he spelled Paine's name without the final "e."). Chalmers never received a degree from the University of Pennsylvania, and "Oldys" was an invented name. His record is that of a shameless liar.

being published at all. They learned that Paine intended to turn over his manuscript to Chapman, a publisher, who had agreed to bring it out as a book in the fall of 1791. Evidently it was to be published on a royalty basis, which was the customary arrangement then, and now, between authors and publishers. This means that the publisher did not buy the book outright, but put it in print and then sold as many copies as the public could be induced to purchase. For each copy sold the author received a certain fixed sum—say one or two shillings—and his recompense as an author would vary, therefore, according to the sales.

After the book had been put in type and was ready to print Chapman asked Paine to come in for a consultation. When he arrived Chapman proposed to buy the book outright, including the copyright, and offered Paine one hundred pounds for it. Paine went away without agreeing to the proposal, and soon thereafter Chapman increased his offer to five hundred pounds, and eventually to a thousand pounds. This last named amount was a huge sum to pay for the author's rights in an unpublished book and the offer aroused Paine's suspicions. He saw clearly that, through acquiring all the rights, including the copyright, Chapman would be able to suppress the book entirely, and keep it from being published at all. Paine thought it over and concluded that behind Chapman's offer there was someone who was trying to kill the publication.

After some reflection he refused the offer of a thousand pounds. He would take that stand, naturally, as there has never been, in all probability, anybody less moved by money and its power than Thomas Paine. It never seemed to mean anything to him personally, and he was quite willing to live in bleak poverty when he could have sold his services at a high figure merely by professing a change in his opinions.

When Paine declined to sell the book for a thousand pounds the true nature of Chapman's proposal came out at once in all its raw crudity. He wrote to Paine on January 17, 1792, that he was unwilling to go on with the publication of the book because the opinions expressed in it were so dangerous that they would get both him and Paine into serious trouble. With this letter he returned the manuscript to Paine. When this was done Chapman had the book already in type and he took the loss which the typesetting entailed.

It is interesting to note, in this connection, that Chapman published Chalmers' (or Oldys') life of Paine, and that the manuscript of that book was in Chapman's establishment while that publisher was endeavoring to buy Paine's rights. In Chalmers' book there are references to opinions expressed in Part II of the *Rights of Man* which had not been published when the Chalmers book appeared, a definite proof that Chalmers had been permitted to read Paine's manuscript while it was in Chapman's hands. Paine turned over the manuscript to J. S. Jordan, a Fleet Street publisher, who printed the book and brought it out in February, 1792, about one year after the same publisher had brought out Part I.

4

The *Rights of Man* was the earliest complete statement of republican principles. It set forth the fundamental ideas on which the American republic was founded, and it was so considered—in the years to come—by Thomas Jefferson, James Madison and Andrew Jackson, three presidents of the United States.

But to the conservatives of the eighteenth century, to all those whose mentality was limited by tradition, by muddy logic, and by a desire to live placidly without disturbing thoughts, Paine's *Rights of Man* was as shocking as the doings of an incendiary who sets houses and towns afire just to see the glowing roofs. The human mind is always slow and doubtful in respect to new ideas which deal with social systems and human relations.

I have read every word of the *Rights of Man* and I can assure my readers who have not perused the book themselves that there is nothing whatever in it that can stir anybody living today into a frenzy of resentment. To the men and women of this generation the ideas therein expressed seem rather old-fashioned. Our civilization has gone rather far beyond what was looked upon as revolutionary in the eighteenth century.

But judge for yourself. Here are some extracts from the second part of the *Rights of Man:*

Formal government makes but a small part of civilized life: and when even the best that human wisdom can devise is established, it is a thing more in name and idea, than in fact. It is to the great and fundamental principles of society and civilization—to the common usage universally consented to, and mutually and reciprocally maintained—to the unceasing circulation of interest, which, passing through its innumerable channels, invigorates the whole mass of civilized man—it is to these things, infinitely more than any thing which even the best instituted government can perform, that the safety and prosperity of the individual and of the whole depends.

.   .   .   .   .   .

One of the great advantages of the American revolution has been, that it led to a discovery of the principles, and laid open the imposition of governments. All the revolutions till then had been worked within the atmosphere of a court, and never on the great floor of a nation. The parties were always of the class of courtiers; and whatever was their rage for reformation, they carefully preserved the fraud of the profession.

.   .   .   .   .   .

In all cases they took care to represent government as a thing made up of mysteries, which only themselves understood: and they hid from the understanding of the nation, the only thing that was beneficial to know, namely, that government is nothing more than a national association acting on the principles of society.

.   .   .   .   .   .

As America was the only spot in the political world where the principles of universal reformation could begin, so also was it the best in the natural world. An assemblage of circumstances conspired, not only to give birth, but to add gigantic maturity to its principles. The scene which that country presents to the eye of the spectator, has something in it which generates and enlarges great ideas. Nature appears to him in magnitude. The mighty objects he beholds, act upon his mind by enlarging it, and he partakes of the greatness he contemplates.

Its first settlers were emigrants from different European nations, and of diversified professions of religion, retiring from the governmental persecutions of the old world, and meeting in the new, not as enemies, but as brothers. The wants which necessarily accompany the cultivation of a wilderness, produced among them a state of society, which countries long harassed by the quarrels and intrigues of governments, had neglected to cherish.

In such a situation man becomes what he ought to be. He sees his species, not with the inhuman idea of a natural enemy, but as kindred; and the example shows to the artificial world, that man must go back to nature for information.

. . . . .

If there is a country in the world, where concord, according to common calculation, would be least expected, it is America. Made up, as it is, of people from different nations, accustomed to different forms and habits of government, speaking different languages, and more different in their modes of worship, it would appear that the union of such a people was impracticable; but by the simple operation of constructing government on the principles of society and the rights of man, every difficulty retires, and all the parts are brought into cordial unison.

There, the poor are not oppressed, the rich are not privileged. Industry is not mortified by the splendid extravagance of a court rioting at its expense. Their taxes are few, because their government is just; and as there is nothing to render them wretched, there is nothing to engender riots and tumults.

. . . . .

Why does Mr. Burke talk of his house of peers, as the pillar of the landed interest? Were that pillar to sink into the earth, the same landed property would continue, and the same ploughing, sowing, and reaping would go on.

The aristocracy are not the farmers who work the land, and raise the produce, but are the mere consumers of the rent; and when compared with the active world, are the drones, a seraglio of males, who neither collect the honey nor form the hive, but exist only for lazy enjoyment.

. . . . .

Whether I have too little sense to see, or too much to be imposed upon; whether I have too much or too little pride, or of anything else, I leave out of the question; but certain it is, that what is called monarchy, always appears to me a silly, contemptible thing. I compare it to something kept behind a curtain, about which there is a great deal of bustle and fuss, and a wonderful air of seeming solemnity; but when, by any accident, the curtain happens to be open and the company see what it is, they burst into laughter.

In the representative system of government, nothing like this can happen. Like the nation itself, it possesses a perpetual stamina, as well of body as of mind, and presents itself on the open theatre of the world in a fair and manly manner. Whatever are its excellencies or its defects, they are visible to all. It exists not by fraud and mystery; it deals not in cant and sophistry; but inspires a language, that, passing from heart to heart, is felt and understood.

We must shut our eyes against reason, we must basely degrade our understanding, not to see the folly of what is called monarchy. Nature is orderly in all her works; but this is a mode of government that counteracts nature. It turns the progress of the human faculties upside down. It subjects age to be governed by children, and wisdom by folly.

· · · · ·

As the republic of letters brings forward the best literary productions, by giving to genius a fair and universal chance; so the representative system of government is calculated to produce the wisest laws, by collecting wisdom where it can be found. I smile to myself when I contemplate the ridiculous insignificance into which literature and all the sciences would sink, were they made hereditary; and I carry the same idea into governments. An hereditary governor is as inconsistent as an hereditary author.

· · · · ·

The representative system takes society and civilization for its basis; nature, reason, and experience for its guide.

Experience, in all ages, and in all countries, has demonstrated, that it is impossible to control nature in her distribution of mental powers. She gives them as she pleases. Whatever is the rule by which she, apparently to us, scatters them among mankind, that rule remains a secret to man. It would be as ridiculous to attempt to fix the hereditaryship of human beauty, as of wisdom.

Whatever wisdom constituently is, it is like a seedless plant; it may be reared when it appears; but it cannot be voluntarily produced.

· · · · ·

We have heard the rights of man called a levelling system; but the only system to which the word levelling is truly applicable, is the hereditary monarchial system. It is a system of mental levelling. It indiscriminately admits every species of character to the same authority. Vice and virtue, ignorance and wisdom, in short, every quality, good or bad, is put on the same level.

Kings succeed each other, not as rationals, but as animals. Can we then be surprised at the abject state of the human mind in monarchial countries, when the government itself is formed on such an abject levelling system? It has no fixed character. Today it is one thing; and tomorrow it is something else. It changes with the temper of each succeeding individual, and is subject to all the varieties of each.

It is government through the medium of passions and accidents. It appears under all the various characters of childhood, decrepitude, dotage, a thing at nurse, in leading strings, or on crutches. It reverses the wholesome order of nature.

It occasionally puts children over men, and the conceits of nonage over wisdom and experience. In short, we cannot conceive a more ridiculous figure of government, than hereditary succession, in all its cases, presents.

·   ·   ·   ·   ·

The revolutions which formerly took place in the world, has nothing in them that interested the bulk of mankind. They extended only to a change of persons and measures, but not of principles, and rose or fell among the common transactions of the moment.

What we now behold, may not improperly be called a "counter revolution." Conquest and tyranny, at some early period, dispossessed man of his rights, and he is now recovering them. And as the tide of human affairs has its ebb and flow in directions contrary to each other, so also is it in this. Government founded on a moral theory, on a system of universal peace, on the indefeasible, hereditary rights of man, is now revolving from west to east by a stronger impulse than the government of the sword revolved from east to west. It interests not particular individuals but nations in its progress, and promises a new era to the human race.

·   ·   ·   ·   ·

In contemplating the whole of this subject, I extend my views into the department of commerce. In all my publications, where the matter would admit, I have been an advocate for commerce, because I am a friend to its effects. It is a pacific system, operating to unite mankind, by rendering nations, as well as individuals, useful to each other. As to mere theoretical reformation, I have never preached it up. The most effectual process is that of improving the condition of man by means of his interest; and it is on this ground that I take my stand.

If commerce were permitted to act to the universal extent it is capable of, it would extirpate the system of war, and produce a revolution in the uncivilized state of governments. The invention of commerce has arisen since those governments began, and is the greatest approach towards universal civilization, that has yet been made by any means not immediately flowing from moral principles.

Whatever has a tendency to promote the civil intercourse of nations, by an exchange of benefits, is a subject worthy of philosophy as of politics. Commerce is no other than the traffic of two persons, multiplied on a scale of numbers; and by the same rule that nature intended the intercourse of two, she intended that of all. For this purpose she has distributed the materials of manufacturers and commerce, in various parts of a nation and of the world; and as they cannot be procured by war so cheaply or so commodiously as by commerce, she has rendered the latter the means of extirpating the former.

.   .   .   .   .

Independence is my happiness, and I view things as they are, without regard to place or person; my country is the world, and my religion is to do good.

Mr. Burke, in speaking of the aristocratical law of primogeniture, says, "It is the standard law of our landed inheritance; and which, without question, has a tendency, and I think," continues he, "a happy tendency, to preserve a character of weight and consequence."

Mr. Burke may call this law what he pleases, but humanity and impartial reflection will pronounce it a law of brutal injustice. Were we not accustomed to the daily practice, and did we only hear of it, as the law of some distant part of the world, we should conclude that the legislators of such countries had not arrived at a state of civilization.

As to preserving a character of weight and consequence, the case appears to me directly the reverse. It is an attaint upon character; a sort of privateering upon family property. It may have weight among dependent tenants, but it gives none on a scale of national, and much less of universal character. Speaking for myself, my parents were not able to give me a shilling, beyond what they gave me in education; and to do this they distressed themselves; yet I possess more of what is called consequence, in the world, than any one in Mr. Burke's catalogue of aristocrats.

The book was dedicated to Lafayette. In this dedication Paine said, in part, "After an acquaintance of nearly fifteen years, in difficult situations in America, and various consultations in Europe, I feel a pleasure in presenting to you this small treatise in gratitude for your services to my beloved America, and as testimony of my esteem for the virtues, public and private, which I know you possess."

Further on Paine said, "When the American Revolution was established I felt a disposition to sit serenely down and enjoy the calm. It did not appear to me that any object could afterwards arise great enough to make me quit tranquillity, and feel as I had felt before. But when principle, and not place, is the energetic cause of action, a man, I find, is everywhere the same.

"I am now once more in the public world; and as I have not a right to contemplate on so many years of remaining life as you have, I am resolved to labor as fast as I can; and as I am anxious for your aid and your company, I wish you to hasten your principles and overtake me."

The unanswerable quality of Paine's arguments was one of their outstanding characteristics. Whatever he wrote was so simple, and yet so convincing, that his enemies felt instinctively there could be no answer except by abuse and intimidation. The chief recourse of those who resented his line of argument was to forbid the sale of his books and to indict him for writing them.

5

No other publication, either before or after the period in which Thomas Paine lived, has ever aroused the storm in England that was brought about by Paine's *Rights of Man*.

Bonfires were made of his books, not merely in a few places, but all over England; and images of Paine himself made of straw were burned at numerous stakes planted on village greens and at country crossroads. Tavern loungers and ex-jailbirds were hired to yell derisively whenever his name was mentioned. Occasionally he was jostled in the street and pushed into the middle of the road by gangs of toughs. Ruffians, most of whom could not even read a child's primer to say nothing of the *Rights of Man,* were hired to threaten Paine with physical violence and to insult him on his daily walks. Paine's enemies paid them in shillings and pence and in free mugs of ale at the taverns.

Someone with an inventive turn of mind conceived an ingenious but silly idea, which was to drive into the heels of shoes a number of nails to make a pattern of the initials "T.P." The enemies of Paine who had gone to all that trouble could then boast that every time they took a step they were treading on Tom Paine.

Medals which closely resembled coins were made by private individuals to bring ignominy upon the author of the *Rights of Man.* I have seen three of these medals. All of them have on one side a man dangling from a gibbet with a church in the background. The inscription around the hanged man reads, "The End of Pain." One of these medals has on the reverse side "The Wrongs of Man." Another shows a monkey dancing, and the inscription is: "We dance; Pain Swings." The third medal carries these words: "May the Knave of the Jacobin Club never Get a Trick."

Beer mugs made of pottery were also used for derisive inscriptions. One of them which is on exhibition at the Paine Museum in New Rochelle, New York, has a poem baked into its clay. The poem runs as follows:

> Prithee, Tom Paine, why wilt thou meddling be
> In Others Business which concerns not thee?
> For while thereon thy dost extend thy career
> Thou dost at home neglect thy own affairs.
> God Save the King.
> Observe the wicked and Malicious Man
> Projecting all the mischief that he can;
> When common Policy will not prevail
> He'll rather venture Soul and all than fail.

George Chalmers' libelous life of Paine appeared in print a few weeks after the publication of Part II of the *Rights of Man*. From what we know now of the situation in respect to Paine at that particular time we may be sure that the Paine-haters who were hiring Chalmers decided to publish his book so that it would closely follow the appearance of the *Rights of Man*. Their purpose was to cast Paine and his writings on the garbage heap of disrepute just when the reading public was getting interested in his latest book, but it failed to work according to plan. The disparagement of Paine was so monstrously overdone that it attracted readers to his *Rights of Man* out of curiosity, if nothing else.

According to Chalmers, Paine was a congenital liar, a crook in all matters concerning money, and so unstable in disposition that even those who had known him a long time could not predict his next move with any assurance of certainty.

He asserts that Paine and his first wife, who was Mary Lambert, slipped away from Sandwich in April, 1760, "carrying the stays of a customer and a stove belonging to the house." He says further that Paine sold the furniture of the Sandwich cottage, although it did not belong to him, and decamped with the proceeds. There is not an atom of proof to sustain these statements; they are lies conceived by Chalmers.

Mary Lambert died soon after she and her husband moved away from Sandwich; Chalmers hinted in his book that her death was caused by ill-treatment on the part of Paine; that she had given premature birth to a child—born dead—and that her husband neglected her in her subsequent illness and forced her to get up and attend to her household duties when she was desperately ill.

This hinted charge of cruelty and neglect is not only untrue in every detail, but it is now—and was then—rather astounding to anyone acquainted with Paine's character. He was at all times kindly, gentle and sympathetic to persons in distress, so much so, indeed, that these traits often seemed to his friends to be carried to needless extremes. But Chalmers, with the notion, apparently, of forestalling any such doubts as to the truth of his charges, wrote of Paine that "the softness of his manner concealed the vileness of his spirit." In fabricating this story of cruelty he reckoned, no doubt, on the fact that only a few of his readers could possibly have any personal acquaintance with Paine, or be in a position to check up on the charges made against him.

He wrote that Paine was dismissed from the excise service because he bought smuggled tobacco and ground it into snuff in his shop in Lewes. That assertion was another falsehood; no such charge was ever made against Paine. The facts concerning his discharge from the service are quite simple and are on record in London. The truth is that he and his wife had made a failure of their shop; neither of them had the merchandising temperament. Paine owed money right and left, and in those days men were jailed for debt. He left Lewes to escape his creditors, and the excise commissioners dismissed him because he was absent without permission.

Nowhere in Chalmers' book does he make any reference to Paine's drinking habits. This is a notable omission, for the lying biographers of Paine who wrote of him in later life, and after his death, are emphatic in declaring that he was a lifelong drunkard. But Chalmers says nothing of the kind, yet who can doubt that if he had heard even the least rumor of excessive liquor drinking he would have made the most of it? And very little intemperance would have been needed, for Chalmers was expert in the art of turning molehills into mountains.

While this campaign of slander was going on the *Rights of Man* was having a large sale. It was the leading best seller in England during that period. By the end of 1793 more than two hundred thousand copies had been bought by the public. The mob violence against Paine was undoubtedly inspired by the government, and one wonders, naturally enough, why the authorities did not stop the sale of the book while they were about it. The answer probably is that such an action would have been a violation of the right of free speech, which would have put the government in a bad light. At first, therefore, it seemed preferable to incite the people to malign Paine in public and in print.

But they picked out the wrong method for accomplishing their purpose. In some respects they did not know Tom Paine, their living contemporary, as well as we know him today. Paine loved public attention, be it good or bad. Naturally he preferred honor and respect in preference to hatred and contempt. Nevertheless he had rather be treated with contempt than not to be noticed at all. In his curiously involved make-up there was more than a trace of masochism, a not uncommon quality that may be often observed in martyrs and saints. The truth is that Paine was a saint in the cause of reason and freedom, and unless he is so considered the record of his life is just a tangle of unrelated impulses.

While the attacks against him and his latest book were going on Paine was living with Thomas Rickman and having a pretty good time—meeting interesting liberals, telling vivid stories of the American Revolution, playing chess with his cronies, and reading books and newspapers. When the tavern loungers yelled after him, uttering catcalls and insulting remarks, he returned to Rickman's house not in despondency but in high spirits. He felt, in such circumstances, that his book was making an impression on the public and was getting under the skin of the conservative government.

CHAPTER XII

Outlawed in England

I

EARLY in May, 1792, J. S. Jordan, the printer who published the *Rights of Man*, was served with a summons to appear in court and face a charge of having printed and circulated seditious literature. He was scared out of his wits, as he had no idea when he took over the job that the book could be in any way objectionable.

Paine was staying just then at Bromley, Kent, with some friends. As soon as he got news of the legal proceedings he hastened to London and assumed the expense of Jordan's defense. But before anything could be done in the matter Jordan lost his courage—if he ever had any—and privately agreed to plead guilty. As the price of his freedom he turned over to the prosecutor's office all the data on Paine and his book that he had acquired during their relationship as author and publisher.

Jordan's status in the matter having become that of a King's witness, he was released and a summons was then served on Paine, at Rickman's home, requiring his presence in court on June 8. He received the summons on May 21, and on the same day a royal proclamation was issued against the writing, printing, selling and circulating of seditious publications such as Paine's *Rights of Man*.

On May 25 there was some discussion of these doings in the House of Commons, and Henry Dundas, Secretary of the Home Office, said in the course of his remarks that the proceedings against Jordan had been instituted because Thomas Paine could not be found at that time. This statement inspired Paine to write a letter to the attorney-general in which he said: "Mr. Paine, Sir, so far from secreting himself, never went a step out of his way, nor in the least instance varied from his usual conduct to avoid any measure you might choose to adopt with respect to him. It is on the purity of his heart, and the universal utility of the principles and plans which his writings contain, that he rests the issue; and he will not dishonor it by any kind of subterfuge."

Paine had no bashful modesty in regard to the value of his own work, but it was not precisely an exhibition of vanity; it was fervor, the conviction and faith that sustained the early Christian martyrs when they were burned at the stake or thrown to the lions. Threats of imprisonment, or of death, did not frighten him at all. He was what we call today a one-idea man, which means that one thought, one purpose, one driving force, filled his mind; and that thought, purpose and force was human freedom and love of truth.

Further on in his letter to Secretary Dundas he says:

The instant that I was informed that an information was preparing to be filed against me as the author of, I believe, one of the most useful and benevolent books ever offered to mankind, I directed my attorney to put in an appearance; and as I shall meet the prosecution fully and fairly, and with a good and upright conscience, I have a right to expect that no act of littleness will be made use of on the part of the prosecution towards influencing the future issue with respect to the author.

The complaint against Paine, on which his indictment was based, covers forty-one handwritten pages. It describes Paine in this fashion:

Thomas Paine, late of London, gentleman, being a wicked, malicious, seditious and ill-disposed person, and being greatly disaffected to our said Sovereign Lord, the now King, and to the happy constitution and government of this kingdom . . . and to bring them into hatred and contempt . . . did write and publish, and caused to be written and published, a certain false, scandalous, malicious and seditious libel. . . .

After this introduction a number of quotations from the *Rights of Man* are set down to show the seditious character of the book. Among them is this sentence: "The time is not very distant when England will laugh at itself for sending to Holland, Hanover, Zell, or Brunswick for men" (meaning William III and George I), "at the expense of a million a year, who understand neither

her laws, her language, nor her interest, and whose capacities would scarcely have fitted them for the office of a parish constable. If government could be trusted to such hands it must be some easy and simple thing indeed; and materials fit for all the purposes may be found in every town and village in England."

Here is another seditious assertion, according to the promoters of the indictment: "All hereditary government is in its nature tyranny. An heritable crown or an heritable throne has no other significant explanation than that mankind are heritable property. To inherit such a government is to inherit the people, as if they were flocks and herds."

On June 8 Paine appeared in the court of the King's Bench, prepared to make his defense, when he learned that the case had been postponed until December.

Just at this time he was sitting daily for his portrait, which was being put on canvas by George Romney, a celebrated portrait painter of the late eighteenth century.

2

The royal proclamation put a stop to the public sale of the Rights of Man, but it did not stop its secret sale, or its circulation from one reader to another. It was, in short, a tremendous advertisement for the book. Thousands of people who were not especially interested in the subject, and who would never have thought of reading the Rights of Man in the natural course of things, were attracted to it by the stir that it had caused, and they bought the paper-covered volume from some hole-in-the-corner dealer who kept his copies hidden under a counter.

The proclamation of the King evoked a large number of congratulatory addresses from the hidebound conservatives and reactionaries who were governing England at that time. They held public meetings (so-called) to pass resolutions and prepare the addresses. These assemblies were dominated by wealthy landowners, or by officeholders who were highly paid for little or no work, or by the officials of boroughs that were controlled politically by members of the House of Lords.

Paine's spirit of combativeness, which was one of his outstanding traits, rose vigorously to meet these attacks. Whenever he learned that a meeting was to be held for the purpose of passing resolutions in commendation of the royal proclamation he wrote a letter to the presiding officer with a request that it be read at the meeting. Also, as a part of this campaign, he distributed hundreds of copies of the *Rights of Man* at his own expense to those who were expected to be present at such gatherings.

Lord Onslow, the Lord Lieutenant of Surrey, summoned a meeting of the gentry of that county, to be held at Epsom, to respond loyally to the proclamation. In this instance Paine sent Horne Tooke, a personal friend, to attend the meeting and make a speech. He sent to Epsom also a hundred copies of the *Rights of Man* and a thousand copies (in printed form) of his letter to Henry Dundas, Secretary of the Home Office, to be given away to those who might be present at the meeting.

Mr. Tooke arose and was allowed to speak, but he had uttered only a few sentences before he was ordered to stop talking and to leave the speaker's stand. He had begun his speech with a characterization of Lord Onslow which was far from flattering. Onslow was a lord of the King's bedchamber at that time. It was an honorary office, with no duties, but with a salary of one thousand pounds a year, and a pension of three thousand pounds upon retirement. In short, Lord Onslow was a parasite of the royal government. Horne Tooke began his speech by calling attention to these facts, and he said also that it was highly improper for such a meeting to be held with a parasite and hanger-on of the Court as presiding officer. After Mr. Tooke was squelched the meeting proceeded to congratulate the government on its suppression of Paine's book.[1]

[1] John Horne Tooke (1736–1812) graduated with honors at Cambridge and entered the Inner Temple as a law student, but his legal studies were discontinued on his father's insistence that he become a clergyman. He consented, and was ordained as a clergyman in 1760, but after a few years he resigned from the ministry, and devoted the rest of his life to the promotion of liberal and democratic ideas. He was a lifelong rebel.

Paine, in his characteristic fashion, thereupon wrote two letters to Lord Onslow, and completed the speech which Horne Tooke intended to deliver. In his first letter he says to the noble lord, in reference to that dignitary's sinecure and pension:

What honor or happiness you can derive from being the principal pauper of the neighborhood, and occasioning a greater expense than the poor, the aged, and the infirm for ten miles round, I leave you to enjoy. At the same time I can see that it is no wonder you should be strenuous in suppressing a book which strikes at the root of these abuses.

The addresses in praise of the royal proclamation against seditious writings inspired Paine to write an angry screed entitled *Letter to the Addressers*. The document thus produced is hardly a letter, even though it is so-called, for it fills eighty pages of print and contains twenty thousand words. It is really a pamphlet in the fighting language of Tom Paine, in which he sets forth his purpose in writing the *Rights of Man*, and then he goes on from there. This is how it begins:

Could I have commanded circumstances with a wish I know not of any that would have more generally promoted the progress of knowledge than the late Proclamation, and the numerous rotten borough and corporation addresses thereon.

They have not only served as advertisements, but they have excited a spirit of inquiry into the principles of government, and a desire to read the *Rights of Man* in places where that spirit and that work were before unknown.

The people of England, wearied and stunned with parties, and alternately deceived by each, had almost resigned the prerogative of thinking. Even curiosity had expired, and a universal languor had spread itself over the land. The opposition was visibly no other than a contest for power, whilst the mass of the nation stood torpidly by as the prize.

In this hopeless state of things, the first part of the *Rights of Man* made its appearance. It had to combat with a strange mixture of prejudice and indifference; it stood exposed to every species of newspaper abuse; and besides this, it had to remove the obstructions which Mr.

Burke's rude and outrageous attack on the French Revolution had artfully raised.

In reading the paragraphs quoted above one is inevitably impressed by Paine's reference to the royal proclamation and the addresses as advertisements for the *Rights of Man*. They were advertisements indeed, and they served to promote prodigiously the underground sale and perusal of Paine's writings.

A few pages further on he says: "Much as the first part of the *Rights of Man* impressed at its first appearance, the progressive mind soon discovered that it did not go far enough. It detected errors; it exposed absurdities; it shook the fabric of political superstition; it generated new ideas; but it did not produce a regular system of principles in the room of those which it displaced.

"And, if I may guess at the mind of the government party, they beheld it as an unexpected gale that would soon blow over, and they forbore, like sailors in threatening weather, to whistle, lest they should increase the wind. Everything on their part was profound silence.

"When the second part of *Rights of Man*, combining Principle and Practise, was preparing to appear, they affected, for a while, to act with the same policy as before; but finding their silence had no more influence in stifling the progress of the work, than it would have in stopping the progress of time, they changed their plan, and affected to treat it with clamorous contempt.

"The speech-making placemen and pensioners, and place-expectants, in both Houses of Parliament, the Outs as well as the Ins, represented it as a silly, insignificant performance; as a work incapable of producing any effect; as something which they were sure the good sense of the people would either despise or indignantly spurn; but such was the overstrained awkwardness with which they harangued and encouraged each other, that in the very act of declaring their confidence they betrayed their fears."

Then comes a very effective bit of book advertising—arousing curiosity, desire for knowledge, self-satisfaction of those who possess the book, etc.—and it runs along in this fashion:

One of the best effects which the Proclamation and its echo the addresses have had, has been that of exciting and spreading curiosity; and it requires only a single reflection to discover that the object of all curiosity is knowledge. When the mass of the nation saw that placemen, pensioners, and borough-mongers, were the persons that stood forward to promote addresses, it could not fail to create suspicions that the public good was not their object; that the character of the books, or writings, to which such persons obscurely alluded, not daring to mention them, was directly contrary to what they described them to be, and that it was necessary that every man, for his own satisfaction, should exercise his proper right, and read and judge for himself.

But how will the persons who have been induced to read the *Rights of Man,* by the clamor that has been raised against it, be surprised to find, that, instead of a wicked, inflammatory work, instead of a licentious and profligate performance, it abounds with principles of government that are uncontrovertible—with arguments which every reader will feel, are unanswerable—with plans for the increase of commerce and manufactures—for the extinction of war—for the education of the children of the poor—for the comfortable support of the aged and decayed persons of both sexes—for the relief of the army and navy, and, in short, for the promotion of everything that can benefit the moral, civil, and political condition of man.

Why, then, some calm observer will ask, why is the work prosecuted, if these be the goodly matters it contains? I will tell thee, friend; it contains also a plan for the reduction of taxes, for lessening the immense expenses of government, for abolishing sinecure places and pensions; and it proposes applying the redundant taxes, that shall be saved by these reforms, to the purposes mentioned in the former paragraph, instead of applying them to the support of idle and profligate placemen and pensioners.

Further on Paine describes the English system of kingly and aristocratic government in a manner that certainly—and automatically—puts him in the class of seditious and ill-disposed persons as defined by the royal proclamation. "Let us suppose," he says, "that government was now to begin in England, and that the plan of government, offered to the nation for its approbation or rejection, consisted of the following parts:"

First—That some one individual should be taken from all the rest of the nation, and to whom all the rest should swear obedience, and never be permitted to sit down in his presence, and that they should give to him one million sterling a year. That the nation should never after have power or authority to make laws but with his express consent; and that his sons and his sons' sons, whether wise or foolish, good man or bad, fit or unfit, should have the same power, and also the same money annually paid to them forever.

Secondly—That there should be two houses of legislators to assist in making laws, one of which should, in the first instance, be entirely appointed by the aforesaid person, and that their sons and their sons' sons, whether wise or foolish, good men or bad, fit or unfit, should forever after be hereditary legislators.

Thirdly—That the other house should be chosen in the same manner as the house now called the House of Commons is chosen, and should be subject to the control of the two aforesaid hereditary powers in all things.

It would be impossible to cram such a farrago of imposition and absurdity down the throat of this or any other nation that was capable of reasoning upon its rights and its interest.

They would ask, in the first place, on what ground of right, or on what principle, such irrational and preposterous distinctions could, or ought to be made; and what pretensions any man could have, or what services he could render, to entitle him to a million a year? They would go further, and revolt at the idea of consigning their children, and their children's children, to the domination of persons hereafter to be born, who might, for anything they could foresee, turn out to be knaves or fools; and they would finally discover, that the project of hereditary governors and legislators was a treasonable usurpation over the rights of posterity. Not only the calm dictates of reason, and the force of natural affection, but the integrity of manly pride, would impel men to spurn such proposals.

In spite of the fact that such publications were banned, the *Letter* was brought out in England by Paine's friend Thomas "Clio" Rickman, who was a bookseller, in co-operation with D. H. Symonds, a printer of Paternoster Row. They decided to take a chance on issuing the publication, but the printing was not completed until late in 1792 and when the pamphlet was eventually offered to the public Paine had returned to France.

There can be no doubt that the government's prosecuting attorneys knew that the *Letter to the Addressers* was being put in type, and that it would be issued as a pamphlet and put on sale or distributed by some undercover method. Before taking action, however, these officials wanted to have printed copies in their hands as evidence; also, their punitive measures were not aimed primarily at Rickman and Symonds, but at Paine, though the printers were prosecuted later for producing Paine's works.

3

While the English mobs, incited by the higher-ups, were burning effigies of Paine, his fame was growing in France. The *Rights of Man*, translated into French, was supplanting the Bible in that land of revolution. It had become the most widely circulated book from Calais to Marseille, and was quoted daily by thousands of people.

On August 26, 1792, the French National Assembly conferred the honorary title of French citizen on Paine, and within a week four departments of France had chosen him to represent them in the National Convention which was soon to meet in Paris for the purpose of devising a republican form of government for the nation. The four departments that elected Paine were Pas-de-Calais, Somme, Puy-de-Dome and Oise. But under the prevailing law a member of the Convention could represent only one department, so Paine had to make a choice. He selected the department of Pas-de-Calais, probably because its body of citizens thoughtfully sent over to England a municipal officer to notify Paine, in formal fashion, that he had been chosen.

The name of the French official was Achille Audibert. He spoke English and had often visited London, so he decided to stay awhile and meet Paine's friends. On September 13 Paine and Audibert attended an evening party where everybody present was anti-royalist, liberal and democratic. The gathering had no special significance politically; it was simply a jolly occasion, devoted to fun, gossip and refreshments.

But Tom Paine was so constituted that he could not remain, even for an hour, in a party of any kind without setting forth his political ideas. They were his whole life; he lived among them. He existed in an unborn universe where freedom, justice, democracy, truth and kindness were the sun, stars and planets —very much in the same manner as other men live in their own worlds of commerce, science, poetry, or greed. During the evening he told the assembled company of a speech he had made the day before at a meeting of the Friends of Liberty, an organization that had a revolutionary purpose, and he repeated parts of his speech. He did not know or did not care that the Home Office sent its spies to meetings of societies suspected of having revolutionary tendencies, and that one or more of such observers were present when he poured out his incendiary remarks before the Friends of Liberty. Their chiefs in the Home Office had decided, after pondering over the notes of Paine's speech, that he had gone too far, that he must be stopped, and they issued a warrant for his arrest.

Paine was unaware of their decision and did not know that the Home Office had given orders to the police to invade Rickman's premises, and to seize him and his papers. It happened, however, that these facts were known to William Blake, the mystic poet, who was a friend of Paine, and who was a guest at the party.

As Paine was getting ready to leave, Blake rose as if to say good-by to him and whispered in his ear, "You must not go home; if you do, you will be going to your death." For a moment Paine was speechless with astonishment. He stared into the poet's face and asked him what he meant by his solemn warning. Blake then told him that the police were waiting to pick him up, and that—if he valued his life—he should leave the country secretly, and at once. Paine welcomed danger, if it happened in a good cause, and his impulse was to go home, await the arrival of the police, and write, while waiting, a justification of his actions and a few additional paragraphs about the stupid tyranny of the British ruling powers. But he was prevented from doing this by the almost frantic opposition of Blake and other friends. The deciding argument was that advanced by Audibert, the French delegate, who said, "You have a great career yet to come in France, so let us go." Paine was moved by this advice and decided to leave the country. He did not return to Rickman's house, but he managed to have some clothes, a little money and all his important papers brought to him in a trunk. He departed for Dover, where he expected to take passage for France.

Accompanying him on this journey were Achille Audibert and Robert Frost, a lawyer, who was one of Paine's close friends. When they reached Dover, where the ship stood in the offing and was ready to sail, they were stopped by port officials who insisted on searching Paine's baggage. They had read the royal proclamation against seditious writings and so, as loyal supporters of the royal government, they thought it was their duty to search the baggage of all outgoing, as well as incoming, travelers for seditious letters and literature.

Tom Paine's wonderful luck stood by him as usual. The very first letter that the inspecting official picked up from the lot that Paine carried in his trunk was from George Washington, President of the United States. The officials read it through with awe; it was a cordial epistle, just one friend writing to another.

That ended the search. The Dover officials were impressed by Paine's apparent importance. They felt that they were getting beyond their depth, and they saw visions of being called down by the bigwigs in London for tampering with state documents and interfering with the movements of persons who should not be annoyed. So they bowed to Paine, begged his pardon and helped him get aboard his vessel. The little cross-channel packet departed, and not too soon. It was still to be seen on the horizon when an emissary of the Home Office, galloping up on a sweating horse, brought to the Dover officials a peremptory order for Paine's arrest. It was too late; if the men of Dover had taken Paine, regardless of his letter from George Washington, their names would have been known in a few days all over the kingdom. So they reflected, no doubt, and decided silently that they would never let such scruples sway them in the future.

When Paine arrived in Calais he was welcomed with the public acclaim that is usually given to returning heroes. Salutes were fired from the batteries and a procession of soldiers and cheering citizens accompanied him to the lodging that had been reserved for him. He stayed in Calais a couple of days as a guest of honor, and then went on his way to Paris, where he arrived on September 19, and took up his residence in White's Hotel on the Rue des Petits Pères.[2]

Paine never returned to England, nor could he have gone back without incurring the penalty of death, for he was tried *in absentia* by the court of the King's Bench, in Guildhall, on December 18, 1793, and found guilty of high treason. As a result of the trial he was declared an outlaw in England and in all the British dominions.

A defense in Paine's behalf might have been made at the trial, with some chance of its being effective, if he had not written an insulting letter to the attorney-general, which was read in court. The following extract from his communication gives an idea of its general tone:

That the Government of England is as great, if not the greatest perfection of fraud and corruption that ever took place since government began, is what you cannot be a stranger to; unless the constant habit of seeing it has blinded your sense. But though you may not chuse to see it, the people are seeing it very fast, and the progress is beyond what you may chuse to believe. Is it possible that you or I can believe, or that reason can make any other man believe, that the capacity of such a man as Mr. Guelph [he means George III, then King of England] or any of his profligate sons, is necessary to the government of a nation? I speak to you as one man ought to speak to another; and I know also that I speak what other people are beginning to think. That you cannot obtain a verdict (and if you do it will

---

[2] Another name for White's Hotel was the Philadelphia House. It had a distinctly American atmosphere. All its clerks, and many of its servants, spoke English, and it made a specialty of English-American breakfasts, instead of the scanty coffee or chocolate and rolls that the French call *le petit déjeuner*. It was praised by sojourners in Paris.

signify nothing) without *packing a Jury*, and we *both* know that such tricks are practiced, is what I have very good reason to believe.

The letter from which the above extract is taken was sent from France to the attorney-general without the knowledge of Thomas Erskine, Paine's leading counsel, and that gentleman was sadly perplexed when the letter was read in court. He insisted that it must be a forgery, but everyone in the court from Lord Kenyon, the presiding justice, down to the last member of the jury knew very well that Paine had written it, for it sounded exactly like him.

In his trunk Paine carried to France the printers' proofs of his *Letter to the Addressers*, which he had just received and had not yet had time to read. He found a way of returning them from Calais and the book was published in England on the last day of that month—September, 1792.

Following his trial and the legal classification of Paine as an outlaw, the English authorities took up the matter of punishing those who had a hand in the printing or circulation of Paine's books. H. D. Symonds was sentenced to two years' imprisonment and fined twenty pounds for selling the *Rights of Man*, in addition to two more years of prison and another fine of one hundred pounds for bringing out the *Letter to the Addressers*.

A dozen or more printers and booksellers were tried and found guilty, but the fines and prison sentences varied from light to heavy. For instance, William Belcher, a bookseller, was sent to prison for only three months for selling the *Rights of Man* and the *Letter*, while J. Ridgway got one year in prison and a hundred-pound fine, and Fische Palmer was sentenced to the Botany Bay penal colony for seven years. "Clio" Rickman, Paine's intimate friend, was indicted but he escaped to France.

The interdiction against the sale of Paine's books continued for years after his death. In 1819 Richard Carlile and his wife, who owned and managed a bookshop in London, were brought into court on a charge of having sold copies of the forbidden works. Paine had then been dead for ten years. Carlile was fined fifteen hundred pounds and sent to prison for three years. Mrs. Carlile got a two-years' sentence in prison and a fine of five hundred pounds.

4

Paine was known by reputation in every part of France, and his distinction as an author and as a champion of human rights was of such a high order that he stood in a class by himself. When he took his seat in the National Convention on September 21 as a deputy from the department of Pas-de-Calais he was given an ovation by his fellow members.

Next day—September 22, 1792—royalty was formally abolished in France by an act of the Convention.

The new French calendar was also adopted that same day. Like many other doings of the revolutionaries the creation of a new mode of reckoning the days, weeks and months seems useless, farfetched and unnecessary, but the leaders of the movement did not so consider it, for they were obsessed by an impulse to make a clean break with the past. Reforming the calendar was a part of the campaign to throw off the influence of the church and royalty by doing away with the observance of holy days, the celebration of historical events and the whole network of traditional associations with dates. For revolutionary France the new life was supposed to begin with the first day of the Year One—and that day was September 22, 1792. Everything that came before that date belonged to an evil, hideous era which should be forgotten by all true patriots.[3]

[3] Under the French Revolutionary calendar the Year One began with the proclamation of the Republic, which was the twenty-second of September, 1792. That was the New Year's Day of the calendar.

There were twelve months in the year—each consisting of thirty days, with five days left over for republican festivals. Each month had three weeks of ten days each. One day a week was a holiday.

The names of the months were: *Vendémiaire* (the vintage month); *Brumaire* (the month of mists); *Frimaire* (the freezing month); *Nivôse* (the snow month); *Pluviôse* (the month of rains); *Ventôse* (the windy month); *Germinal* (when plants begin to germinate); *Floréal* (the month of flowers); *Prairial* (the time of hayfields); *Messidor* (the harvest moon); *Thermidor* (the hot season); *Fructidor* (the month of fruits).

The French Revolution had begun as a protest against an obsolete national system in which all the power—and nearly all the wealth—was in the hands of the King and the nobles. Within such an economic and social frame the millions of people who composed the nation and carried on the whole of its productive effort had no rights or privileges of a political nature. They were serfs, in fact if not in name.

The primary aim of those who inspired the Revolution at the beginning was not to overthrow the government or to dethrone the King, but simply to institute reforms which would give the people a part in governmental affairs. In other words, they stood for manhood suffrage, for a congress or parliament in which all classes of the population would be represented, for laws which would apply to all citizens equally, irrespective of social classification; and for a civilization characterized by justice, intelligence and liberty.

If the ruling class—meaning, the King and the nobles—had met these demands even halfway the French Revolution would have come to a peaceful end without much bloodshed. Of this there can hardly be a reasonable doubt. But the King and his satellites were too stupid to adopt such a course. They were hardened Tories, trained from childhood to look upon the ordinary run of humanity as a class of servants, useful as workers but without any claim to consideration in national affairs.

It is true that some concessions were granted by the King and the ruling class when the mobs began to roar beneath the palace windows and to run wild in the streets, but these concessions were given grudgingly and with bad grace, for the noble lords —so renowned for their exquisite courtesy—had no manners at all when it was a matter of dealing with the common people.

In the meantime King Louis XVI and his advisers were secretly plotting with foreign governments and urging them to invade France.

As time passed the revolutionaries crushed all opposition and became the rulers of France. The King, Queen and their retainers were confined in the Temple awaiting their fate, whatever it might be. Nearly all the members of the nobility were refugees, living shabbily in the other countries of Europe.

With the success of the Revolution, its leaders and their respective followers began to group themselves into two opposing political parties. One of these was composed of rabid, uncompromising and bloodthirsty radicals. They were called Jacobins, a name derived from the Jacobin Club in Paris, a political organization.

The Jacobins were really Communists in thought and action. They advocated the nationalization of the estates of the nobility and the clergy, the redistribution of wealth, the abolition of the church, and the destruction—by massacre or the guillotine—of all those who opposed them.

The bulk of the Jacobin party belonged to the lowest element of the people. Their leaders, cruel and rapacious, were gangsters at heart and in action, although some of them—Robespierre, Marat and Danton, for example—were men of intellect and education. Under revolutionary symbols and catchwords they intended, undoubtedly, to set up a despotism of their own.

The opposition party was known as the Girondins, a name that came from the Gironde, a department of southwestern France of which Bordeaux is the capital. But the party was national, notwithstanding its local designation. There were Girondins all over France, and Jacobins also. The Girondins were what we would call Liberals today. They stood for the republican form of government; they believed in the private ownership of property, and argued that the government should be limited in its authority over industry and human affairs generally. The Girondins were opposed to violent measures in any form, and certainly to wholesale executions on the guillotine.

The two parties were usually called by their nicknames. The Jacobins were the "Mountain," or the "Mountaineers," because they sat on the higher tiers of seats in the National Convention and looked down on the Girondins who were grouped on the level of the hall. The Girondins were called the "Plain," or the "Marsh," in the common speech of the time.

Tom Paine was a Girondin, naturally and of course, for the ideas of that party coincided almost precisely with his own. He took his seat, on becoming a member of the Convention, with his fellow Girondins in the "Plain."

The Convention selected, on October 11, a committee composed of its members to draft a constitution for the proposed French republic. For this purpose nine deputies were named: Sieyès, Paine, Brissot, Pétion de Villeneuve, Vergniaud, Gensonné, Barère, Danton, Condorcet. Paine was unfamiliar with the French language, though he could understand it if it were spoken very slowly. But at least four members of the committee could speak English, and they acted as interpreters. The four were Brissot, Condorcet, Danton and Barère. Brissot and Paine were old friends; Brissot had lived in America for some time and had met Paine there.

Only two of the members of this committee of nine survived the Reign of Terror. The two were Sieyès, who saved himself by changing sides; and Paine, who was saved by another instance of the good luck that seemed to hang around him like a protective cloud. Condorcet, faced by hopeless ruin, committed suicide. Danton met his death on the guillotine—and so did others who served on the committee for drafting a constitution. One of the members—Pétion de Villeneuve—disappeared and was generally supposed to have left France, until one day when his decomposing body, half-eaten by wolves, was found lying in a forest.

The drafting committee met daily for several months and a republican constitution was finally evolved from its deliberations. When it was submitted to the Convention it was not accepted as it stood, for dozens of amendments and changes were proposed. Eventually an amended document that satisfied a majority of the members was adopted as the basic law of the land. The date of its adoption by the Convention was June 25, 1793, but it was immediately suspended on account of the war in which France was then engaged with England, Austria, Prussia, Holland and Spain.

One of the first acts of the Convention was to bring Louis XVI before it for trial on a charge of high treason. He had invited Austria and Prussia to send their armies into France and had turned over to hostile foreign governments much of the confidential information concerning the national armed strength that had come to him as head of the State. There was no doubt whatever as to the truth of these accusations, so his conviction was virtually certain from the beginning of the trial.

Paine made a strong and long-continued effort to save the King's life, for he believed that the execution of Louis XVI would contribute nothing to the cause of human freedom, but would be only an exhibition of savagery. Royalty as an institution had been abolished in France, so what good could be gained by killing Louis Capet, former King but only a helpless individual at the time of the trial? Paine took that stand, and many delegates in the Convention agreed with him, but not enough of them to carry the point at issue. On November 20 he spent the evening in his rooms writing an argument for sparing the King's life. He proposed to send the deposed King to America to live the rest of his days as a private citizen.

The address was translated into French the next morning (November 21) by the Marquise de Condorcet and Paine gave it to the secretary of the Convention to be read. It is too long to be given here in its entirety, but the following extracts carry the flavor of it:

Let then those United States be the guard and the asylum of Louis Capet. There, in the future, remote from the miseries and crimes of royalty, he may learn, from the constant presence of public prosperity, that the true system of government consists not in monarchs, but in fair, equal and honorable representation. In recalling this circumstance, and submitting this proposal, I consider myself a citizen of both countries. I submit it as an American who feels the debt of gratitude he owes to every Frenchman. I submit it as a man who, albeit an adversary of kings, forgets not that they are subject to human frailties. I support my proposal as a citizen of the French Republic, because it appears to me the best and most politic measure that can be adopted.

In another part of his address he made this excellent point:

It has already been proposed to abolish the penalty of death, and it is with infinite satisfaction that I recollect the humane and excellent oration pronounced by Robespierre on the subject, in the constituent Assembly. Monarchial governments have trained the human race to sanguinary punishments, but the people should not follow the examples of their oppressors in such vengeance. As France has been the first of European nations to abolish royalty, let her also be the first to abolish the punishment of death, and to find out a milder and more effectual substitute.

The Jacobins in the Convention—and they constituted a majority of the membership—were determined to put the former King to death, so it is hardly probable that Paine's argument, even under favorable conditions, would have saved his life; but it so happened the conditions on that particular day were extremely unfavorable. A locksmith who had been employed by the royal household to do some work in the Tuileries palace went to the Jacobin leaders and told them that on the King's orders he had built a secret safe in the wall of the King's chamber, and that this hiding place for documents was so concealed that it looked precisely like the rest of the wall and could be found only by one who knew the trick of locating it and opening it.

The workman was taken at once to the palace, the safe was found and opened, and its contents proved, without a doubt, that the King, before he had been deposed, was in secret correspondence with the enemies of his country.

The safe was opened on November 20, and its contents were shown to the Convention the next day, just before Paine's address was read. It is hardly possible to conceive a worst conjunction of circumstances.

The trial of Louis Capet proceeded at a slow pace, day after day and week after week. The evidence thus produced would fill volumes. Now and then a vote was taken on the prisoner's guilt or innocence, but they were only test votes and not final. In all of them the majority voted the ex-King guilty. Marat was the leader of those who advocated the execution of Louis. Whenever the roll was called to record the sentiment of the Convention concerning the ex-King Thomas Paine rose when his name was reached and shouted in French: "I vote for the detention of Louis until the end of the war, and after that his perpetual banishment." Paine had gone to the trouble of learning this sentence in French perfectly, so it would be understood by all who heard him.

On January 19, 1793, the Convention voted to put Louis Capet to death, but the leaders decided not to be too hasty, and decided to have a final vote the next day. Before the final vote was taken—on January 20—Paine mounted the tribune with Bancal, an English-speaking delegate who had been a friend of Benjamin Franklin, and was now a supporter of Paine. The address which had been prepared by Paine and translated into French was read by the secretary of the Convention. He was interrupted by Marat, bloodthirsty leader of the Jacobins, who declared that Paine was incompetent to vote on the question, as he was a Quaker and opposed to the death penalty in any case.

When the excitement had subsided, the secretary continued to read Paine's speech. Here are a few quotations that express the general sentiment of the address:

My language has always been that of liberty and humanity and I know by experience that nothing so exalts a nation as the union of these two principles, under all circumstances. I know the public mind of France, and particularly that of Paris, has been heated and irritated by the dangers to which they have been exposed; but could we carry our thoughts into the future, when the dangers are ended, and the irritations forgotten, what today seems an act of justice may then appear an act of vengeance. . . . If, on my return to America, I should employ myself on a history of the French Revolution, I had rather record a thousand errors dictated by humanity, than one inspired by a justice too severe. . . .

France has but one ally—the United States of America. That is the only nation that can furnish France with naval provisions, for the kingdoms of northern Europe are, or soon will be, at war with her. It happens, unfortunately, that the person now under discussion is regarded in America as a deliverer of their country. I can assure you that his execution will there spread universal sorrow, and it is in your power not thus to wound the feelings of your ally. Could I speak the French language I would descend to your bar, and in their name become your petitioner to respite the execution of the sentence on Louis.

Marat, livid with rage, interrupted the reading of the speech at this point and declared that it was not in the language of Thomas Paine; and that whatever had been written by him had been improperly translated with intent to deceive the Convention as to Paine's real opinions. It was soon proved, however, by comparison with the English version in Paine's handwriting that the speech had been correctly translated. While this heated discussion was going on Paine sat in silence and took no part in it.

Of the 721 members voting on the subject of the King's punishment, 387 voted unconditionally for death, and 334 for his imprisonment. There were no votes for Paine's proposal to banish the King for life. As a matter of fact, that alternative was not put formally before the Convention; the only thing a deputy had to decide in his own mind was whether the King should be executed, imprisoned or set free.

On January 21, 1793, the day after the vote was taken, Louis XVI was carted to the guillotine and beheaded.

5

The Jacobins were growing in power, and rapidly assuming control of all the functions of the government. They had little sympathy with republican ideals and preferred a dictatorship under Jacobin control. The mere existence of opinions contrary to their own was a mortal offence which should be punished by the death of the offender, so the guillotine was brought into service. One must admit that there is a finality about the practice of head-chopping that appeals to those who cannot bear contradiction. Cut off your opponent's head and that puts an end to his loud-mouthed objections, his logical, convincing arguments, and his vote-winning maneuvers. To men who thought

in the manner of Robespierre, Danton and Marat it seemed that
France would be always torn by dissensions and disagreements
until a large number of the dissenters were put to death. Such
a conception of the matter—bloody, and cruel and barbarous
as it may be—is still very much alive and dynamic in the middle of the twentieth century. We have all seen it at work within
the last few years in Russia, Germany, Italy and other countries.

Thus began the Reign of Terror. Members of the Convention
were not immune. All the Girondins in that important legislative body were under suspicion and in danger. On October 3,
1793, twelve Girondin deputies were beheaded in Paris and in
Bordeaux half a dozen others met the same fate. During the
early months of 1794 deputies of the party were arrested daily.
Twenty-two Girondins were removed from the Convention in
one day.

More than three hundred members of the Convention had
voted against the execution of Louis XVI. The Jacobins looked
upon all of them as traitors, and Marat—addressing a radical
club in Paris—urged everyone present to recall from the Convention "all of those faithless members who had betrayed their
duties in trying to save a tyrant's life."

Thomas Paine, as one of the leaders of that section, lost his
influence day by day and was suspected by the Jacobin leaders
of being, first of all, an English spy. His enemies claimed that
his outlawry by the British Government was a pretence, and
that it had been done to give him a high standing in the councils
of the French revolutionaries where he would be able to observe their activities from the inside and report them, by some
secret means of communication, to their enemies across the Channel. But, of course, this view of Paine's presence was not unanimous. He had friends who knew better and never lost their
faith in him. Among them Danton must be included, surprising
as that fact may seem.

In a long letter to Danton, written on May 6, 1793, Paine
discusses with admirable common sense some of the problems
that were then facing the nation. He urged Danton to propose

to the leaders of the Convention the removal of the capital from Paris temporarily, if not permanently, to take it outside the range of the Parisian mobs. These ragamuffins swarmed daily into the galleries of the Convention and made so much noise with their yelling, cheering and singing that the speakers on the floor could not be heard.

He wrote, in this same letter to Danton:

There ought to be some regulation with respect to the spirit of denunciation that now prevails. If every individual is to indulge his private malignancy or his private ambition, to denounce at random and without any kind of proof, all confidence will be undermined and all authority be destroyed. Calumny is a species of Treachery that ought to be punished as well as any other kind of Treachery. It is a private vice productive of public evils; because it is possible to irritate men into disaffection by continual calumny who never intended to be disaffected.

It is therefore, equally as necessary to guard against the evils of unfounded or malignant suspicion as against the evils of blind confidence. It is equally as necessary to protect the characters of public officers from calumny as it is to punish them for treachery or misconduct. . . .

Calumny becomes harmless and defeats itself when it attempts to act upon too large a scale. Thus the denunciation of the Sections [of Paris] against the twenty-two deputies falls to the ground. The departments that elected them are better judges of their moral and political characters than those who have denounced them. This denunciation will injure Paris in the opinion of the departments because it has the appearance of dictating to them what sort of deputies they shall elect. Most of the acquaintances that I have in the Convention are among those who are in that list, and I know there are not better men or better patriots than what they are.

As time passed Paine, with infinite sadness, saw the French Revolution turn into a murderous crusade. The guillotine in Paris stood in the square that is now called the Place de la Concorde, and it was kept busy all day. Frequently men and women were executed on flimsy accusations that should not have been considered for a moment—on hearsay evidence, on mere suspicion, on lies that had an ulterior motive.

In Lyon the troops of the revolutionary army shot down the people in droves on the pretence that the whole community was in revolt. At Nantes the guillotine was abandoned in favor of drowning, a method that enabled the executioners to handle a hundred or more people at the same time. Boats were built with hinged bottoms which could be opened at sea so that all those who were standing in the vessel might be dropped into the water.

On April 20 of that year, 1793, Paine wrote to Thomas Jefferson, his lifelong friend, a letter in which he gave a gloomy description of affairs in France. Its last two paragraphs are given here:

Had this revolution been conducted consistently with its principles, there was once a good prospect of extending liberty through the greatest part of Europe; but I now relinquish that hope. Should the Enemy by venturing into France put themselves again in a condition of being captured, the hope will revive; but this is a risk that I do not wish to see tried, lest it should fail.

As the prospect of a general freedom is now much shortened, I begin to contemplate returning home. I shall await the event of the proposed Constitution, and then take my final leave of Europe. I have not written to the President, as I have nothing to communicate more than in this letter. Please to present him my affection and compliments, and remember me among the circle of my friends. Your sincere and affectionate friend,

Thomas Paine.

P.S. I just now received a letter from General Lewis Morris, who tells me that the house and Barn on my farm at New Rochelle are burnt down. I assure you I shall not bring enough money to build another.

The New Rochelle house to which Paine refers was occupied by a tenant when it was destroyed by fire. No description of the house now exists, but it was said to have been handsome and spacious. In the letter quoted above he tells Jefferson that he may return soon to America, but it was nine years after that letter was written before he came home. The cottage at New Rochelle that is now shown to sightseers was erected, on Paine's order, by a contractor in 1793, and Paine lived in it for awhile after his return from France in 1802.

Paine was no longer an important figure in the Convention. He was the victim of many lies, for the big popular party was the Jacobin and its leaders had never forgiven him for trying to save Louis Capet's life. Although he had barely enough income to keep himself alive there was a story current that he was secretly in the pay of the former French royal family as well as the recipient of money from sources in London.

In the "Plain" of the Convention—meaning the rows of benches on the level lower floor—he was at times the only delegate, for nearly all the Girondin deputies had been forced to resign by the midsummer of 1793, or they had been sent to prison, or to the guillotine.

On June 7 Robespierre called upon the Convention for drastic action against foreigners in France who belonged to enemy nations. Not long afterward a law was passed ordering their imprisonment, but it was understood that the act was not to be enforced in respect to Thomas Paine (of English origin) and Anacharsis Cloots (a Prussian), the only foreigners who were members of the Convention.[4]

Marat, the Jacobin leader, was murdered in his bath on July 13, 1793, by Charlotte Corday, a comely young woman who had never laid eyes on Marat until that moment. She was seized, quickly tried and convicted, and sent to the guillotine.

The Convention voted, in September of that year, to create a Committee of Public Safety and turn over to it most of the authority of the Convention, though the Convention would still remain in existence in an advisory capacity.

This newly formed Committee, destined to become famous as the directing power of the Reign of Terror, consisted of

---

[4] Cloots was a Prussian who had come to France with the hope of persuading the French revolutionists to incite an international overthrow of all rulers. He was wealthy, with an income of one hundred thousand livres a year. He believed that Humanity and God are one and the same, and he was a humanitarian of the most pronounced type. In 1794, before the end of the Terror, he met his death on the guillotine.

twelve members. Robespierre belonged to it and might be considered its most important member, but there were others who distinguished themselves in the field of terrorism. There was for instance, Bertrand Barère, the so-called "Anacreon of the Guillotine," and Jacques Nicolas Billaud-Varenne—both of whom were human tigers. The youngest member of the Committee, Antoine Louis Saint-Just, became widely known as "The Angel of Death."

It may be interesting to note that not one of the twelve members of this all-powerful Committee of Public Safety was a workman or a peasant, or had ever made a living by manual labor. Six members were lawyers by profession, one was a playwright, one a business man, two had been army officers, one was a nobleman by birth, and another—strange as it may seem—was a Protestant clergyman.

The mobs, which were such a conspicuous feature of the Revolution, were composed mainly of working people, but the inspiration, encouragement and leadership came from the middle classes. It was they who resented bitterly the crushing impact of the royal regime—the overbearing nobles; the arrogant officials; the owners of vast estates, who, in their way, were as despotic as sultans. All of these favored nobles lived in spacious chateaux or luxurious city mansions, while the homes of those among the King's subjects who furnished the talent, ideas and executive ability to carry on the nation's work were humble by comparison with the palaces of their lordly neighbors. Nor could these enterprising men of the bourgeoisie ever hope to reach highly honored positions in the government, for such places belonged to the crowd of courtiers who surrounded the King.

The laboring element that composed the mobs lived in such filth, misery and destitution that it was not difficult to incite them to rebel and to commit bloody atrocities wholesale. Their moral standards, like their standards of living, were of the lowest, naturally enough, for they had been brought up from childhood in a world where cruelty and oppression were not exceptional, but merely the common occurrences of daily life.

This sanguinary turn of the Revolution was extremely distressing to Tom Paine. He did not believe that the cause of liberalism could be advanced by the practice of murder and destruction. All his violence lay in the sharp and smashing logic of his ideas. His purpose was to convince people, not to destroy them.

He seldom went any more to the meetings of the Convention, for nearly all his friends had been expelled or imprisoned, and when he rose to speak his voice was drowned by yells, catcalls and hissing from the gallery.

6

Although he had fallen out of favor with most of the intensely radical leaders of the revolutionary movement—the leaders of the mob and the feeders of the guillotine—Paine still had a large circle of friends, French, American and English, residing in Paris. Before France declared war against England in February, 1793, he was on familiar terms with various eminent Englishmen in Paris. One of them was Lord Lauderdale, with whom he dined once a month. Lord Edward Fitzgerald, son of the Duke of Leinster, was another constant companion and an enthusiastic admirer. Until Fitzgerald had to leave France on account of the war he and Paine had rooms together in the hotel. On October 30, 1792, he wrote to his mother, "I lodge with my friend Paine, we breakfast, dine and sup together. The more I see of his interior, the more I like and respect him. I cannot express how kind he is to me; there is a simplicity of manner, a goodness of heart, and a strength of mind in him, that I never before knew a man to possess." [5]

[5] Lord Edward Fitzgerald, who was in his twenty-ninth year when he lived with Paine in Paris, had been a young officer in the British army in America during the last year of the American Revolution. He acquired, during that period, a love of human freedom that moved him to action during the rest of his short life. In Paris in 1792 he was still an army officer on furlough, but his openly expressed sympathy with the French Revolution brought about his expulsion from the British army. In 1796 he joined the Irish Rebellion and became a colonel. He received a mortal wound, was captured and died in captivity in 1798, at the age of thirty-five.

Paine's callers at the Philadelphia House grew in number as the weeks passed. Before long they had become so numerous that he could hardly find time to write, so he decided to change his place of residence and to keep his new address secret except to a few friends.

In the early summer of 1793 he took rooms in a mansion at No. 63 Faubourg St. Denis. The house at that number was famous, for it had been the residence of Madame de Pompadour when she was the courtesan favorite of Louis XV.[6]

His new home seems, at this distance in time, to have been very agreeable. In a letter to Lady Smythe, one of his cherished friends, he said:

The house, which was enclosed by a wall and gateway from the street, was a good deal like an old mansion farm-house, and the courtyard was like a farm-yard, stocked with fowls,—ducks, turkeys, and geese; which, for amusement, we used to feed out of the parlor window on the ground floor. Beyond was a garden of more than an acre of ground, well laid out, and stocked with excellent fruit trees. . . .

My apartments consisted of three rooms; the first for wood, water, etc.; the next was the bedroom; and beyond it the sitting room, which looked into the garden through a glass door. I used to find some relief by walking alone in the garden, after dark, and cursing with hearty goodwill the authors of that terrible system that had turned the character of the Revolution I had been proud to defend.

I went but little to the Convention, and then only to make my appearance, because I found it impossible to join in their tremendous decrees, and useless and dangerous to oppose them. My having voted and spoken extensively, more so than any other member, against the execution of the king, had already fixed a mark upon me; neither dared any of my associates in the Convention to translate and speak in French for me anything I might have dared to have written. . . . Pen and ink were then of no use to me; no good could be done by writing, and no printer dared to print; and whatever I might have written, for my private amusement, as anecdotes of the times, would have been con-

---

[6] The house stood on the ground now occupied by the Gare du Nord. But the street numbering has been changed and No. 63 is now on the other side of the street. The garden of that era is now an engine shed.

tinually exposed to be examined, and tortured into any meaning that the rage of party might fix upon it. And as to softer subjects, my heart was in distress at the fate of my friends, and my harp hung upon the weeping willows.

Although he lived during this period at No. 63 Faubourg St. Denis he arranged with the management of the Philadelphia House to let him have the use of two rooms twice a week to hold "levees," or informal parties where he received anyone who cared to call on him. Many of those who came were foreigners who wanted him to intercede with the government in their behalf, not knowing that he was out of favor himself. Others sought him to discuss his books or to learn what he thought of the future of France—and of civilization.

Among his close friends who resided at the house in the Faubourg St. Denis, or who called on him there, were Nicolas and Madame de Bonneville, Joel Barlow, Mary Wollstonecraft, Mr. and Mrs. Christie, the Marquis de Condorcet and his wife. The gracious Marquise translated some of Paine's writings into French for publication in that language. Another guest was "Clio" Rickman, who had escaped from London in a hurry, without money or baggage, when he had been indicted on the charge of sedition for having published Paine's *Rights of Man*.

"It was summer," Paine wrote to Lady Smythe, "and we spent most of our time in the garden, passing it away in those childish amusements that serve to keep reflection from the mind,—such as marbles, Scotch hops, battledores, etc., at which we were all pretty expert. In this retired manner we remained about six or seven weeks, and our landlord went every evening into the city to bring us the news of the day and the evening journal."

CHAPTER XIII

The Age of Reason

I

DURING the whole of 1793 Paine lived in imminent danger. It surrounded him on all sides, and he walked in it as one walks in a fog without knowing what lies ahead. He realized clearly that he had lost the confidence of the Jacobin leaders who had seized the revolutionary movement and were turning it into a bloody massacre. And he, himself, no longer had any faith in them or in their professions of liberty, equality and human rights.

The difficulties that surrounded him in France were made more complicated and far more dangerous by the presence there of an American who should have had Paine's welfare in his heart and mind. That individual was Gouverneur Morris, who had succeeded Jefferson as the American minister to France. George Washington and his administration selected Morris to represent this country in France at a period in history when they could have hardly made a worse choice. He was recalled in 1794 at the request of the French Government. By that time he had done a great deal of harm to Tom Paine.

Morris had long detested Paine and all his doings, but he had the adroitness of a clever hypocrite, and the ability to conceal his real opinions when such concealment seemed desirable. When he was the American minister in Paris he had Paine as a guest at his table, not once but many times, yet his diary—to be found today in almost any large public library—shows that his comments concerning his guest were like the spatterings of mud flung against a white wall. He characterized Paine as a mere adventurer from England, ignorant even of grammar and polite usage. These, and even more derogatory comments, were made also, in all probability, to officials of the French Government.

Between Thomas Paine and Gouverneur Morris there lay an abyss of disagreement which it would have been impossible to bridge, for the reason that their respective conceptions of life and society were fundamentally different. Morris, for instance, thought that suffrage should be restricted to men who owned land, as a necessary safeguard "against the dangerous influence of those people without property or principle," to quote his own words. Note that he connects property and principle; they go together. If you have no property you are an unprincipled knave as a matter of course.

At the time of the formation of the Constitution of the United States he proposed an aristocratic Senate, all the members to be appointed by the President and selected from a list of rich men. The House, he argued, should be democratic—its members elected by those who had the right to vote; that is to say, by people of property. The plutocratic Senate and the semi-democratic House would hold each other in check, which means that no popular reform measure would ever become a law.

Later in life Gouverneur Morris lost faith in the republican system and in the Union itself. He thought that the territories in the West should never be raised to statehood, but should be governed as provinces and allowed no voice in the councils of the nation. It would be wise, he said, to curtail our western frontier and permit the Indians in that region to have independent sovereignties under British protection.

His distinctly British leaning led Morris to adopt a number of un-American ideas. He declared, for example, that the British had a right to take seamen by force from American ships and use their services on British vessels. The war debt incurred in fighting the British in the War of 1812 should be repudiated, he argued, for the American nation had no valid reason for going into the war.

When Morris became the American minister at Paris in 1792 he soon learned that Paine was such an important figure, not only in the Convention but among Frenchmen of all classes, that he was generally looked upon as the real representative of the American Government. In comparison with the author of the *Rights of Man* Gouverneur Morris appeared to them a mere figurehead. This conception, mistaken as it was, irritated Morris intensely, for his vanity was colossal, and he set out to do whatever he could to correct the impression by depreciating Paine, not publicly but quietly and secretly.

The lofty estimation of Paine in the minds of the public began to sink downward slowly but persistently in the early months of 1793.

Gossip was soon floating around that the so-called gladiator for humanity, freedom and democracy was not all he seemed to be; that he was at heart—and in purpose—a traitor playing a treacherous role in France, no matter how noble his intentions may have been when he aroused the spirit of independence in America with his *Common Sense* or when he started an uproar in England with the *Rights of Man*.

Such was the tone of those who spread the gossip.

Furthermore, they cautioned their listeners to be watchful and careful when dealing with Paine, for who can be sure of this renegade Englishman, a man without family, home or country? He has outlived his welcome in America. No doubt about that. When they began to find out the truth about him over there he left the country. Now France is learning, a little at a time, that he is an impostor.

Many of our patriotic citizens have followed closely the doings of Paine as a member of the Convention, and they feel sure that he is in the pay of the British Government, and is here acting as a spy in the councils of our own glorious Revolution; and that he is a traitor to both France and America. The outlawing of this unprincipled adventurer by the English court means nothing. It was a trick—*a coup de théâtre*—to make us welcome him.

Don't forget the fact that Paine was bitterly opposed to the punishment of the infamous Louis Capet. He made more than one speech in the Convention in his effort to save the scoundrel. Paine urged the Convention to send Louis, the convicted traitor, to America. What a wonderful solution of the matter that would have been! After that anybody might practice treason just to get the sea voyage. And in America Louis Capet would have lived on the riches of the land while plotting to return.

There is a lot of deception in Tom Paine. He pretends to be in sympathy with our revolution, but does he really mean it, or is he just playing a part?

These slanderous comments, and others like them—made in whispers and innuendoes—ran through Paris.

2

The long struggle between the Jacobins and the Girondins came to an end in the summer of 1793, and the clamorous, bloody-minded Jacobins were the victors. With the Girondins out of the way, the Jacobins had no longer any restraining influence to check their destructive impulses.

Twenty-one of the Girondins who were members of the Convention were guillotined in one day, October 31, but Paine had not at that time been arrested or even formally charged with any offence. He knew, however, or felt instinctively, that his time was short, and he began, around the first of November, to write a book that had been maturing in his mind for months. During November and December he seldom left the house in the Faubourg St. Denis, for he felt that he could not spare the time to visit his friends, and most of his daily walks were taken in the garden belonging to the mansion. He expected daily—morning, noon and night—to hear the fatal rap on his door, and to find, upon opening it, a squad of soldiers with a summons that would remove him forever from this world and all its doings.

The book that he wrote in such circumstances is called *The Age of Reason,* and during the past hundred and fifty years it has stirred up innumerable controversies, sermons, maledictions, feuds and hornets' nests of one kind or another.

The Age of Reason has been given at least a score of foul names. The "Devil's Prayer Book" is one, and another, widely current a hundred years ago, is "The Bible of Atheism." It would be difficult, if not impossible, to discover any book in any language that has had more lies circulated about it. All of this must seem puzzling and curious to readers who are familiar with *The Age of Reason*, for Paine was not an atheist but a Deist, and his purpose in writing the book was to combat atheism. In a letter to Samuel Adams he said:

It has been my intention, for several years past, to publish my thoughts upon religion. I am well aware of the difficulties that attend the subject; and, from that consideration, had reserved it to a more advanced period of life. I intended it to be the last offering I should make to my fellow-citizens of all nations; and that at a time when the purity of the motive that induced me to it could not admit of a question, even by those who might disapprove the work.

My friends were falling as fast as the guillotine could cut their heads off, and as I expected, every day, the same fate, I resolved to begin my work. I appeared to myself to be on my death bed, for death was on every side of me, and I had no time to lose. . . . The people of France were running headlong into atheism, and I had the work translated in their own language, to stop them in that career, and fix them to the first article of every man's creed who has any creed at all and that first article should be—*I believe in God*.

Paine was expelled from the Convention late in December. He was not present at the time for he had ceased to attend the meetings. The act of expulsion canceled the exception from the law concerning foreigners which had given him immunity while he was still a member of the Convention.

When the news of his expulsion came to him he had finished writing, only a few hours before, the last page of Part I of *The Age of Reason*. Here is an extract from that final page:

The Creation we behold is the real and ever-existing word of God, in which we cannot be deceived. It proclaims his power, it demonstrates his wisdom, it manifests his goodness and beneficence.

The moral duty of man consists in imitating the moral goodness and beneficence of God, manifested in the creation toward all his creatures. That seeing, as we daily do, the goodness of God to all men, it is an example calling upon all men to practice the same toward each other; and, consequently, that everything of persecution and revenge between man and man, and everything of cruelty to animals is a violation of moral duty.

From some source, never revealed, he was informed that he would be put under arrest that very night. He had expected that to happen, and he had become accustomed to the thought, but he was anxious over his manuscript. Would it be destroyed at sight by those who came to take him in charge, or would it be shown to those higher up and eventually lost? He did not know what its fate might be if it should fall into their hands, so he decided to turn it over for safekeeping to Joel Barlow, a well-known American who was then living in Paris. Barlow was an admirer of Paine's writings and they had become intimate friends.[1]

Though Paine made his home in the Faubourg St. Denis his official residence was the Philadelphia House and he went there as soon as he learned that he was to be put under arrest. He carried his manuscript with him, for he expected to meet Barlow at the hotel. It was not where Barlow lived—he had rooms elsewhere—but he spent hours every day at the Philadelphia House, which was a favorite resort of the Americans in Paris.

Within an hour after Paine's arrival at the hotel a squad of

---

[1] Joel Barlow (1754–1812) was a native of Connecticut, and a graduate of Yale. He was good-looking, sprightly, witty and a good companion. During the American Revolution he had served in the Continental Army. Entered business, and in 1788 was sent to Europe to sell shares, or acreage, in an Ohio land company. The scheme was a failure, but he remained in Europe for seventeen years.

In 1790 he met Paine in London, and two years later he wrote his *Advice to the Privileged Orders*—an echo of Paine's *Rights of Man*. The British suppressed the book and proscribed the author. Barlow sought refuge in Paris. Among the French he was popular, and the Convention made him an honorary citizen.

The American Government appointed him consul to Algiers in 1795. He held the office ten years, then came back to America and lived on an estate near Washington. His mansion, called "Kalorama," was famous for its beauty. James Madison appointed him minister to France. He died in Poland while returning from Russia in 1812, and is buried near Warsaw. He was a man of distinction.

gendarmes came with orders to take him in custody. They treated him courteously, but they made a thorough search of his room to discover incriminating papers. Nothing of the kind was found. They were then about to proceed to his living quarters at No. 63 Faubourg St. Denis to make a further search, when their prisoner informed them that Joel Barlow had some papers belonging to him. The statement was untrue, but he made it for the purpose of getting in touch with Barlow so that he might turn over to him the manuscript of *The Age of Reason.*

Acting on this supposed information the party proceeded to Barlow's rooms on the left bank of the Seine. They got there around three o'clock in the morning, an hour of the night when even feverish revolutionary Paris was slumbering. As soon as they had succeeded in waking Barlow he declared that he had no documents belonging to Paine, and the latter apologized to the officers, saying that he had made a mistake. Nevertheless, they searched every foot of the premises without result. Paine then gave his manuscript to Barlow, making no concealment of the matter, and asked him to have it printed. The captain of the gendarmes immediately seized the manuscript and ruffled its pages, but he did not know enough English to read it, so some one in his party translated a few paragraphs and read them to him. He seemed bored and said that Barlow might keep the manuscript, as it seemed to be merely a religious tract.

They started out then to go across the river again to make a search of Paine's rooms at No. 63 Faubourg St. Denis. It was broad daylight by that time, and the gendarme captain thought they should have breakfast before going further. That decision was agreeable to all, so the guards and their prisoner went into a café and ate. With them was Joel Barlow, who had slipped into his clothes while his quarters were being searched. He intended to accompany his friend Paine until he entered the prison.

They found the Faubourg St. Denis house entirely deserted. For the past week Paine had been its only occupant. All the others who lived there, including the landlord, had been arrested and jailed, or had taken refuge in flight. A search of Paine's quarters revealed nothing and no further effort to find incriminating papers was made. By mid-afternoon he was an occupant of a cell in the Luxembourg prison, where he was destined to remain for more than ten months.

His room, or cell, was on the ground floor of the prison, and it was damp and cold. In the same cell were three other men: Joseph Vanheule of Bruges, and Michael Robyns and Charles Bastini of Louvain.

Joel Barlow carried out faithfully his instructions in respect to *The Age of Reason*. He put the manuscript in the hands of Barrois, a printer of Paris, whose shop assistants were experienced in using English. The first edition of Part I was brought out early in 1794. Part II was written partly while Paine was in prison, and was finished after his release. It was published in 1795. Both parts are now printed and bound together.

The book has had an enormous sale during the one hundred and fifty years of its existence, and has been translated into many languages.

3

If you lack the time or the opportunity to read *The Age of Reason* in its entirety the following extracts, taken verbatim from its text, will give you a clear idea of the character of the book and Paine's method of handling the subject with which it deals. His doubts that the Bible was the word of God began in his childhood. He says:

I well remember, when about seven or eight years of age, hearing a sermon read by a relation of mine, who was a great devotee of the Church, upon the subject of what is called *redemption by the death of the Son of God*.

After the sermon was ended I went into the garden, and as I was going down the garden steps, (for I perfectly remember the spot), I revolted at the recollection of what I had heard, and thought to myself that it was making God Almighty act like a passionate man, that killed his son when he could not revenge himself in any other way;

and, as I was sure a man would be hanged that did such a thing, I could not see for what purpose they preached such sermons.

This was not one of that kind of thoughts that had anything in it of childish levity; it was to me a serious reflection, arising from the idea I had that God was too good to do such an action, and also too almighty to be under any necessity of doing it. I believe in the same manner at this moment; and I moreover believe that any system of religion that has anything in it which shocks the mind of a child cannot be a true system.

Here is his comment on the Biblical account of the birth of Christ:

When also I am told that a woman called the Virgin Mary said, or gave out, that she was with child without cohabitation with a man, and that her betrothed husband, Joseph, said that an angel told him so, I have a right to believe them or not; such a circumstance requires a much stronger evidence than their bare word for it; but we have not even this—for neither Joseph nor Mary wrote any such matter themselves; it is only reported by others that they said so—it is hearsay upon hearsay, and I do not choose to rest my belief upon such evidence.

But he did not look upon Christ as an impostor, or as a selfish seeker for power.

Nothing that is here said can apply, even with the most distant disrespect, to the real character of Jesus Christ. He was a virtuous and an amiable man. The morality that he preached and practised was of the most benevolent kind; and though similar systems of morality had been preached by Confucius, and by some of the Greek philosophers many years before, and by the Quakers since; and by many good men in all ages, it has not been exceeded by any.

Jesus Christ wrote no account of himself, of his birth, parentage, or anything else; not a line of what is called the New Testament is of his own writing. The history of him is altogether the work of other people; and as to the account given of his resurrection and ascension, it was the necessary counterpart to the story of his birth. His historians, having brought him into the world in a supernatural manner, were obliged to take him out again in the same manner, or the first part of the story must have fallen to the ground.

Many of us who have read the New Testament thoughtfully have often wondered why Christ did not cause His doctrine to be written in his lifetime, and why so many of the ideas expressed in His name appeared only after His crucifixion. Paine wrote on this topic:

Had it been the object or the intention of Jesus Christ to establish a new religion, he would undoubtedly have written the system himself, *or procured it to be written in his lifetime*. But there is not a publication extant authenticated with his name. All the books called the New Testament were written after his death. He was a Jew by birth and by profession; and he was the Son of God in like manner that every other person is—for the Creator is the Father of All.

The first four books, called Matthew, Mark, Luke and John, do not give a history of the life of Jesus Christ, but only detached anecdotes of him. It appears from these books that the whole time of his being a preacher was not more than eighteen months; and it was only during this short time that those men became acquainted with him. They make mention of him at the age of twelve years, sitting, they say, among the Jewish doctors, asking and answering questions. As this was several years before their acquaintance with him began, it is most probable they had this anecdote from his parents.

From this time there is no account of him for about sixteen years. Where he lived, or how he employed himself during this interval is not known. Most probably he was working at his father's trade, which was that of a carpenter.

Paine did not look upon the Bible as the Word of God, nor did he believe that it had been inspired by God, but that it had been conceived and written by the prophets and apostles as a pious fiction. He considered it a human document, a literary production of the same class as the dialogues of Plato or the annals of Herodotus. Its authors wrote it, Paine thought and said, for the purpose of inspiring awe and fear.

He wrote, on the first page of Part II of *The Age of Reason:*

It has often been said, that anything may be proved from the Bible, but before anything can be admitted as proved by it, the Bible itself must be proved to be true; for if the Bible be not true, or the truth of it be doubtful, it ceases to have authority, and cannot be admitted as proof of anything.

It has been the practice of all Christian commentators on the Bible, and of all Christian priests and preachers, to impose the Bible on the world as a mass of truth and as the word of God; they have disputed and wrangled, and anathematized each other about the supposed meaning of particular parts and passages therein; one has said and insisted that such a passage meant such a thing; another that it meant directly the contrary; and a third, that it meant neither one nor the other, but something different from both; and this they have called understanding the Bible.

.   .   .   .   .

Now, instead of wasting their time and heating themselves in fractious disputations about doctrinal points drawn from the Bible, these men ought to know, and if they do not, it is civility to inform them, that the first thing to be understood is whether there is sufficient authority for believing the Bible to be the word of God or whether there is not.

There are matters in that book, said to be done by the express command of God, that are as shocking to humanity and to every idea we have of moral justice as anything done by Robespierre, by Carrier, by Joseph le Bon, in France, by the English government in the East Indies, or by any other assassin in modern times. When we read in the books ascribed to Moses, Joshua, etc., that they (the Israelites) came by stealth upon whole nations of people, who, as history itself shows, had given them no offense; that they put all those nations to the sword; that they spared neither age nor infancy; that they utterly destroyed men, women and children; that they left not a soul to breathe—expressions that are repeated over and over again in those books, and that, too, with exulting ferocity—are we sure these things are facts? Are we sure that the Creator of man commissioned these things to be done? And are we sure that the books that tell us so were written by His authority?

It is not the antiquity of a tale that is any evidence of its truth; on the contrary, it is a symptom of its being fabulous; for the more ancient any history pretends to be the more it has the resemblance of a fable. The origin of every nation is buried in fabulous tradition; and that of the Jews is as much to be suspected as any other.

To charge the commission of acts upon the Almighty, which, in their own nature and by every rule of moral justice, are crimes, as all assassination is, and more especially the assassination of infants, is matter of serious concern. The Bible tells us, that those assassinations were done by the express command of God. To believe, therefore, the Bible to be true, we must unbelieve all our belief in the moral justice of God; for wherein could crying or smiling infants offend? And to read the Bible without horror, we must undo everything that is tender, sympathizing, and benevolent in the heart of man. Speaking for myself, if I had no other evidence that the Bible is fabulous than the sacrifice I must make to believe it to be true, that alone would be sufficient to determine my choice.

But while Paine ridiculed the absurd fictions of the Bible, which should not deceive an intelligent person for a moment, he believed nevertheless in God, in a future life, and in the eternal kindness and all-embracing love of the Creator. He believed that the true Word of God is shown only in Nature—in the forests and the fields, in sunshine and rain, in the living creatures of the earth, and he calls the choicest gift of God to man the Gift of Reason.

But some, perhaps, will say: Are we to have no word of God—no revelation? I answer, Yes; there is a word of God; there is a revelation. THE WORD OF GOD IS THE CREATION WE BEHOLD: and it is in this word, which no human invention can counterfeit or alter, that God speaketh universally to man.

.   .   .   .   .

It is only in the CREATION that all our ideas and conceptions of a word of God can unite. The Creation speaketh an universal language, independently of human speech or human language, multiplied and various as they may be. It is an ever-existing original, which every man can read. It cannot be forged; it cannot be counterfeited; it cannot be lost; it cannot be altered; it cannot be suppressed. It does not depend upon the will of man whether it shall be published or not; it publishes itself from one end of the earth to the other. It preaches to all nations and to all worlds; and this word of God reveals to man all that is necessary for man to know of God.

Do we want to contemplate his power? We see it in the immensity of the Creation. Do we want to contemplate his wisdom? We see it in the unchangeable order by which the incomprehensible whole is governed. Do we want to contemplate his munificence? We see it in the abundance with which he fills the earth. Do we want to contemplate his mercy? We see it in his not withholding that abundance even from the unthankful. In fine, do we want to know what God is? Search not the book called the Scripture, which any human hand might make, but the Scripture called the Creation.

The only idea man can affix to the name of God is that of a first cause, the cause of all things. And incomprehensible and difficult as it is for a man to conceive what a first cause is, he arrives at the belief of it from the tenfold greater difficulty of disbelieving it. It is difficult beyond description to conceive that space can have no end; but it is more difficult to conceive an end. It is difficult beyond the power of man to conceive an eternal duration of what we call time; but it is more impossible to conceive a time when there shall be no time.

In like manner of reasoning, everything we behold carries in itself the internal evidence that it did not make itself. Every man is an evidence to himself that he did not make himself; neither could his father make himself, nor his grandfather, nor any of his race; neither could any tree, plant, or animal make itself; and it is the conviction arising from this evidence that carries us on, as it were, by necessity to the belief of a first cause eternally existing, of a nature totally different to any material existence we know of, and by the power of which all things exist; and this first cause man calls God.

The three paragraphs given below set forth Paine's conception of the clergy and the priesthood.

It is possible to believe, and I always feel pleasure in encouraging myself to believe it, that there have been men in the world who persuade themselves that what is called a pious fraud might, at least under particular circumstances, be productive of some good. But the fraud being once established, could not afterward be explained, for it is with a pious fraud as with a bad action, it begets a calamitous necessity of going on.

The persons who first preached the Christian system of faith, and in some measure combined it with the morality preached by Jesus Christ, might persuade themselves that it was better than the heathen mythology that then prevailed. From the first preachers the fraud went on to the second and to the third, till the idea of its being a pious fraud became lost in the belief of its being true; and that belief became again encouraged by the interests of those who made a livelihood by preaching it.

But though such a belief might by such means be rendered almost general among the laity, it is next to impossible to account for the continued persecution carried on by the Church for several hundred years against the sciences and against the professors of science, if the Church had not some record or some tradition that it was originally no other than a pious fraud, or did not foresee that it could not be maintained against the evidence that the structure of the universe afforded.

He had much to say about the collections of myths and fables that make up most of the Old Testament. One of his comments is given here:

Take away from Genesis the belief that Moses was the author, on which only the strange belief that it is the Word of God has stood, and there remains nothing of Genesis but an anonymous book of stories, fables and traditionary or invented absurdities, or of downright lies. The story of Eve and the serpent, and of Noah and his Ark, drops to a level with the Arabian tales, without the merit of being entertaining; and the account of men living eight to nine hundred years becomes as fabulous as the immortality of the Giants of the Mythology.

Besides, the character of Moses, as stated in the Bible, is the most horrid that can be imagined. If those accounts be true, he was the wretch that first began and carried on wars on the score or on the pretense of religion; and under that mask, or that infatuation, committed the most unexampled atrocities that are to be found in the history of any nation.

Paine was a professed Deist. He says so emphatically in *The Age of Reason*. He had, so he declares,

The most clear and long-established conviction that the Bible and the Testament are impositions upon the world, that the fall of man, the account of Jesus Christ being the Son of God, and of his dying to appease the wrath of God, and of salvation by that strange means are all fabulous inventions, dishonorable to the wisdom and power of the Almighty; that the only true religion is Deism, by which I then meant, and mean now, the belief of one God, and an imitation of His moral character, or the practice of what are called moral virtues—and that it was upon this only (so far as religion is concerned) that I rested all my hopes of happiness hereafter. So I say now—and so help me God.

.   .   .   .   .

Deism teaches us, without the possibility of being deceived, all that is necessary or proper to be known. The creation is the Bible of the Deist. He there reads, in the handwriting of the Creator himself, the certainty of His existence and the immutability of His power, and all other Bibles and Testaments are to him forgeries.

The probability that we may be called to account hereafter will, to a reflecting mind, have the influence of belief; for it is not our belief or our disbelief that can make or unmake the fact. As this is the state we are in, and which it is proper we should be in, as free agents, it is the fool only, and not the philosopher, or even the prudent man, that would live as if there were no God.

But the belief of a God is so weakened by being mixed with the strange fable of the Christian creed, and with the wild adventures related in the Bible, and with the obscurity and obscene nonsense of the Testament, that the mind of man is bewildered as in a fog. Viewing all these things in a confused mass, he confounds fact with fable; and as he cannot believe all, he feels a disposition to reject all.

But the belief of a God is a belief distinct from all other things, and ought not to be confounded with any. The notion of a Trinity of Gods, has enfeebled the belief of one God. A multiplication of beliefs acts as a division of belief; and in proportion as anything is divided it is weakened.

If Tom Paine were living today he would be called a Unitarian, for his religious belief was closely along that line.

He wrote: "I believe in one God, and no more; and I hope for happiness beyond this life.

"I believe in the equality of man; and I believe that religious duties consist in doing justice, loving mercy, and endeavoring to make our fellow-creatures happy."

4

Gouverneur Morris could hardly restrain a public exhibition of his pleasure at Paine's incarceration, but he realized that such a display of satisfaction on his part would not seem to be quite in harmony with his role as American minister, so he expressed himself only privately in conversation and in letters.

On January 21, 1794, when Paine had been a resident of the

Luxembourg prison about three weeks, Morris wrote to Thomas Jefferson, who was then our Secretary of State:

> Lest I should forget it, I must mention that Thomas Paine is in prison, where he amuses himself with publishing a pamphlet against Jesus Christ. I do not recollect whether I mentioned to you that he would have been executed along with the rest of the Brissotins if the advance party had not viewed him with contempt. I incline to think that if he is quiet in prison he may have the good luck to be forgotten, whereas should he be brought much into notice, the long suspended axe might fall on him. I believe he thinks that I ought to claim him as an American citizen; but considering his birth, his naturalization in this country, and the place he filled, I doubt much the right, and I am sure that the claim would be, for the present at least, inexpedient and ineffectual.

This short reference to Paine is full of shrewdly calculated misstatements, written by Morris with the intention of deceiving Jefferson.

Let us take them up in order.

The Age of Reason was not against Jesus Christ. On the contrary, Paine called Christ "a virtuous and amiable man" and praised his teachings.

Morris declares that Paine would have been executed with the rest of the Brissotins "if the advance party had not viewed him with contempt." It is a false statement. Nobody viewed Paine with contempt; but the bloodthirsty Jacobin leaders viewed him with intense dislike. They did not send him to the guillotine at once because they were anxious to keep on friendly terms with the United States and they felt, in the early months of 1794, that his execution would cause a storm of resentment to arise in the young nation across the sea. Robespierre knew very well that Morris was an inveterate enemy of Paine, but he was not at all sure that the slanders circulated by Morris had any basis in fact. Until he could find out the truth he meant to keep Paine in prison.

There is no doubt that Paine was still an American citizen, although Morris prefers to call him a naturalized Frenchman. Paine did not ask for French citizenship; it was conferred upon him as an honor, and on the same day the Convention made citizens of George Washington, James Madison, Alexander Hamilton and several other Americans.

Paine had never been a candidate for membership in the Convention; he was elected without making speeches or soliciting votes. He was looked upon as a foreigner while he was a member of the legislative body.

The fact that he was an American citizen was his salvation while he was in prison in 1794 when the Girondins with whom he was associated were being sent to the guillotine in droves, like cattle to a slaughterhouse.

The Americans residing in Paris made an effort to free him by an appeal to the Convention in the January following his arrest. Their communication, in which they set forth Paine's work for liberty and human rights in both America and France, was answered by Vadier, then president of the Convention. His letter is too long to be given here in full, but one paragraph reads as follows:

You demand of us, citizens, the liberty of Thomas Paine; you wish to restore to your hearths this defender of the rights of man. One can only applaud this generous movement. Thomas Paine is a native of England; this is undoubtedly enough to apply to him the measures of security prescribed by the revolutionary laws. It may be added, citizens, that if Thomas Paine has been the apostle of liberty, if he has powerfully cooperated with the American Revolution, his genius has not understood that which has regenerated France; he has regarded the system only in accordance with the illusions with which the false friends of our revolution have invested it. You must with us deplore an error little reconcilable with the principles admired in the justly esteemed works of this republican author.

It is difficult, if not impossible, to grasp the meaning of this vague comment on Paine's activities, as written by the president of the Convention. What does he mean by "illusions"? Paine had no illusions about the course of events in France. He was not in sympathy with the tyranny and cruelty which characterized the Reign of Terror, and he saw clearly that the Revolution had changed its course. It was no longer a fight for freedom, but had become an instrument of oppression, a campaign against the whole people directed by thugs and cutthroats.

It was believed in England, by many people and for a long time, that Paine had been executed after having been imprisoned for several months in the Luxembourg. His journey in a cart to the place of execution was described in a thrilling fashion by the author of a pamphlet which had a large sale. He was sent to the guillotine—according to this account—on September 1, 1794. As he stood on the scaffold he confessed his wickedness, and said, "I have written and spoken nothing but lies in my life."

Not long thereafter the children of England were chanting a nursery rhyme which ran in this fashion:

> Poor Tom Paine! There he lies:
> Nobody laughs and nobody cries.
> Where he has gone or how he fares
> Nobody knows and nobody cares.

5

The daily life in the Luxembourg prison was not as harsh and unpleasant as one might expect, but this statement is only a deduction growing out of Paine's silence concerning the matter. He had no eye, and apparently no perception, for the details of living. He was the sort of man who might live, eat and sleep in a room for a year or more without thinking of its furniture, or the pictures on the wall. He liked comfortable living, as nearly everybody else does, but he did not think a lot about it. He lived in a world of ideas, not among pots and pans, hats and neckties. Nevertheless, if the prisoners in the Luxembourg had been half-starved, or beaten, or treated with cruelty he would have put the facts on paper. But as he says nothing of the kind in his notes or letters we may reasonably infer that the prisoners were treated well.

Most of the prisoners in the Luxembourg considered them-

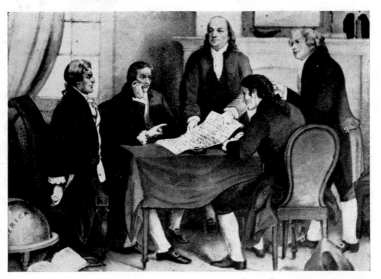

DRAFTING THE DECLARATION OF INDEPENDENCE

The title of this picture is not literally correct, for the Declaration of Independence was drafted by Thomas Jefferson alone — a work which occupied his time for seventeen days. In writing the Declaration he followed closely the ideas expressed by Paine in Common Sense. When his task was accomplished Jefferson submitted the document to a committee of the Continental Congress for approval. A meeting of the Committee on a day In June, 1776, is shown in the picture on this page.

Jefferson sits at the extreme left; next to him is Alexander Hamilton. Benjamin Franklin and John Adams are shown standing, and the sitting man in front of the picture is Roger Sherman, of Connecticut.

JAMES MONROE

FROM A PAINTING BY CHAPPELL

*This picture shows James Monroe as he appeared in
1795, when he was the American Minister to France.*

selves under the sentence of death, even though no sentence of any kind had been given them. During the Reign of Terror there was not much formality about trials, convictions and sentences. The prisoners had been picked up, as a rule, and sent to the Luxembourg without trial or without a hearing in court or before a judge or jury. There they remained until they were sent to death under the knife of the guillotine. It was all quite fortuitous and haphazard. Now and then prisoners were given their freedom without ever learning who had accused them in the first place, or with what they had been charged, or why they had been set free.

It seems from various accounts that the prisoners were allowed to visit one another and to sit in the cells of their friends for hours at a time. Paine soon got on friendly terms with all the Englishmen in the prison. (There were no other Americans.) To Dr. Bond, an English surgeon, who was a prisoner, Paine read the pages of Part II of *The Age of Reason* as he wrote them. Among the prisoners was General O'Hara, who had been one of the officers under Lord Cornwallis when the British army was surrendered to the Americans at Yorktown on October 19, 1781. Those who are familiar with the history of the American Revolution will recall, no doubt, that Cornwallis pleaded illness on that fateful day and sent General O'Hara to make the surrender in his stead. This subordinate was instructed by Cornwallis to surrender to the Marquis de Rochambeau, who commanded the French troops, and not to General Washington, but the French general declined to accept the surrender, as Washington was commander in chief of the combined forces. O'Hara then turned to Washington, who had General Lincoln take Cornwallis' sword as the token of surrender.

O'Hara and his suite were in France when the British declared war against the French, and they were sent to the Luxembourg as prisoners of war. There all of them made friends with Tom Paine, English outlaw, hater of kings, American patriot, French revolutionist, and disbeliever in the Bible. Prisons create strange friendships.

In a few months General O'Hara was informed by the

French authorities that his liberation was at hand. That was good news for him, but it carried with it a large chunk of perplexity, for the General's money was all gone. He had had only a small sum when he was sent to prison and he had spent all of it, buying little luxuries which were not furnished to the prisoners. He was told that he was set free on condition that he leave France at once. At that time there were no Englishmen in Paris who were out of prison, and no English funds to be obtained at the banks.

He told Paine of his troubles and forthwith his hearer assured him that he would furnish the funds to take him to England. One may readily imagine the gaping astonishment of O'Hara as he listened to this assurance. Paine? Money? Is he crazy? Why, the man is as poor as a church mouse. Where did he get any money and how does he keep it in prison?

But Paine's promise was genuine and he carried it out. When he entered the prison he had two hundred pounds of English money on his person and he was afraid that it would be taken from him, for he did not believe that he could keep it concealed day after day, perhaps for months. So he looked around for a hiding place for the Bank of England notes and found that it would be possible to secrete them in the lock of the door of his cell. In those days the locks were enormous in size, and the keys were correspondingly huge. Paine saw that the banknotes might be folded into a tight wad and pushed into the lock in such a way that the movements of the key would have no interference, so he thrust his money into the hiding place one day while his cellmates were out taking the air in the courtyard. No one besides himself knew where his small fortune was hidden.

He managed to extricate the tight little wad of paper money by pulling it out through the keyhole, and after the dust was brushed off and the bills smoothed out he turned over the whole sum to General O'Hara, presumably as a loan. The two hundred pounds enabled the General and his suite to get back to England.

This curious event brings up a number of queries. Where, when and from whom did Paine get the money that he concealed in such a strange hiding place? No one knows the answer. A hundred and fifty years have gone by and the facts are buried under the oblivion of time. Paine was always poor, from the cradle to the grave. Some of his books—notably the *Rights of Man* and *The Age of Reason*—produced large royalties, but he gave away their earnings, usually to associations that had been formed to promote the ideals of democracy and freedom. His generosity was profuse. Whenever he happened to have any funds in hand he was ready and willing to help others who were in need of money. It is surprising, therefore, to learn that he possessed two hundred pounds in English banknotes when he was a prisoner in the Luxembourg.

The money may have been contributed by the eighteen American residents of Paris who wrote and presented to the Convention the petition for Paine's freedom a few days after he had been sent to prison. All the signers of the petition were business men who were in France as representatives of American commercial interests, and they were all well-to-do. They could have raised two hundred pounds without making any great sacrifice. When they realized that their eloquent plea to the Convention had failed to set Paine free, the idea may have occurred to them that he might possibly escape from the prison by bribing the jailers, and the money might have been raised for that purpose. It would have been easy enough to get the money to him, for Benoit, the head jailer of the prison during the first six months of 1794, was a kindly, tolerant official who allowed the prisoners many liberties, including a standing permission to receive visitors at all times. The money might have been slipped to Paine on one of those occasions.

Or the two hundred pounds could have come from Joel Barlow. He possessed considerable wealth and was a fervent disciple of Tom Paine. Another reasonable supposition is that the Paine-ites in England quietly raised the money and sent it to him secretly. The fact that it was in notes of the Bank of England lends color to that view of the matter.

But why did Paine turn it over to General O'Hara?

That is another field for guesswork. The most reasonable

answer may be set forth in a few words. O'Hara had been very friendly to Paine while they were both in prison, and Paine had acquired a great liking for the jovial, courageous Irishman who could be cheerful even though he lived in a cell. Paine did not expect to regain his freedom; he felt that he might be summoned to the guillotine any day, so why hold on to the money? He could not get any benefit from it, but it would be an immense help to O'Hara, who could walk out of the prison with a pocketful of money and pay his way home instead of being penniless in the land of his enemies.

6

Events moved swiftly. At the beginning of the summer of 1794 the French Revolution was no longer a movement of civilized people who sought liberty and democracy. It may be justly compared to a mad dog that runs helter-skelter through the streets, foaming at the mouth and attacking people. The Revolution had become hysterical and rabid—a condition that is likely to develop in any overthrow of governmental institutions that is accomplished by force.

Maximilien Robespierre was, at this hectic period, the chief figure in the revolutionary picture. As the leader of the Jacobins he had become head of the government, or of the butcher shop that went by that name. He was, in other words, the chief tyrant and know-it-all of the French nation during its Reign of Terror. But do not picture him as a calm, godlike creature with a stern serenity shining from his countenance. He was as hysterical, jittery and tense as a frightened child. There was no quality of statesmanship in his make-up. To repress criticism by the death of the critic was his method of carrying on national affairs, and it must be said that such a policy has its points. If you have the power and the cruel inclination to kill everybody who holds a different opinion from your own you will certainly put an end to argument for a while.

But new enemies spring up and it is difficult to keep pace with them. So it was with Robespierre, and as underground and secret opposition grew stronger his repressive measures became more and more insensate and cruel. Here is a case in point, one of many: On May 25—the year was 1794—a young woman whose name was Cecile Renault called at Robespierre's quarters and asked to see him. She was not permitted to enter but was immediately arrested on suspicion. When searched she was found to have two knives concealed in her clothing. Maybe she intended to stab the tyrant as Charlotte Corday killed Marat, or maybe not, but the police—acting under orders—rounded up her entire family and all her relatives, as well as her friends, and sent them to the guillotine in one big party. There were forty persons in the group, and on their last journey they were clothed in red shirts, which was the traditional garb of convicted parricides. The evidence against them, or any one of them, was flimsy and utterly unconvincing.

Among the multitude of victims that passed through the Luxembourg prison on their way to the guillotine were Hérault de Séchelles who, as President of the National Assembly, had welcomed Paine to France; Anacharsis Cloots, the only foreigner other than Paine who had been a member of the Convention; Camille Desmoulins, the fiery young orator who stirred the people to action in the early days of the Revolution; and Georges Jacques Danton, one of the great figures of that era in France. He and Paine were friends. One day, shortly before he was led to his execution, Danton shook hands with Paine and said, "That which you did for the happiness and liberty of your country I tried in vain to do for mine. I have been less fortunate, but not less innocent. They will send me to the scaffold; very well, my friend, I shall go gaily."

The Revolution turned against Robespierre himself in July, 1794. As a dictator and despot he had built up a huge and powerful coterie of enemies who had resolved to overthrow him and put him to death. For months they waited silently for the opportune moment. It came at last; in July, 1794, Robespierre was deposed by force, tried peremptorily before a makeshift court that deliberated while a mob yelled for the tyrant's life. He was executed on the twenty-ninth of that month.

Among the memoranda of things to be done that were found on the top of his desk was a sheet of paper with these words on it: *"Demander que Thomas Payne soit décrete d'accusation, pour les interêts de l'Amerique autant que de la France."* ("Demand that a writ accusing Thomas Payne be issued, in the interests of America as much as of France.")

In the interests of America as much as of France! Gouverneur Morris and the scandalmongers had won their point. They had convinced Robespierre that Thomas Paine was a traitor to America and France, and in the pay of the British. Morris had told him, no doubt, that the execution of Paine would not disturb the friendly relations that existed between the Americans and the French, and that many of "the best people" in America looked upon Paine as an unprincipled trouble-maker.

CHAPTER XIV

Monroe Rescues Paine

I

ROBESPIERRE's curt order to bring Paine to judgment was disregarded for a time by his successors. They had no great admiration for the men in jail, but they hardly felt inclined to carry out the instructions of a person whom they had just sent to the guillotine.

They did, however, get around to Thomas Paine (or "Payne," as they spelled it) in the course of a few weeks, and his name was set down on the list of those who were to be executed the next day.

His escape from this virtual certainty of death is as strange and exciting as anything that one is likely to read in a fictional adventure story. Here is an account of it in his own words:

One hundred and sixty-eight persons were taken out of the Luxembourg in one night, and a hundred and sixty of them guillotined the next day, of which I knew I was to be one; and the manner I escaped that fate is curious, and has all the appearance of accident. The room in which I lodged was on the ground floor, and one of a long range of rooms under a gallery, and the door of it opened outward and flat against the wall; so that when it was open the inside of the door appeared outward, and the contrary when it was shut. I had three comrades, fellow prisoners with me, . . . when persons by scores and by hundreds were to be taken out of the prison for the guillotine it was always done in the night, and those who performed that office had a private mark or signal by which they knew what rooms to go to, and what number to take. We, as I have said, were four, and the door of our room was marked, unobserved by us, with that number in chalk; but it happened, if happening is the proper word, that the mark was put on when the door was open and flat against the wall, and thereby came on the inside when we shut it at night; and the destroying angel passed by it.

The death mark was on the door, but inside, and when the hurrying wardens came through at dawn, looking for the fatal signs there was nothing to be seen on that door, so they went on their way. One hundred and sixty-eight condemned persons are a multitude, and in the confusion of herding them together and checking their names on the list a few might be missing without their absence attracting attention.

The marvelous good luck which had protected Paine on many occasions was still potent. But though he was alive the walls of the prison were around him, and it could only be a question of time before his name would come up again.

Like most prisons of that era the Luxembourg was a breeding ground for disease, owing to undernourishment, lack of fresh air and exercise, and the continual presence of prison filth. In August Paine was prostrated by a malignant fever which kept him in bed for weeks. "I was not in a condition to be removed," he wrote later, "or to know what was passing, or of what had passed, for more than a month. It makes a blank in my remembrance of life."

While he was going through this long period of unconsciousness the physician of the prison, who was one of Paine's friends, expected him to die at any moment. The fever was followed by a painful abscess in his side. He lost weight, his hair turned white, his brilliant eyes became dull and leaden, and in time his appearance had only a ghost-like resemblance to the Tom Paine of former days.

2

Meanwhile the career of Gouverneur Morris as an American diplomat in Paris was coming to an end. In the early summer of 1794 the Washington administration recalled him at the request of the French, and James Monroe was sent to take his place.

Monroe was amazed when he arrived in August and learned that Paine was still in prison. In the letters written by Morris to his friends in America, as well as in his official communications to the President and Secretary of State, he had seldom

London Feb.ry 13th 1792

Sir

An opportunity immediately offering, I have had a Doz Copies of my new Work put up for the purpose (the work being not yet published) to present to you and Mr Jefferson. I hope the fifty Copies which were sent to Portsmouth (England) to the Care of Mr. Greene of my former work; have come safe to your hands

wishing you every happiness

I remain your much obliged
Obedient Helle Servant

Thomas Paine

George Washington
President of the
United States.

LETTER OF THOMAS PAINE TO GEORGE WASHINGTON
REGARDING THE "RIGHTS OF MAN."

PAINE PLEADING FOR THE LIFE OF LOUIS XVI IN THE FRENCH
NATIONAL ASSEMBLY

*The statue for which this was the model was finished by Gutzon Borglum in
1937 and was to have been set up in the Parc Montsouris in Paris. But
before it could be erected the Nazis had invaded France, and the statue was
hidden in a secret place. With Paris again in French hands, this strikingly
impressive image of Tom Paine will be set on its pedestal in the park at some
time in the near future.*

mentioned Paine, and only casually, as when he wrote that the author was in prison where he amused himself by composing a pamphlet against Jesus Christ. In another letter he wrote to the Secretary of State that Paine had asked him to take his case up with the French authorities on the ground that he was an American citizen and therefore should not be included in the provisions of the act against enemy aliens. Morris did not think such action would be effective, or so he wrote, because Paine had forfeited his American citizenship.

In the course of this correspondence with the State Department Morris remarked that the less said about Paine the better, for it would be unwise to stir up a dispute between America and France over such a person. The French authorities, Morris declared, had probably overlooked Paine in prison, but if he were made the subject of controversy he might be taken out to execution. In short, if we read between the lines, it is perfectly clear that the aim of Gouverneur Morris was to expedite his trip to the guillotine, quietly and without fuss, and without more than a faint and purely formal objection from the American Government.

James Monroe was disposed to give Paine every aid within his power, but he had no instructions concerning the matter, and he hardly knew what to do. On September 10 Paine wrote Monroe a letter from which the following extracts are taken:

They who propagate the report of my not being considered as a citizen of America by government, do it to the prolongation of my imprisonment, and without authority; for Congress, as a government, has neither decided upon it, nor yet taken the matter into consideration; and I request you to caution such persons against spreading such reports.

I know not what opinions have been circulated in America. It may have been supposed there, that I had voluntarily and intentionally abandoned America, and that my citizenship had ceased by my own choice. I can easily conceive that there are those in that country who would take such a proceeding on my part somewhat in disgust. The idea of forsaking old friendships for new acquaintances is not agreeable.

I am a little warranted in making this supposition by a letter I received some time ago from the wife of one of the Georgia delegates, in

which she says, "your friends on this side the water cannot be recon-
ciled to the idea of your abandoning America." I have never abandoned
America in thought, word, or deed, and I feel it incumbent upon me to
give this assurance to the friends I have in that country, and with whom
I have always intended, and am determined, if the possibility exists, to
close the scene of my life. It is there that I have made myself a home.
It is there that I have given the services of my best days.

.   .   .   .   .   .

France does not claim me for a citizen; neither do I set up any claim
of citizenship in France. The question is simply, whether I am or am
not a citizen of America. I am imprisoned here on the decree for im-
prisoning Foreigners, because, say they, I was born in England. I say
in answer, that, though born in England, I am not a subject of the English Government any more than any other American is who was born,
as they all were, under the same government, or that the citizens of
France are subjects of the French monarchy, under which they were
born. I have twice taken the oath of abjuration to the British king and
government, and of Allegiance to America. Once as a citizen of the
State of Pennsylvania in 1776; and again before Congress, administered to me by the President, Mr. Hancock, when I was appointed Secretary in the office of foreign affairs in 1777.

To this communication Monroe responded on September 18
with a letter in which he told Paine that he would immediately
do something to bring about his release. "It is unnecessary for
me to tell you," Monroe said in this letter, "how much all of
your countrymen, I speak of the great mass of the people, are
interested in your welfare. . . . The crime of ingratitude has not
yet stained, and I trust never will stain, our national character."

Further on he said, "To liberate you will be an object of my
endeavors, and as soon as possible." But it took weeks to free
the prisoner, not on account of any great objection on anybody's
part, but solely because of the difficulty that Monroe encountered in getting the matter considered by those in authority.
France was governed at that time by a tangled net of commit-
tees who hardly knew themselves where their responsibility began or ended.

On November 2 Monroe wrote a letter to the Committee of

General Surety in which he asked for Paine's release on the ground that he was an American citizen and that no charge had been made against him. He had addressed the proper committee at last, and at a time when its members were in the frame of mind to consider such matters.

Paine was set free four days later. He had been in prison ten months and nine days. Monroe took him to his own residence, as Paine had no home and not a penny to his name. He was so feeble that he could barely walk. Mrs. Monroe had him put to bed while her husband sent one of his servants for a physician. After examining the patient the doctor said that he would probably recover, and that he was suffering chiefly from the effects of poor nutrition and general lack of attention. The abscess, he thought, would heal if properly treated.

His condition did improve considerably within the next few weeks. He was able to sit up and write, and it was there in James Monroe's house that he finished the second part of *The Age of Reason*. But after a time he had a relapse, and it looked as if it was to be his last illness. Monroe wrote to a friend in Virginia that he did not expect Paine to live. "Latterly his symptoms have become worse," he wrote, "and the prospect is now that he will not be able to hold out more than a month or two at the furthest. I shall certainly pay the utmost attention to this gentleman, as he is one of those whose merits in our Revolution were most distinguished."

It was not a hopeful comment, but Paine had a good constitution, and was well cared for, so in the course of time he was up and going about his affairs. That spell of illness, lasting for months, left permanent effects. He never recovered his hearty robustness, and for the remaining years of his life he weakened quickly when engaged in any activity that required much exertion, either physical or mental.

3

Paine had many friends in Paris. Among them were the Barlows, Joel and his wife; Robert Fulton, famous builder of the steamboat *Clermont*; Peter Whiteside of Philadelphia; Achille Audibert, the deputy from the department of Calais who had aided Paine in his escape from England, and who had remained a devoted friend; Nicolas Bonneville and Marguerite, his wife; and Sir Robert and Lady Smythe.

The Marquis de Lafayette had been a close friend of Tom Paine during the American Revolution, and their intimacy was renewed when Paine went to France. Adrienne—wife of the Marquis—shared her husband's liking for him. When Paine was released from prison neither Lafayette nor his wife was on hand to greet him. The Marquis was at that time immured in the fortress prison of Olmutz in Austria, and Madame Lafayette was in the prison of La Force in Paris, where she expected to be led out to execution any day. Her family had suffered greatly during the Reign of Terror; her aged grandmother, her mother and her sister had been sent to the guillotine. The story of the trial and execution of those three women is a tale of barbarism that reminds one of some hideous dream.

James Monroe obtained the release of Madame Lafayette from La Force on January 22, 1795. While she was still in prison, but allowed to receive visitors, she wrote this friendly letter to Paine:

19 Brumaire, Paris.—I was this morning so much agitated by the kind visit from Mr. Monroe, that I could hardly find words to speak; but, however, I was, my dear Sir, desirous to tell you, that the news of your being set at liberty, which I this morning learnt from General Kilmaine, who arrived here at the same time with me, has given me a moment's consolation in the midst of this abyss of misery, where I shall all my life remain plunged. Gen. Kilmaine has told me that you recollected me, and have taken great interest in my situation; for which I am exceedingly grateful.

Accept, along with Mr. Monroe, my congratulations upon your being restored to each other, and the assurances of these sentiments from her who is proud to proclaim them, and who well deserved the title of citizen of *that second country*, though I have assuredly never failed, nor shall ever fail, to the former. Salut and friendship.

Sir Robert Smythe and his lady were close friends of Paine. They were English expatriates, and evidently people of considerable wealth. Sir Robert was a well-known banker, with a handsome establishment in Paris, and a country house at Versailles. Although he bore a title he was bitterly opposed to the royal pattern of government, to kings and nobles, and he wanted the whole world to know it. At a dinner given to Paine at the Philadelphia House on November 18, 1792, Sir Robert Smythe and young Lord Edward Fitzgerald formally renounced their titles. Sir Robert proposed a toast, "A speedy abolition of all hereditary titles and feudal distinctions." All the guests at this dinner were English or American, and the news of the doings of Smythe and Fitzgerald soon drifted over to London with the result that Lord Fitzgerald was expelled from the British army.

Paine's acquaintance with Lady Smythe began on the day when he was arrested, which was December 27, 1793, and they happened to meet in circumstances that were curious and interesting. It was a feverish day, a time of desperate haste, for Paine had heard that Robespierre's minions were coming for him that very day, and he wanted to finish the writing of Part I of *The Age of Reason* before they arrived. He was hard at work, in his cluttered room, when a visitor was announced. He thought he would give the intruder about five minutes of his time, but he changed his mind when he saw that the caller was a charming English lady, who was somewhat embarrassed because she had come to ask a favor of a man whom she had never met. She was Lady Smythe and she had come to ask Paine to intervene on behalf of an Englishman of rank who had been arrested. She was then unaware of the turn in Paine's affairs which deprived him of all influence of any kind.

He told her that he could do nothing, and explained why he was powerless. She was startled and sorry when she learned from him that he expected to be in prison himself within a few hours. Paine was charmed by her soft, gentle voice and her sympathy. He laid aside his work, important as it was, and spent an hour listening to Lady Smythe and talking with her about French affairs. As he sat there, in the lady's radiant presence, he was embarrassed—as men often are in such circumstances—because he had not brushed up a bit and changed his shirt before she came. His room was a litter of books, scraps of food, dust and soiled clothes, but Lady Smythe did not seem to notice the disorder of the room, nor the snuff which Paine had neglected to brush from the front of his waistcoat. She had long admired his books, and she was so delighted at meeting him that she had no eye for such things.

Not long thereafter Paine received a letter, through the kindness of Benoit, the jailer, which was signed "A Little Corner of the World." It was a missive of sympathy. Other letters bearing the same signature came from time to time. Their writer had a poetical turn of mind, and the letters were evidently intended to beguile the dull hours of prison life. Paine soon suspected that Lady Smythe was writing them and he replied, signing his epistles "The Castle in the Air," but he was not altogether certain of the identity of his unknown correspondent until he was set free and met the lady at Monroe's house. None of this correspondence is now in existence.[1]

While he was living with the Monroes his acquaintance with Lady Smythe and her husband grew into a firm and lasting friendship. During that period he addressed a poem to the lady, calling it *The Castle in the Air to the Little Corner of the World*. Perhaps it is worth reproducing here, as it gives some glimpses of Paine's inner self at that period of his life.

> In the region of clouds, where the whirlwinds arise,
>   My Castle of Fancy was built;
> The turrets reflected the blue from the skies,
>   And the windows with sunbeams were gilt.
>
> But a storm that I felt not had risen and rolled,
>   While wrapped in a slumber I lay;
> And when I looked out in the morning, behold,
>   My Castle was carried away.

[1] It was probably consumed in the fire that destroyed Paine's papers.

It passed over rivers and valleys and groves,
    The world it was all in my view;
I thought of my friends, of their fates, of their loves,
    And often, full often, of YOU.

At length it came over a beautiful scene,
    That nature in silence had made;
The place was but small, but 't was sweetly serene,
    And chequered with sunshine and shade.

I gazed and I envied with painful good will,
    And grew tired of my seat in the air;
When all of a sudden my Castle stood still,
    As if some attraction were there.

Like a lark from the sky it came fluttering down,
    And placed me exactly in view.
When whom should I meet in this charming retreat,
    This corner of calmness, but—YOU.

Delighted to find you in honor and ease,
    I felt no more sorrow nor pain;
But the wind coming fair, I ascended the breeze,
    And went back with my Castle again.

Paine always had a poetic impulse stirring within him. Even as a child he wrote verse now and then, as—for instance—the little quatrain concerning the sad fate of John Crow which appears in the first chapter of this book. But, of course, he was not a true poet; he was simply a versifier—a man who had great things to do in the world who sometimes turned to rhyming.

Another lady with whom he was on very friendly terms was Mrs. Barlow, wife of the imaginative, dynamic Joel. One day she told him that while he was writing against religious superstitions he was, at the same time, setting up a new religion of Love which would arouse both bigotry and enthusiasm, and be even more dangerous to its devotees than the Scriptures with all their imbedded superstitions. Her remarks inspired Paine to write these verses and send them to Mrs. Barlow:

Oh, could we always live and love,
   And always be sincere,
I would not wish.for heaven above,
   My heaven would be here.

Though many countries I have seen,
   And more may chance to see,
My LITTLE CORNER OF THE WORLD
   Is half the world to me.

The other half, as you may guess,
   America contains;
And thus, between them, I possess
   The whole world for my pains.

I'm then contented with my lot,
   I can no happier be;
For neither world I'm sure has got
   So rich a man as me.

Then send no fiery chariot down
   To take me off from hence,
But leave me on my heavenly ground—
   This prayer is *common sense*.

Let others choose another plan,
   I mean no fault to find;
The true theology of man
   Is happiness of mind.

In the spring and summer of 1796 Paine was a frequent visitor at the home of the Smythes at Versailles. They were fond of him, and he had a standing invitation to come whenever he pleased and stay for a day or a week or a month. On these sojourns in the country he was outdoors for a large part of the time, taking long walks through the woods or riding horseback. He was an accomplished horseman of the daring kind; he liked to leap over fences and ditches rather than to amble along the roads.

There was only one drawback to these visits. The Smythes moved in a wealthy social set and they made a point of observing the formalities of elegant life. Paine, as a guest of distinction, was expected to meet their friends, to dress for dinner, and to spend the evenings in light chitchat. He detested that sort of thing, so he usually made only short visits, though his liking for the Smythes was not diminished because they lived in a social sphere that was very different from the one he preferred. He was more at ease in the taprooms of taverns, but Sir Robert Smythe and his lady were inclined to spend their evenings in a drawing room decorated with tapestry and paintings, listening to the music of a harpsichord and commenting in gentle speech on current happenings.

4

For twenty years George Washington had been one of Tom Paine's demigods. He thought of the Father of Our Country as the potential leader in a world-wide crusade for human freedom, of which the American Revolution was only the first act. The revolt against tyranny, despotism and royal prerogatives which had begun in the American Colonies would in the course of time spread throughout the world, and Washington would lead it—or so Paine hoped and believed.

This conception did not portray Washington as he really was; it was simply a revelation of the poetic idealism that lay deep under Paine's matter-of-fact manner.

As we look upon Paine's career and study carefully his contact with other men—with friends and enemies—there was only one other person who evoked a feeling of admiration and reverence equal to that which he gave to Washington, and that person was Benjamin Franklin. In Paine's estimation Franklin was a living epitome of all the useful knowledge in the world. He knew the inner secrets of matter, of force and energy, or Paine thought he did, but that alone would not have endeared him to the author of *Common Sense*. It was his encouragement of Paine's efforts to express himself in print, and the sympathy shown by the aged philosopher for the poor and oppressed, that stirred Paine emotionally and caused him to love Franklin as one loves a helpful father. But Franklin died in 1790, and there remained only Washington to whom Paine could turn with a feeling that the world-famous leader was his lifelong friend, and that if he ever found himself in deadly peril he could rely on Washington's aid.

When Paine was sent to prison the story of his misfortune, and of his grave danger, crossed the Atlantic as speedily as news could travel in that century of slow movement. Washington, then President of the United States, was made aware of the facts. He did nothing, however, in Paine's behalf. At that time nearly the whole of the civilized world was at war against the French, but the American nation remained on friendly terms with them, despite the atrocities perpetrated in the name of liberty by their runaway revolution, with its guillotine and its unruly mobs. Our people had not forgotten the powerful aid given by France to the struggling Colonies in their War for Independence, and consequently their affection for the French was still a glowing emotion.

There can be hardly a doubt that a courteous request from George Washington for the release of Thomas Paine on the ground of his American citizenship would have brought a ready and favorable response.

Robespierre evidently expected such a message from the President of the American republic and saved Paine from the guillotine while he was waiting. But no such message came, and the only attention Paine's imprisonment received in American official quarters was expressed in the weak and purely perfunctory communications from Gouverneur Morris, which were written in such a fashion that they invited refusal.

What was the reason for the silence of George Washington? Why did he abandon Thomas Paine, who had so courageously supported him and the American cause during the dark days of Valley Forge? Had he forgotten that the clear, brave words of Paine's *Crisis* pamphlets had inspired the army even amid its defeats and disasters?

These questions naturally arise when Paine's imprisonment is a subject of consideration, but there is no direct answer to them, for Washington never discussed the matter publicly. Nevertheless, they may be answered by drawing inferences from the surrounding circumstances.

When Paine was sent to prison John Jay was in England, where he had been sent by Washington to negotiate a new treaty, if possible, with the British Government, one which would relieve the American nation of several extremely vexatious situations that had been dragging along for years. When the War for Independence had been brought to a victorious close, and the independence of the Colonies was acknowledged, a number of unsettled matters were left still dangling in the air. Under the terms of the treaty the new American republic had acquired all the territory north of Florida (then held by Spain) and south of the Great Lakes. But, regardless of the treaty, the British continued to hold on to their military posts in a wide expanse of territory that includes today the states of Ohio, Indiana, Illinois and Michigan. They declared that they intended to keep their armed forces in that region until the Americans complied with an article of the treaty which provided for the reimbursement for the loss of property belonging to the Loyalists in the Colonies that had been seized by the Americans during the war. The total amount was large, and when the treaty was confirmed the states had been asked to make an accounting and to compensate the Loyalists—most of whom had then left the country—for the seizure of their property.

None of the states complied with that recommendation, so for several years an anomalous and dangerous situation existed throughout the region that we call today the Central States. Both the British and the Americans were exercising authority in the same territory.

It was not long after the war, however, before a stream of American settlers began to move into the territory and take up land. This led to further complications. Did the American laws apply in that region, or did the British military authorities have the final word? No one could say with certainty. Moreover, the

British military had no love for the Americans, and the Indians were encouraged by them, on various occasions, to resist with force the occupation of the land by the incoming settlers.

Another matter of bitter controversy which disturbed the friendly relations of Great Britain and her alienated child, the United States, had to do with the commercial relations of the Americans and the people of the British West Indies. The English Navigation Acts had been planned and put in force for the purpose of diverting all, or most, of the commerce of British overseas possessions into the hands of English merchants. These restrictions had ruined the flourishing trade that the American Colonials had formerly carried on with the West Indian islands.

The negotiations for a new treaty concerning these and other points of dispute were going on while Paine was in the Luxembourg prison. Let us not overlook the fact that Paine was an outlaw in England, where he had been convicted of treason, and that his writings had so deeply offended the ruling class of that country that his name, when mentioned among them, was greeted with anger and contempt. They hated Paine so bitterly that they were pleased to learn that even the French—with whom they were at war—had acquired a dislike for him and had sent him to prison, with the guillotine as his ultimate destination.

Though it is a conclusion reached by inference there can be hardly a doubt of George Washington's conviction that the freeing of Paine at his request, or demand, would have a harmful effect on John Jay's negotiations. To the English mind such an action would seem to be an insult, or so Washington thought, and he did nothing.

He was probably swayed by other reasons also. One of them is that Paine had sought trouble by taking part in a revolution in a foreign country in which he had no interest. He could not even speak its language, and he was acquainted personally with only a few of its people. To a man of Washington's practical outlook and temperament it seemed to be the exploit of a venturesome fool—so let him take the consequences.

Washington seems to have been in doubt also as to the extent of his authority in such cases. Had he the right, as the country's Chief Executive, to involve the nation in a quarrel with a friendly power over an individual who had gone, of his own free will, to a foreign land to join in activities which led to his imprisonment? And there was also some question as to Paine's citizenship. Gouverneur Morris, Minister of the United States at Paris, had informed the American Government in an official communication that Paine had no right to claim citizenship in this country; that he had abandoned his American citizenship and had become a citizen of France. Washington felt that he had to accept the word of Morris in this matter, for he was on the ground and knew the facts.

So nothing was done until James Monroe took over the official position held by Morris. He obtained the release of Paine without much trouble. The French were really glad to find an excuse for setting him free.

During the months of Paine's imprisonment his friendship for George Washington slowly turned to hate and his admiration shriveled into contempt. Furthermore, he was angry with himself for having believed in Washington's word, and for having honored and trusted him.

The long days, weeks and months in prison went by with Paine expecting every day some cheering message from Washington, or the news that the President of the United States had demanded that he be given his freedom. Then—as he imagined the scene—there would be the tramp of heavy feet on the stone floor of the corridor, a key turning in the lock, the door swinging open and before it a smiling prison official, bowing and holding out a written paper to Thomas Paine, prisoner. And the officer, resplendent in his shining gold-braided uniform, would say, "You are given your freedom, Monsieur Paine, as an act of courtesy to President Washington, who has requested it."

But no such scene took place; it was only a daydream. When Paine was finally set free he hastened to James Monroe to thank that Minister for what had been done in his behalf, and then he learned, to his sad astonishment, that Monroe had come to France without any instructions concerning Paine. In his last conference with Washington, before leaving America, Paine's name had not been mentioned, and—as a matter of fact—Monroe did not know that Paine was in prison until he arrived in France. Everything that was done thereafter to bring about Paine's release had been on Monroe's own initiative.

On Washington's next birthday, which was February 22, 1795, Paine wrote him a letter of bitter reproach. It was an exceedingly injudicious document, but it was not sent—at that time—for Monroe, after reading it at Paine's request, induced him not to send it. Nevertheless, it did reach Washington much later in circumstances which will be set forth presently. The following extract from it shows its character and style:

As it is always painful to reproach those one would wish to respect, it is not without some difficulty that I have taken the resolution to write to you. The danger to which I have been exposed cannot have been unknown to you, and the guarded silence you have observed upon that circumstance, is what I ought not to have expected from you, either as a friend or as a President of the United States.

You knew enough of my character to be assured that I could not have deserved imprisonment in France, and, without knowing anything more than this, you had sufficient ground to have taken some interest for my safety. Every motive arising from recollection ought to have suggested to you the consistency of such a measure. But I cannot find that you have so much as directed any enquiry to be made whether I was in prison or at liberty, dead or alive; what the cause of that imprisonment was, or whether there was any service or assistance you could render. Is this what I ought to have expected from America after the part I had acted towards her? Or, will it resound to her honor or to yours that I tell the story?

I do not hesitate to say that you have not served America with more fidelity, or greater zeal, or greater disinterestedness, than myself, and perhaps with not better effort. After the revolution of America had been established, you rested at home to partake its advantages, and I ventured into new scenes of difficulty to extend the principles which that revolution had produced. In the progress of events you beheld yourself a president in America and me a prisoner in France: you folded your arms, forgot your friend, and became silent.

As everything I have been doing in Europe was connected with my wishes for the prosperity of America, I ought to be the more surprised at this conduct on the part of her government. It leaves me but one mode of explanation, which is, that everything is not as it ought to be amongst you, and that the presence of a man who might disapprove, and who had credit enough with the country to be heard and believed, was not wished for. This was the operating motive of the despotic faction that imprisoned me in France (though the pretence was, that I was a foreigner); and those that have been silent towards me in America, appear to me to have acted from the same motive. It is impossible for me to discover any other.

Seven months later—on September 20, 1795—Paine, then ill and at death's door, wrote Washington another letter. This second epistle was sent in care of Franklin Bache—a grandson of Paine's deceased friend, Benjamin Franklin.

There exists considerable doubt as to whether Washington ever received this letter, for he never mentioned it in his correspondence with Monroe. Such an omission seems quite improbable in the circumstances if Washington had actually received the letter that Paine wrote. It is possible that Franklin Bache read the letter and destroyed it, thinking that it would do more harm than good.

The letter is given below in full:

Sir,—I had written you a letter by Mr. Letcombe, French consul, but, at the request of Mr. Monroe, I withdrew it, and the letter is still by me. I was the more easily prevailed upon to do this, as it was then my intention to have returned to America the latter end of the present year (1795;) but the illness I am now suffering prevents me. In case I had come, I should have applied to you for such parts of your official letters (and your private ones, if you had chosen to give them) as contained any instructions or directions either to Mr. Monroe, to Mr. Morris, or to any other person, respecting me; for after you were informed of my imprisonment in France it was incumbent on you to make some enquiry into the cause, as you might very well conclude that I had not the opportunity of informing you of it.

I cannot understand your silence upon this subject upon any other ground, than as connivance at my imprisonment; and this is the manner in which it is understood here, and will be understood in America, unless you will give me authority for contradicting it.

I therefore write you this letter, to propose to you to send me copies of any letters you have written, that I may remove this suspicion. In the Second Part of *The Age of Reason*, I have given a memorandum from the handwriting of Robespierre, in which he proposed a decree of accusation against me "for the interest of America as well as of France." He could have no cause for putting America in the case, but by interpreting the silence of the American government into connivance and consent.

I was imprisoned on the ground of being born in England; and your silence in not enquiring the cause of that imprisonment, and reclaiming me against it, was tacitly giving me up. I ought not to have suspected you of treachery; but whether I recover from the illness I now suffer, or not, I shall continue to think you treacherous, till you give me cause to think other wise. I am sure you would have found yourself more at your ease had you acted by me as you ought; for whether your desertion of me was intended to gratify the English government, or to let me fall into destruction in France that you might exclaim the louder against the French Revolution; or whether you hope by my extinction to meet with less opposition in mounting up the American government; either of these will involve you in reproach you will not easily shake off.

In reflecting upon the unhappy situation which these letters reveal we should keep in mind the important fact that Washington had not been informed fully of Paine's predicament. He had relied on the statements of Gouverneur Morris—naturally, of course—as Morris was the official American representative. But Washington was not fully aware of the hatred and malice which moved Morris in all his relations with Paine.

No answer to Paine's letters came from Washington and, after waiting more than six months, Paine decided to publish the letters and to expand the subject so that the pamphlet in which the letters were to appear would contain also a great deal concerning his relations with Washington and an estimate of that gentleman's claim to distinction. The result was a pamphlet of

many pages, published in Philadelphia, in 1796, under the title
—*Letter to George Washington.*[2]

The publication of this pamphlet by Paine was an utterly
tactless procedure. Much of the criticism of George Washington expressed in it is merely a rehash of statements made by his
political enemies, with only a thin tincture of truth in them. But
Paine did not know this, and even when the information on
which his assertions were based was actually true, Paine overemphasized the facts.

The pamphlet did no harm to George Washington's reputation for he stood so high as a national hero, leader, and prophet
that he was far above criticism. But it did a great deal of harm
to Tom Paine, who had already a host of critics and ill-wishers.
They used his *Letter to Washington* to prove that their low
opinion of Paine and his ideas was a correct estimate of his
proper place in the world. Just an ill-bred gutter-snipe, they
said, who lashes out at men and ideals that are too lofty for his
comprehension. Not long ago it was the Bible and Christ and
the Christian religion that got his jeers of derision; now it is the
revered Father of Our Country who receives his blast of contempt.

The extracts from the *Letter to Washington* which are
printed below will give the reader a clear idea of the tone of
the pamphlet:

Elevated to the chair of the Presidency, you assumed the merit of
everything to yourself, and the natural ingratitude of your constitution
began to appear. You commenced your Presidential career by encouraging and swallowing the grossest adulation, and you traveled America
from one end to the other to put yourself in the way of receiving it. You
have as many addresses in your chest as James II. As to what were your
views, for, if you are not great enough to have ambition, you are little
enough to have vanity, they cannot be directly inferred from expressions
of your own; but the partisans of your politics have divulged the secret.

---

[2] In the ten-volume set of Paine's
Works, published by the Thomas Paine
National Historical Association, the
Letter to George Washington occu-
pies sixty-one pages and contains
twelve thousand words.

One of his comments on the failure of Washington to intercede with the French for his release from prison is expressed in
this paragraph:

Mr. Washington owed it to me on every score of private acquaintance, I will not now say, friendship; for it has some time been known
by those who know him, that he has no friendships; that he is incapable
of forming any; he can serve or desert a man, or a cause, with constitutional indifference; and it is this cold, hermaphrodite faculty that imposed itself upon the world and was credited for a while, by enemies as
by friends, for prudence, moderation and impartiality.

And here is a comment on Washington's administration that
sounds like an editorial in a newspaper of today:

Monopolies of every kind marked your administration almost in the
moment of its commencement. The lands obtained by the Revolution
were lavished upon partisans; the interest of the disbanded soldier was
sold to the speculator; injustice was acted under the pretence of faith;
and the chief of the army became the patron of the fraud. From such
a beginning what else could be expected than what has happened? A
mean and servile submission to the insults of one nation; treachery and
ingratitude to another.

To understand Paine's attitude in his denunciation of his former friend we must realize that his character was so clean-cut
and sharply decisive that he was unable to distinguish any middle ground between right and wrong. Obviously he was unable
to perceive that George Washington could possess many excellent qualities and yet be lacking in others. If we study carefully
his whole career we cannot fail to note that when Paine's mind
was made up on any subject he never wavered even a hair's
breadth from his fixed conclusion. This is a characteristic of
martyrs everywhere and at all times. It is also a quality of
heroes. But it is likely to create as many enemies as friends—if
not more. And Paine was well supplied with enemies, and they
were extremely active.

He was fully aware that he was a forthright and tactless person, and that he was so by preference. Tact, as we all know, is a device for concealing one's real opinions; it is simply a repression of the quality of frankness. And it is, also, merely another name for courtesy. But Paine was not tactful and was glad of it. He held such verbal devices in contempt. His mind did not work that way. The *Letter to Washington* is an example of his outspoken manner.

It would seem, at first sight, that Paine with his stubborn convictions, his abrupt mannerisms and his utter lack of tact, would readily make a fool of himself and become a laughing stock in the estimation of the public. Many a worthy cause has been lost because its leaders made themselves ridiculous or were turned into comic figures by their opponents.

Not so in the case of Tom Paine. What he wrote or said on controversial questions had the indestructible merit of common sense, and his criticisms did not merely touch the surface, but went through skin and flesh and bone to the heart of the matter. His arguments inspired dismay and fury rather than laughter.

None of his enemies ever tried to laugh him off the stage or to make him a subject of jests. No, their reaction was quite different, and may be described as the gnashing of teeth and the shaking of fists. Their chief resource in combat with Paine was Slander and Abuse—and in the long run it produced an effect on the public mind that exists even to this day.

When the letters to Washington were printed as a pamphlet in America, and widely circulated, the abuse and lies that were poured out on Paine's head were so numerous that, if printed here, they would fill this entire volume. As an example of their tone and substance one is given below. It is taken from *Porcupine's Gazette*, which was a weekly newspaper edited and published by William Cobbett, an Englishman who had sought a refuge in the United States from the persecution that hounded him in England.

Mr. Cobbett's opinion of Thomas Paine was expressed in these words:

How Tom gets a living, or what brothel he inhabits, I know not. Nor does it signify to anybody here or elsewhere. He has done all the mischief he can in the world, and whether his carcase is at last to be suffered to rot in the earth, or to be dried in the air, is of little consequence. Wherever or whenever he breathes his last, he will neither excite sorrow nor compassion. No friendly hand will close his eyes, not a moan will be uttered, not a tear will be shed. Like Judas he will be remembered by posterity. Men will learn to express all that is base, malignant, treacherous, unnatural, and blasphemous, by one single monosyllable—Paine.

Now and then, in the course of a lifetime, one comes across facts that seem so incredible, and so contradictory to human experience, that they would be dismissed as pure fiction if they were not supported by incontestable proof. Among them must be included the relationship of William Cobbett to Tom Paine and his works. You have just read what Cobbett wrote of Paine in 1796. But in the last chapter of this book you will read of Cobbett's change of heart—of his utter devotion to Paine, of his endeavors to follow in Paine's footsteps, of his efforts to create a shrine, or memorial, in honor of Paine.

5

Love of America was an inseparable part of Paine's existence. It was so deeply seated in his nature that it might be defined as a form of mysticism. He felt that his nation, the United States and its people, were destined to be the guiding stars of mankind; that America would eventually free the whole world of despotism and cruelty. Paine would have died for America— willingly, gladly—if his sacrifice were needed.

He planned to return to America some day. The sooner the better, but one thing after another prevented him for years from carrying out his resolution. In 1796 James Monroe was recalled to America, and Paine resolved to sail home with him. Monroe did not leave France at once; he decided to leave in the spring of the next year, that is, in 1797. Paine hoped to accompany the Monroes on their journey.

His plans to return to America came to naught. He went to Havre with the Monroe party, but when they arrived at the port and learned that British war vessels were patrolling the Channel and searching all neutral ships he realized that they would never permit him to continue the voyage. Though England and the United States were not at war it was virtually certain that he would be taken off the ship and sent in irons to London.

Monroe advised him not to take the risk. The vessel sailed without him, and as he stood on the shore and saw its white sails melt into the distant horizon a feeling of deep sadness settled upon his mind and heart. For the first time in his life he felt that he was an outcast, that people in general looked upon him as a nuisance and would like to hear no more of him. He had upset too many accepted notions, or so he thought in that hour of depression, to hold the love and respect of men and women.

There is nothing strange in such misgivings. They occur at times to most of the valiant fighters for truth, when they look back over their careers and wonder if their lives would not have been much pleasanter if they had taken everything as it came, without argument or dispute, and had greeted the world every morning with a smile.

He was then sixty years old, tired and homesick. He had climbed the ladder of years until he had reached a point where he felt that life was slipping away from him, and that the vivid world in which he lived would sink into the past just as the ship which he was then watching would drop out of sight.

After his return from Havre Paine made his home with his friends Nicolas and Marguerite Bonneville, who lived at No. 4 Rue de Théâtre Français. He lived with them more than five years, until he left Paris in 1802 to return to America. To Paine they were more than friends or acquaintances; they were home folks, and he behaved toward them as if he were a member of the family.

Nicolas Bonneville, then thirty-seven years of age, was an editor and publisher, but one gathers the impression, in reading today of his troubles, that he was not much of a success in a business way, though he was evidently a man of education and culture. He spoke English and German fluently, and had translated a number of books from those languages into French.

He had owned and edited various newspapers, all of them revolutionary and vehement. The best known of these journals is the one that he was publishing when Paine went to live with the Bonneville family. It was called *Bien Informé*.

The Bonnevilles had been married three years when Paine joined them, and they had one child—a son. Another son was born the next year and his parents asked Paine to act as the child's godfather. The boy was christened Thomas Paine Bonneville. This incident gave the maligners of Paine an opportunity to fling a cartload of mud. The story that Paine had seduced Marguerite Bonneville was passed around, and many who had heard it believed that the boy who bore Paine's name was actually his son.

There is not a word of truth in these assertions. Paine would never do such a thing as have a sexual affair with the wife of a friend, for he was not that kind of man. And Marguerite Bonneville was certainly not that kind of woman. She was a staid, plump, homely, housewifely person who had a lofty conception of womanly virtue.

Paine was a paying guest, a boarder, while he lived with the Bonnevilles, and whenever they were hard up for cash, which was not seldom, he furnished additional sums to meet their expenses.

Where did the money come from?

That is a legitimate question, but a puzzling one, and we can only guess at the answer. Paine earned considerable money from his books, but his habitual practice was to give it away or turn it over, before he received it, to various organizations that advocated views similar to or identical with his own. During the whole of his career as an author the money that he actually received from his writings and used to supply his own needs would not have supported him for a year. My readers will understand that this is only an estimate and not a proved fact. It is deduced from the circumstances.

He owned a house and nearly three hundred acres of land in

New Rochelle, a gift of the State of New York. While he was absent in Europe the house and land were leased to a farmer. How much income came to him from the rental is not known at this late day; his records were destroyed by fire after his death. But we may safely assume that the rent of his land in New Rochelle—and of his tiny cottage in Bordentown, New Jersey—were not sufficient to pay his living expenses, even though he lived in an extremely simple manner.

While he was in the Luxembourg prison the British Government seized a thousand pounds that was owing to Paine as profits on the English edition of *The Age of Reason*. This seizure was quite legal, as Paine had been adjudged an outlaw in England and was therefore not entitled to any property whatsoever. That was apparently the only money he possessed outside the prison. Within the prison he had two hundred pounds carefully hidden but, as you know, he gave this sum—or maybe lent it—to General O'Hara on the latter's release. This money may have been repaid to Paine after he was set free, but if so there is no mention of it in Paine's notes or letters. We know, however, that he was without money at the time of his release, and that his expenses were paid by James Monroe.

For about eighteen months he lived in Monroe's house as a guest. Moreover, during that time Monroe supplied him with cash for his daily expenses and for the purchase of clothes, books, etc. The total amount was two hundred and fifty louis d'or, or $1,188 in American currency. It appears that this sum was not considered a loan or a gift by either Monroe or Paine, but was paid to the latter for his services in aiding Monroe in the conduct of his mission, as Paine was familiar with French affairs. The money advanced to Paine was a personal outlay on Monroe's part, and was not a charge against the legation.[3]

[3] Near the end of his life Monroe had a series of misfortunes which deprived him of all, or most, of his resources. Thereupon Congress passed an act, as of April 7, 1831, to repay from the United States Treasury the funds advanced by Monroe to Paine. Monroe accepted the money, but he said at the time that "no claims were ever presented on my part, nor is any indemnity now desired." Monroe was devoted to Paine.

Besides this sum from James Monroe, he may have received gifts from well-to-do friends and admirers like Sir Robert Smythe and Joel Barlow as well as from other Englishmen and Americans then living in Paris. However, that is merely a guess. His New Rochelle farm increased greatly in value while he was in Europe, but he did not sell any land until he returned to America, nor did he mortgage his farm. All it produced, apparently, was its rental while he was abroad.

Madame Bonneville, in her conversations with William Cobbett, gave an interesting account of Paine's daily life while he was living in her house. She said that he had two rooms. One of them was his bedchamber, and he used the other room as a study. In it were a few articles of furniture—a desk and some chairs—and the walls were lined with bookshelves from floor to ceiling. He had a great variety of books, said Madame Bonneville, but they had to do chiefly with science, government and history, which were the three subjects in which he was deeply interested. He seldom read a novel.

He always rose late, had a meager breakfast and read newspapers throughout the morning. "Though he understood but little of the French when spoken," said Madame Bonneville, "he could read it very well, and he did not fail to collect all the material information relative to politics, in which subject he took most delight. When he had finished his morning's reading he used to carry back the journals to my husband, and they then had a chat on the topics of the day."

In the house he was never idle, according to his landlady. If not writing he was busily employed in tinkering with mechanical devices and trying to improve them. He had many callers, some of whom came out of mere curiosity, just to look at a man whose writings had caused such a stir in the world.

"He treated such visitors with civility," said Madame Bonneville, "but with little ceremony, and, when their conversation was mere chitchat, and he found that they had nothing to say to him, he used to retire to his own pursuits, leaving them to entertain themselves."

During this period Robert Fulton lived in Paris with the

Barlows. Joel Barlow introduced Fulton to Tom Paine and they spent many an evening together, for both of them were fascinated by machinery and new inventions. Paine worked with Fulton for months helping him to perfect his steamboat.

In all these reminiscences Madame Bonneville does not say —or even hint—that Paine was a heavy drinker. If he had nothing better to do he would go to the Irish Coffee House in the Rue Condé after dinner and spend the evening there. Evidently he did not return home in a drunken state at any time, or his landlady would have mentioned the fact in her frank observations on his manner of living.

One of his unexpected visitors was Napoleon Bonaparte, who called on Paine one day in the autumn of 1797, soon after his return from his victorious Italian campaign. Bonaparte had become a national hero; his military exploits were the subject of daily and enthusiastic discussion; and when he went about the city he was always followed by a group of admirers. One may imagine Madame Bonneville's amazement and the suppressed excitement in her home when she went to the door to receive a visitor and found General Bonaparte, who asked to see Monsieur Paine. Behind him, in the street, stood a group of onlookers.

He told Paine that he had been greatly influenced by the *Rights of Man* and slept every night with the book under his pillow. He said, "A statue of gold should be erected to you in every city in the universe."

Napoleon Bonaparte was a skillful liar and he frequently exercised his talent in that direction, but he never lied without a definite reason and with the expectation of accomplishing something of benefit to himself. In this instance his purpose was not revealed on his first visit. With Nicolas Bonneville sitting between them as interpreter Bonaparte and Paine discussed the problems of mankind and the young French general agreed with the sixty-year-old author on everything. On leaving he asked Paine to dine with him some day soon and remarked that he would like to have the benefit of his advice. He made a favorable impression on Paine, not only by his courteous manner and his keen intelligence but mainly because of his professed belief in the ideals of democracy.

But Bonaparte was merely putting on an act. He cared nothing for democracy and human rights but was absorbed wholly in his visions of the future power and glory of Napoleon Bonaparte. At their next meeting he told Paine that he was planning an invasion of England to free the English people from the tyranny under which they were groaning. He wanted information about England and asked many questions.

In case the proposed invasion was actually made, would Paine accompany the French army as a spokesman to the people of England? Yes, Paine would do that—provided the invasion had no other purpose than to bring liberty to his former countrymen. Why, of course; that was the idea behind the whole project. So Bonaparte assured him.

There were other meetings of Paine and Bonaparte, but the atmosphere of friendliness and understanding that surrounded them at first gradually became cooler and cooler. Paine had begun at their second meeting to suspect Bonaparte's intentions and his suspicion deepened as time went on. He did not care to take any part, however small, in a world-conquering program. His sympathy went out to people, and he did not see how their condition would be improved by merely exchanging one despotic ruler for another.

Their acquaintance—or friendship, if one may call it that—came to an end, and thereafter Paine always referred to Bonaparte as "that French charlatan." The term that Bonaparte applied to Paine is not recorded, but it was probably quite as uncomplimentary.

CONTEMPORANEOUS SILHOUETTE OF
COLONEL JOSEPH KIRKBRIDE
COURTESY OF RODMAN GILDER

Colonel Kirkbride was Paine's neighbor in Bordentown, New Jersey, and was for many years his staunch friend.

CHAPTER XV

The Last Sad Years

I

Tom Paine was a forerunner of Abraham Lincoln. Paine stood for manhood suffrage, and so did Lincoln. Paine argued for the abolition of Negro slavery years before Lincoln was born. Paine was an advocate of universal education, of free schools for all children and so was Lincoln. Paine believed that women should be classed as men's equals in human affairs, and that was also Lincoln's idea.

In their respective attitudes toward life and human welfare, even toward religion since Lincoln was as much a Deist as Jefferson, and in their intellectual processes, there was a close kinship between Lincoln and Paine. But there was also an important difference. Lincoln was a politician, or statesman, and he knew when to be silent and when to speak out. He could be soft in manner and pleasing in speech when facing his adversaries, and he won many of them over to his side, time and again, by such methods.

But Tom Paine had only contempt for those who did not agree with him and that attitude was seldom concealed. He spoke out harshly and clearly, in season and out of season. There can be hardly a doubt that, within the depths of his unconscious self, he had a need for martyrdom. It would be difficult indeed to find another important person in history who was so wholly lacking in shrewdness.

Paine had an unshakable belief that if once men understood his ideas and were honest, no more was necessary. But Lincoln felt that no matter how good an idea was, it had to be put into practice slowly and gradually.

To determine the character and extent of Paine's sins I have done a good deal of digging into the past; the result is wholly negative. He was certainly not a thief, a forger or a swindler, and was never charged with any of these crimes. He gave away most of his earnings and lived all his life in a state that was close to poverty. He never seduced a woman, never showed a trace of cruelty to man or beast, and never evaded an obligation that he had undertaken. That he never cursed or swore at anybody or anything was one of his outstanding traits that attracted attention, as it would, naturally enough, in an age when swearing was a second language in almost every man's vocabulary. Moreover, Paine was notable in respect to obscene stories. There is no record of his telling one at any time or place, but it was a well-known fact during his lifetime that if anyone started to relate a vulgar yarn Paine would rise and excuse himself, saying pleasantly that he had forgotten an appointment, or giving some other reason for leaving the room.

He loved children and had a way of amusing them with his stories and games. He was liked by women, also, for his gentle manner appealed to them. But many men disliked him, not with mild distaste, but with hearty hate. Why? Because he had opinions which ran counter to most of the accepted and traditional ideas of his time, and he often made comments that irritated his hearers, for what he had to say was opposed to their cherished beliefs, and his statements were so logical and convincing that they aroused anger rather than argument. His beliefs were based on sharp and pure logic. They were never softened by sentimentality. Even intelligent and open-minded people like to have their beliefs eased on feather beds of emotional vagueness. For these Paine had no comfort. Sometimes he lost his temper—as when he learned now and then that he was being lied about—and on such occasions he would fall into a gloomy, angry silence which he might keep up for hours.

His extraordinary frankness was a serious hindrance to himself and to his career. When he did not like a person, or a plan, or a house, or anything else his immediate impulse was to say so in unmistakable terms, and that is what he frequently did. One who has followed his career closely cannot help feeling that many times a little clever and tactful lying would have been a great help to him.

Paine was not an atheist, for he believed in God and immortality, while atheism is a denial of the existence of God and of life after death. He has been called a sinner, a liar and a hypocrite, and he has been denounced for these shortcomings many times in print and in the pulpit.

He has been called a hater of Christ, but the assertion is not sustained by the facts. He thought that Christ was a "virtuous and amiable" man, and that his teachings are excellent. But he did not believe that Christ had been born of a virgin mother or that he was more closely related to God than are people in general.

In 1797 Paine helped to establish a church in Paris which would make the love of mankind its basic belief and field of action. In association with a number of his friends, he founded in January of that year the church of Theophilanthropy, a name which is compounded of three Greek words meaning *God, Love and Man*. They called it a church, but it really was an ethical society, and it happens to have been the first one of its kind. The room in which the Theophilanthropists held their meetings was made to resemble the interior of a church. It had an altar covered with flowers and on the walls were framed texts, some of which were taken from the Bible, others from philosophical works. Poems put into musical form were sung in place of hymns. The lectures, or sermons, had to do with the primary virtues and the relations of men and nations to one another, and their purpose was to encourage the brotherhood of man.

The church of Theophilanthropy existed nearly five years. The treaty, or Concordat, signed by the Pope and Napoleon on July 15, 1801, made Roman Catholicism the official and only religion of the French people, and Napoleon agreed to suppress all other forms of worship, including the tiny little congregation of Theophilanthropists.

2

One of Paine's close friends was Thomas Jefferson, and many letters passed between them. In October, 1800, while Jefferson was Vice-President of the United States, and was to be inaugurated as President in a few months, Paine wrote him a long letter concerning French affairs and, near the end of the epistle, stated that he was anxious to return to America. He said also that he would like to make the trip on an American warship, if a vessel of that character was due to visit France. The French and British war was still going on, and Paine was almost certain that the British—who were searching all neutral ships—would take him off any merchant vessel on which he might engage passage.

On March 18, 1801, Jefferson, who had then become President, wrote to Paine that the frigate *Maryland* was sailing to France at an early date to convey John Dawson, an agent of the American Government. Jefferson adds:

You expressed a wish to get passage to this country in a public vessel. Mr. Dawson is charged with orders to the captain of the Maryland to receive and accomodate you back if you can be ready to depart at such short warning. Rob. R. Livingston is appointed minister plenipotentiary to the republic of France, but will not leave till we receive the ratification of the convention by Mr. Dawson. I am in hopes you will find us returned generally to sentiments worthy of former times. In these it will be your glory to have steadily labored, and with as much effect as any man living. That you may long live to continue your useful labors, and to reap the reward in thankfulness of nations, is my sincere prayer. Accept assurances of my high esteem and affectionate attachment.

The *Maryland* went to France and returned to America, but Tom Paine did not sail on that ship. At the last moment he decided not to go on a war vessel, and his decision was made on account of an article that had appeared in a Baltimore newspaper and had reached him in Paris just before it was time for the *Maryland* to sail. The article in the newspaper was an attack on President Jefferson because he had permitted Tom Paine to use a vessel of the American navy for his traveling. Why not turn the navy over to any Tom, Dick or Harry who wants to knock about the world? That was the tone of the article in the anti-Jefferson paper. The writer of it also remarked that Paine had left these shores many years ago and had never returned,

even for a visit; was he still an American citizen? After Paine
had read the article he unpacked his bags and made up his mind
to wait. He did not want to do anything that would arouse
criticism of his friend Jefferson.

The war between France and England came to an end early
in 1802, and thereafter the British frigates no longer stood outside the French ports to search ships of neutral nations. There
was nothing to deter Paine from taking passage on any suitable
vessel, and he made his plans accordingly.

Sir Robert Smythe died in 1802, and Paine felt deeply the
loss of his best friend in France. He wrote that he thought of
America day and night, and that he desired urgently to come
home.

He wanted the Bonneville family to come to America with
him and settle here. They were pleased with the idea, and would
have made their arrangements to accompany him on the same
ship, but they learned, to their surprise, that Nicolas Bonneville would not be permitted to leave France. Since his imprisonment for having called Napoleon a "Cromwell" in his paper,
Bien Informé, he had been under surveillance, and his paper
had been suppressed. He earned his living by working here and
there in printing offices, and by writing pieces and translating
books from foreign languages into French. His income from
these activities was only a pittance and his family was almost
destitute. Paine thought that both the Bonnevilles could obtain
work in America, and he stood ready to lend them money for
their passage across the ocean, as well as funds to carry them
along for a while after they had landed on the other side.

When they found out that Nicolas Bonneville would not be
allowed to depart they decided that Madame and the three
children should sail anyway, and her husband should join them
later. But they did not come with Paine. He had been in America for the better part of a year before Madame Bonneville and
her family arrived.

Paine landed at Baltimore on October 30, 1802. He had been
away from America for fifteen years, and much had happened
since his departure. The War for Independence had become only

a memory, for more than twenty years had gone by since the surrender of Cornwallis. A new generation had grown up and a swarm of new ideas had supplanted those that were current and powerful in the early days when the whole nation had been grateful to Thomas Paine for his inspired utterances in the cause of freedom.

The pursuit of wealth had taken the place of the pursuit of liberty, and Paine had no place in its activities or in its aims. His maligners had had it all their own way for years and the public that never thinks, but forms its conclusions on impressions, had a mental picture of a dirty, drunken, lying rascal when Paine's name was mentioned.

"He cursed God," men in barrooms would say in awe-stricken tones to other men as they drank their ale and cider.

"Then he's bound for hell," someone else would remark.

"He claims there ain't no hell."

"Oh, he does, ye say? Well, he'll be frying in it before long, and then he'll wish he'd acted decent here in this world."

Sentiments of this nature were not limited to the uneducated. The *New England Palladium*, a Federalist newspaper of high standing, had been informed before Paine arrived that Thomas Jefferson had invited him to return. Thereupon, the sedate *Palladium* burst into this comment:

What! Invite to the United States that lying, drunken, brutal infidel, who rejoiced in the opportunity of basking and wallowing in the confusion, devastation, bloodshed, rapine, and murder, in which his soul delights?

The real reason for the movement to discredit Paine was not because of his Deism or on account of his dissection of the Bible in *The Age of Reason;* they were used only as convenient arguments to evoke popular detestation. The underlying cause may be found in Paine's political and economic views, also in his opposition to Negro slavery. The country had become an oligarchy, with wealth and land as the determining factors of leadership. Only a small fraction of the male population could qualify as voters. The men elected to all important offices were either men of wealth or they possessed a far-reaching influence among the wealthy. The poor—the farm hands, the mechanics of the towns and cities, the clerks in the shops—none of these had anything to say about the problems of the nation, the state, or the city. Trade unions were forbidden by law, and there was no regulation of working hours or living conditions.

That was the situation in 1802, and for about thirty years thereafter. Paine, with his enlightened views, his frequently expressed arguments for human rights, and his intense sympathy for the common people, would be like a firebrand in a powder mill if he were not stopped. And the most effective way to stop him—so they thought—would be to lay stress on his atheism, his hatred of religion, his detestation of prayer and worship, his leaning toward all that is evil. People could understand such arguments.

Then, too, his faults must be magnified; he must be made to appear as if he were drunk every day—drunk and staggering, with slobber dribbling from his mouth—as if he went about unshaven, unclean, in clothes so dirty they stank. This program, if carried out, would cause even the lowest ditch-digger to shun Tom Paine as if he were the devil—or so his enemies thought.

But Paine had friends, and many of the newspaper comments about his arrival were favorable to him. He went to Washington soon after he had landed at Baltimore. The *National Intelligencer* said in its account of his arrival in the capital: "Thomas Paine has arrived in this city, and has received a cordial reception from the Whigs of Seventy-six and the Republicans of 1800, who have the independence to feel and avow a sentiment of gratitude for his eminent revolutionary services."

3

From Baltimore Paine sent a letter to President Jefferson in which he announced his arrival and said that he would be in Washington in a few days.

When he reached Washington he took a room in a hotel and

after he had brushed up a bit he went over to the Executive Mansion and called on the President.[1] They had a long talk about French affairs and then the conversation shifted to America. Jefferson thought Paine ought to disregard the venomous slurs and diatribes that were appearing in the press, and Paine decided to follow his advice, but soon after his first visit to the Executive Mansion he began a series of articles under the general title, *Letters to Citizens of the United States*. There were seven of these. Five of them appeared in the *National Intelligencer*, one in the Philadelphia *Aurora* and one in the Trenton *True American*. In them Paine discussed public affairs. They were strongly Jeffersonian, or Republican, in tone, and bitterly anti-Federalist.

In the first article—printed in the *National Intelligencer* in Washington, November 15, 1802—he said:

The French Revolution was beginning to germinate when I arrived in France. The principles of it were good, they were copied from America, and the men who conducted it were honest. But the fury of faction soon extinguished the one and sent the other to the scaffold. Of those who began that Revolution, I am almost the only survivor, and that through a thousand dangers. I owe this not to the prayers of priests, nor to the piety of hypocrites, but to the continued protection of Providence.

But while I beheld with pleasure the dawn of liberty rising in Europe, I saw with regret the lustre of it fading in America. In less than two years from the time of my departure some distant symptoms painfully suggested the idea that the principles of the Revolution were expiring on the soil that produced them.

John Adams had called Paine "a worthless fellow" and had

[1] Washington was merely a village at that time, though it had been laid out on a magnificent scale. In 1802 there were about 3200 inhabitants in the place. The name White House was not given to the President's home until after the War of 1812. During that conflict Washington was captured by the British and they set fire to the Executive Mansion for the purpose of burning it down. But the fire was extinguished by a heavy rain, and after the British had gone the Mansion was given a coat of white paint to hide the black smudges left by the smoke from the fire. Hence the name White House. In those days Pennsylvania Avenue ran through a swamp that lay between the Capitol and the Executive Mansion.

treated his opinions with scorn and derision on many occasions. In his second *Letter* Paine had a lot to say about John Adams. The following extract may give you a fair idea of his comments:

I have had doubts of John Adams ever since the year 1776. In a conversation with me at that time, concerning the pamphlet *Common Sense*, he censured it because it attacked the English form of government. John was for independence because he expected to be made great by it; but it was not difficult to perceive, for the surliness of his temper makes him an awkward hypocrite, that his head was as full of kings, queens and knaves, as a pack of cards. But John has lost the deal.

When a man has a concealed project in his brain that he wants to bring forward, and fears that he will not succeed, he begins with it as physicians do by suspected poison, trying it first on an animal; if it agrees with the stomach of the animal he makes further experiments, and this was the way John took. His brain was teeming with projects to overturn the liberties of America and the representative system of government, and he began by hinting it in little companies.

The secretary of John Jay, an excellent painter and a poor politician, told me, in presence of another American, Daniel Parker, that in company where he himself was present, John Adams talked of making the government hereditary, and that as Mr. Washington had no children, it should be made hereditary in the family of Lund Washington.

John had not impudence enough to propose himself in the first instance, as the old French Normandy baron did, who offered to come over to be king of America, and if Congress did not accept his offer, that they would give him thirty thousand pounds for the generosity of it; but John, like a mole, was grubbing his way to it under ground. He knew that Lund Washington was unknown, for nobody had heard of him and that as the President had no children to succeed him, the Vice-President had, and if the treason had succeeded, and the hint with it, the goldsmith might be sent for to take measure of the head of John or of his son for a golden wig.[2]

[2] It is an historical fact that John Adams did not believe that government by the people and for the people would work out successfully. He favored a governing aristocracy. In his *Defence of the Constitution* he wrote: "The proposition that the people are the best keepers of their own liberties is not true. They are the worst conceivable, they are no keepers at all; they can neither judge, act, think, or will, as a political body."

Paine called the American maligners of himself the Terrorists of the New World and likened them to the French terrorists under Robespierre. He thought and said that the only reason they did not attempt to crush all opposition by force, for the purpose of turning the American republic into a harsh despotism, was their fear that such drastic measures might fail and react upon themselves. So they did the next best thing; they set out to undermine confidence in the leaders of the people by spreading lies about them and he—Paine himself—stood at the top of their list.

So he says in his third *Letter*, from which the following paragraphs are quoted:

When Robespierre had me seized in the night and imprisoned in the Luxembourg (where I remained eleven months), he assigned no reason for it. But when he proposed bringing me to the tribunal, which was like sending me at once to the scaffold, he then assigned a reason, and the reason was, for the interests of America as well as of France. *"Pour les intérêts de l'Amerique autant que de la France."*

The words are in his own handwriting, and reported to the Convention by the committee appointed to examine his papers, and are printed in their report, with this reflection added to them, "Why Thomas Paine more than another? Because he contributed to the liberty of both worlds."

There must have been a coalition in sentiment, if not in fact, between the Terrorists of America and the Terrorists of France, and Robespierre must have known it, or he could not have had the idea of putting America into the bill of accusation against me.

Yet these men, these Terrorists of the New World, who were waiting in the devotion of their hearts for the joyful news of my destruction, are the same banditti who are now bellowing hypocrisy about humanity and piety, and often about something they call infidelity, and they finish with the chorus of *Crucify him, crucify him.* I am become so famous among them, they cannot eat or drink without me. I serve them as a standing dish, and they cannot make up a bill of fare if I am not in it.

But there is one dish, and that the choicest of all, that they have not presented on the table, and it is time they should. They have not yet accused *Providence of Infidelity.* Yet according to their outrageous piety, she must be as bad as Thomas Paine; she has protected him in all his dangers, patronized him in all his undertakings, encouraged him in all his ways, and rewarded him at last by bringing him in safety and in health to the Promised Land.

The seventh *Letter to Citizens of the United States*, which was the last of the series, is an outline for a League of Nations. The original draft of this suggestion was sent in Paine's own handwriting to Thomas Jefferson on October 6, 1803, to which Jefferson replied: "These papers contain precisely our principles, and I hope that they will be generally recognized here."

Paine did not call the compact that he proposed a "league," but an "Association of Nations." It was to be, he wrote, "an unarmed Association for the protection of the rights and commerce of nations that shall be neutral in time of war."

The first article for his "Association of Nations" was that a neutral nation did not and could not surrender its rights because of other nations at war.

Article 2 provided for the absolute freedom of the seas of neutral nations, "without being seized, searched, visited or any ways interrupted, by the nation or nations with which that nation is at war."

Article 3 provided for a boycott against any of the offending nations in the following manner: that, "if any belligerent power shall seize, search, etc.," then, "the powers composing this Association . . . will cease to import . . . any goods, wares or merchandise . . . of the power so offending against the Association . . ."

Article 4 provided for a boycott against the aggressor nations. It states that, "The powers composing this Association shall be shut against the flag of the offending nations."

Article 5 is a further extension of the boycott, and provides for the payment of reparations by the withholding of the payments of debts to the offending nations until proper reparation be made for the offense against the members of the Association. Paine's specific language regarding this provision is "that no remittance . . . shall be made by any of the citizens or subjects . . . of any of the powers composing this Association . . . to the citizens or subjects of the offending nations . . . until reparation be made."

Article 6 provided for the notification of any of the violations of the rights of the individual members to the other members of the Association to be published by them as a declaration to the offending nation that "the penal articles of this Association shall be put into execution against the offending Nation."

Article 7 provided for the time element required for the payment of reparations.

Article 8 provided for the design of the "flag to be carried at the mast-head conjointly with the national flag of each nation composing this Association" by being "composed of the same colors that compose the rainbow, and arranged in the same order as they appear in that phenomenon."

Article 9 provided for the use of this flag by the nation which "is a member of the Association and a respecter of its laws."

Article 10 provided for the neutrality of the peaceful nations in their intercourse with the belligerent powers by providing that, "We, therefore, the powers composing this Association, declare that we will, each one for itself, prohibit in our dominions the exportation or transportation of military stores . . . and all kinds of iron and steel weapons used in war. Excluding therefrom all kinds of utensils and instruments used in civil or domestic life . . ."

Paine also provided that, immediately upon the outbreak of war, the members of the Association shall meet as quickly as possible.

These articles of Paine's "Association of Nations" were to be the law of nations at all times or until a "Congress of Nations shall meet to form some laws more effectual." He also provided that "immediately on the breaking out of war between any two or more nations, deputies be appointed by all neutral nations . . . to meet in congress in some central place to take cognizance of any violation of the rights of neutral nations."

He also provided that "The Association of Nations have a

President for a term of years and the presidency to pass by rotation to each of the parties composing the Association."

Nothing came of this proposal conceived by Paine, it is needless to state, for in this matter he was more than a hundred years ahead of the period in which he lived.

Paine had known Thomas Jefferson for more than twenty years. He admired him and believed that he was one of only a few men of high position who had a sincere desire to serve the people as a whole rather than a special class. He hoped to have many long leisurely talks with the President, and he was sorely disappointed when he learned that he must arrange for his interviews with Jefferson's secretaries; that he was limited as to length of time he might remain in conversation with him, since Mr. Jefferson had to see many callers in the course of a day. A few days after he reached Washington he had a rather lengthy interview with Jefferson and after that occasion the conversation when they met consisted of not much more than *How d'ye do* and *Good-by*. Paine had brought over from Paris a number of mechanical models which he wanted to show to Jefferson and discuss with him, so he had them sent to the Executive Mansion. When he had waited more than a month and nothing happened, he wrote to the President in these words:

I will be obliged to you to send back the Models, as I am packing up to set off for Philadelphia and New York. My intention in bringing them here in preference to sending them from Baltimore to Philadelphia, was to have some conversation with you on those matters and others I have not informed you of.

But you have not only shown no disposition towards it, but have, in some measure, by a sort of shyness, as if you stood in fear of Federal observation, precluded it. I am not the only one who makes observations of this kind.

Paine did not seem to understand that Jefferson, as the chief executive of a nation, had but little time to spare. It was not the President's intention, however, to treat his old friend with discourtesy. Evidently he thought Paine had stopped in Washington just to look around and make some social calls, but as soon as he received the letter that is quoted here he invited him to come over to the Executive Mansion as a house guest. Paine accepted the invitation and lived at the Mansion for about two weeks, until the time of his departure from Washington. In the evenings, after the last guest had gone home, Jefferson and Paine would sit before the cozy fire in the President's study, discussing the affairs of men and nations.

Jefferson was a widower and the hostess of the Executive Mansion was his daughter Maria—now Mrs. Eppes. She was no stranger to Tom Paine; he had known her in Paris when she was living there while her father was the American Minister to France. She wanted to hear the news about her friends and acquaintances across the sea, and Paine told her all he knew, which was not a great deal, for he could hardly be called a social lion and frequenter of drawing rooms in Paris or anywhere else.

On Christmas Day of the previous year (1802) Paine had written Jefferson a note in which he suggested that the United States purchase Louisiana from the French. Jefferson sent for him the next day and whispered to him privately and confidentially that negotiations for the purchase had been under way for some time. In January, when Paine became a guest of the President, it looked as if the deal with Napoleon would go through, and that the United States would find itself with a vast new territory to manage. Jefferson told Paine that he wanted advice on how to handle the problems that would surely arise as soon as the region west of the Mississippi was transferred to the American nation. That was one of the constantly recurring topics of discussion in the evening talks.

Another uncertainty which Jefferson brought up had to do with his own right to make such a transaction. Neither Congress nor the President was given any authority, express or implied, under the Constitution, to purchase foreign territory. The Constitution says nothing at all on the subject. Paine advised Jefferson to assume the authority—that, as a matter of common sense, the President possessed the power to do whatever might be of indisputable benefit to the country. After discussing the matter from every standpoint Jefferson said that he agreed with that conclusion.

Both he and Paine thought the Federalists—anti-Republicans —in Congress might try to obstruct the purchase, as they had made a practice of opposing nearly every important measure that had the support of Jefferson's party. But in this case, when the matter came before Congress, the issue did not arise. The purchase of the Louisiana Territory was of such undoubted and extraordinary benefit to the nation that even the most rabid political adversary of Thomas Jefferson did not have the courage to oppose it.

Paine met many people while he was a guest at the Executive Mansion, for Jefferson's dinners and social gatherings were largely attended. Some of those who met Paine wrote their impressions of him, and not one of them said he was filthy, or a drunkard, or that his manners were bad. On the contrary, they were impressed by his interesting conversations and his anecdotes. He was good-humored, polite, and attentive. Also—he was always clean-shaven, neatly dressed, his face washed, his hair combed and brushed.

His stay at the Executive Mansion was pleasant in every way. The President supplied a horse on which Paine rode around the countryside on fine days, and now and then he and Jefferson would take walks, strolling arm in arm, like old cronies.

4

In February, 1803, Paine started for New York. He broke his journey by stopping at Bordentown, New Jersey, to visit his old friend, Colonel Joseph Kirkbride, and to look over the tiny cottage he owned in that village. The Colonel gave him a hearty welcome, and so did John Hall, the mechanic who had helped him build the model of his iron bridge he had carried to France in 1787.

Hall called on Paine as soon as he heard that his former employer was in Bordentown, and here is the entry in his journal for that day:

Had a ride to Bordenton to Mr. Paine at Mr. Kirkbride's. He was well and aperd jollyer than I had ever knowne him. He is full of whims and skeams and mechanicall inventions. and is to build a place or shop to carry them out, and wants my help.

Paine had stopped in Philadelphia on his trip from Washington and met some friends there, but Dr. Benjamin Rush, who had stood by him and encouraged him in years gone by, did not call on him and let it be known that he would refuse to see him. In explanation of his attitude Dr. Rush said, "His principles avowed in *The Age of Reason* were so offensive to me that I did not wish to renew my intercourse with him."

The Doctor was not the only one who treated Paine with studied discourtesy. He was to experience many such insults in the years to come. One day while he was Colonel Kirkbride's guest his host took him across the river to call on Samuel Rogers, who was the Colonel's brother-in-law and an old friend of Paine. As they walked into the house Rogers turned his back, refused to shake hands with Paine, or to speak to him, because he was the author of *The Age of Reason*.

As soon as it became known generally in Bordentown that Paine was spending a week or two in the community the preachers of the various denominations began to preach sermons on Infidel Paine, his sins and his future punishment in the glowing fires of Hell. In those days sermons consisted largely of descriptions of the tortures that sinners were to expect in the hereafter. Paine's writings were said to be "a sin against the Holy Ghost," for which there is no forgiveness.

In March (1803) Paine left Bordentown and went to New York. He planned to take the stage at Trenton, and Kirkbride drove him over to the place where the stagecoach awaited its passengers. Everyone who bought a ticket was required to give his name, and when the stage driver heard the name of Thomas Paine he snatched the ticket from Paine's hand and shoved the passage money back to him. "Ye can't go in my stage," he exclaimed. "Last year my horses wuz struck by lightning and killed and I ain't taking no more chances."

The driver said just that, and meant it. As he sold tickets to other passengers he glanced fiercely at Paine now and then as if he did not like to have him standing near, for he might attract a stroke of lightning even if he were not going in the stagecoach. Paine might have been marooned indefinitely in Trenton if Colonel Kirkbride had not taken him to New York in his private carriage.

When Paine arrived he went at once to the City Hotel and engaged a room. He stayed there a few weeks, but he found the hotel too dear for his limited means, so he moved to Wilburn's boarding house at 16 Gold Street. Not many days after he reached New York he went up to New Rochelle to look over his property. The farm was rented to a farmer who cultivated it. He lived in the cottage that had been built on Paine's order by a contractor in 1793, after the house that formerly stood on the land had been destroyed by fire.[3]

Madame Bonneville and her three young sons, Benjamin, Thomas and Louis, arrived at Norfolk, Virginia, in August, 1803. Paine had been expecting them for several months, but Madame Bonneville had delayed her departure from France in the hope that her husband would be allowed to come with them. The French authorities would not permit him to leave the country, however, and finally she decided to come, anyway, and bring her children.

The Bonneville family was absolutely penniless, so Paine agreed to pay for their passage and keep them supplied until Madame Bonneville could find a way of earning money. That was something of a rash promise on his part, for the expense was much larger than he had anticipated, but he kept his word though he had to borrow money to do it. She wrote to Paine from "Mrs. Hunt's Boarding House, Norfolk, Va." to let him know that she and the children were in America at last, and also to inform him that she needed twenty-two pounds and ten shil-

[3] The cottage erected in 1793 still stands, and a picture of it is shown in this volume. It is now the property of the Huguenot and Historical Association of New Rochelle, and is open for the inspection of visitors, and is very interesting. It contains relics of Paine's personal life.

lings to pay for their passage, as she owed that sum to the captain of the ship.

Paine, in his reply, told her that the money would be sent at once. He said further:

> I have written to Col. Kirkbride, of Bordentown, in the State of New Jersey, who will expect your coming there, and from whom you will receive every friendship. I expect to be there myself in about a month or five weeks.
>
> If you are in want of money to continue your journey to Bordentown, I will be obliged to any of my friends in Norfolk to supply you, and I will remit it to them as soon as I am informed of it. I can depend on your economy in the use of it, and you and the poor boys can rest upon my friendship. I am not personally acquainted with Col. Newton, of Norfolk, but I find he is a friend of Mr. Madison, the Secretary of State, and if Col. Newton will be so kind as to supply you with what money you may want, I will repay it immediately into the hands of Mr. Madison, or remit it to him thro' the Postmaster.
>
> I suppose your best way will be to come up the bay by the packet to Baltimore, and from thence to Philadelphia and Bordentown. . . . Embrace the poor boys for me and tell them they will soon see me at Bordentown. I shall write again to Col. Kirkbride to inform him of your arrival.

Colonel Kirkbride had told Paine, before Madame Bonneville had sailed from France, that he could find plenty for her to do in Bordentown—meaning that she would do well there as a teacher of French—and that is why Paine arranged for her to go there instead of coming to New York. He invited her to occupy his Bordentown cottage, which was then without a tenant.

The Colonel made good on his promise to get pupils for her. In a few weeks she had as many of them as she could handle, but she did not get along very well with the folks in the village. When she had been in Bordentown about a month Paine went there to see her. She told him that she was bored by the place and the people and wanted to leave. As she spoke only a few words of English, and nobody in her neighborhood spoke French, her social life was limited to the classroom. Paine listened to her tale of boredom, but he did not know what to say except to advise her to stay until something more agreeable could be found.

She was, however, a strong-willed woman, accustomed to deciding for herself. A couple of months later, during the winter of 1804, Paine returned to his boarding house on Gold Street after a walk to find Madame Bonneville there. She had arrived with her baggage and her children and had taken lodgings as a regular guest. She was through with life in Bordentown, she said. Further conversation brought out the fact that she had left bills unpaid in the New Jersey village, and as Paine was her sponsor he had to arrange for their payment. He decided, however, that he would not be responsible for her bill at Wilburn's, and he notified the proprietor to that effect, and also informed Madame Bonneville that she would have to look out for them herself.

She did fall behind in her payments and when she left in the early summer of 1804 to accompany Paine to New Rochelle and keep house for him she still owed Wilburn thirty-five dollars. He sued Paine for that amount, and Paine won the suit, for the complainant was unable to prove that Paine had assumed any responsibility for the debt. But as soon as the case was decided in his favor Paine turned around and paid Wilburn the money. Few men, if any besides Paine, would have done that, but to him it was a perfectly natural action, and it illustrates his temperament, or nature, or eccentricity, or whatever one cares to call it.

Paine took over the New Rochelle farm in 1804, the lease of his tenant having expired, and he went there to live. Madame Bonneville accompanied him with two of her boys. Young Thomas, who was Paine's godson, was at a boarding school in Connecticut, and it was not long before her two other boys were sent to boarding school in New Rochelle.

Madame Bonneville remained at New Rochelle only a few months. As a housekeeper she displayed an astonishing incompetence, which is not easy to understand, for she certainly managed her husband's household in Paris. Paine thought she would do better as a teacher, and so he wrote to a friend, Colonel Fellows, with this comment:

It is certainly best that Mrs. Bonneville go into some family as a teacher, for she has not the least talent of managing affairs for herself. She may send Bebia [4] up to me. I will take care of him for his own sake and his father's, but that is all I have to say.

In a letter to Jefferson Paine described his farm in this fashion:

It is a pleasant and healthy situation, commanding a prospect always green and peacable, as New Rochelle produces a great deal of grass and hay. The farm contains three hundred acres, about one hundred of which is meadow land, one hundred grazing and village land, and the remainder woodland. It is an oblong about a mile and a half in length. I have sold off sixty-one acres and a half for four thousand and twenty dollars. With this money I shall improve the other part, and build an addition 34 feet by 32 to the present building.

On Christmas Eve of 1804 an attempt was made to murder Paine by a disorderly fellow who was well-known in New Rochelle for his vicious habits. His name was Christopher Derrick or Dederick. He was a farm laborer who had done some work on Paine's land. In the course of his employment he had drawn not only all his pay, but forty-eight dollars besides. He could not reimburse Paine, as he had no money, but he agreed to build a stone fence on Paine's land. That was the understanding, but Derrick never even started the work.

Then Paine was surprised to receive a request from a New Rochelle merchant to pay for a considerable amount of goods that Derrick had obtained from his store by saying that they

[4] Bebia was the pet name for Madame Bonneville's son Benjamin. He graduated at West Point, became an army officer, fought in the Mexican War and the Civil War, and retired as a general. He died in 1878. His account of an exploring expedition to the Rocky Mountains was edited by Washington Irving, and is still considered a work of merit.

were intended for Mr. Paine and should be charged to him. Thereupon Paine sought Derrick out and gave him a tongue lashing.

Derrick bore the reproof meekly, for he was sober and depressed, but on Christmas Eve he was drunk, in high spirits, and without meekness, fear or ordinary common sense. So he borrowed a gun and went to look for Thomas Paine. At eight o'clock, or thereabouts, on that evening, Paine was sitting at his desk, which was placed close to a window in a room on the ground floor of his house. There was a lighted candle on the desk and the head and upper part of Paine's body could be seen clearly by anyone standing on the ground just outside the window.

Derrick crept up quietly, stood just outside the window and fired at Paine point-blank. The muzzle of the gun was not more than ten feet from Paine's head when it was fired. Something must have happened at that instant to depress the muzzle, for the bullet passed through the outer wall just a few inches below the window sill and missed its target altogether. Paine suspected Derrick on account of the threats he had made and he was soon picked up, but when the case came to trial Paine refused to press the charge.[5]

In this incident we see another providential escape from death —the third one in Paine's life so far as we know, but there may have been others of which we have never heard. He escaped from the officers of the British Crown at Dover, when they were searching for him with a warrant for treason which would have meant his death; then there was the incident at the Luxembourg prison; and now we see him saved again.

5

The New Rochelle house was uncomfortable in winter, and by Christmas Paine had had about enough of its chilly drafts and

---

[5] Visitors to the Paine cottage at New Rochelle may see the hole that was made by the bullet just below the window sill. It is large enough to permit one to run a thumb through it.

rattling windows and cold rooms. In January, 1805, he closed the house and went to New York to stay until spring. Madame Bonneville also went to the city where she became a French teacher, but she and Paine did not live in the same house.

Paine boarded at the home of William Carver at 36 Cedar Street. Carver had introduced himself in 1803, soon after Paine had come to New York. He said that he was a native of Lewes, in England, and that he had been brought up in that town. When Paine was an excise officer Carver had often seen him, he said, which was probably true; but Paine did not recall Carver, who was a mere boy in the early 1770's. He had been brought up as a farrier—he shod horses and took care of them—but after coming to America he called himself a veterinary.

Carver and his family were illiterate, with all the objectionable traits of small, mean minds. Like many other persons, he thought Paine was wealthy, and he planned, undoubtedly, to make himself the heir of the affluent author, so he became a Deist and an admirer of Paine's books, none of which he had read, for he read with such effort and so slowly that reading played no part in his pursuits or pleasures.

In the course of time Carver learned that Paine was not rich, but poor, and that whatever property he possessed would go to Madame Bonneville and her children when he died. Thereupon he turned against Paine—at first slyly and secretly, later openly. Some of the most outrageous lies concerning Paine's personal life were created by him.

Paine stayed again at Carver's house for a while in 1806. That was during the period of Carver's pretended friendship. But in 1807, when his hypocrisy was revealed and he had to come out in the open, Carver asserted that Paine had been so filthy in his personal habits that he was a nuisance in the house, that he was drunk every day and all day, and that nothing in the way of food or service ever pleased him.

A few days before Paine died, in 1809, Carver wrote to him and humbly begged his forgiveness for the lies he had told. Some of them had appeared in print, in James Cheetham's newspaper, *The American Citizen*, and elsewhere. Carver said his words had been twisted; also that he had been a little angry with Paine about something—he said that he had forgotten what it was—and that his temper got out of control and that he had said more than he intended.

That was his excuse; it seems too flimsy to be taken seriously, and Carver must have made it up to ease his sense of guilt. My own guess is that Carver was paid for his vicious lies and that the money came from reactionary leaders who feared the effect of Paine's radical ideas on the people. The best way to counteract them was, they thought, to discredit Tom Paine personally—to picture him as a drunkard who wallowed in filth and never did a real day's work, and who hated churches, God and the Bible.

It is an old story: if one's opponent has the best of an argument—if his facts are correct, his logic is sound and his conclusions are irrefutable—then what shall one do? Why, the answer is simple: just pick up a brickbat and hurl it at him, and follow up the attack with stones and clubs, accompanied by loud yells of abuse and vulgarities. That is precisely what Paine's enemies did away back in 1807, and also what they are doing today.

There is an interesting similarity between Carver in his repentant phase and the change that William Cobbett underwent in his attitude toward Paine, though Carver and Cobbett were miles apart in their respective stations in life. Carver was a half-illiterate stableman who called himself a veterinary, while Cobbett was a widely read English journalist whose fiery comments on men and their doings usually kept him up to his neck in hot water. In the preceding chapter of this book there is a quotation from his reply to Paine's *Letter to George Washington*. He printed his reply as a series of articles in *Porcupine's Gazette*, a periodical that he owned and edited during his sojourn in the United States (1792 to 1800). Perhaps it may not be considered tiresomely repetitious to quote again a few sentences of that historic tirade.

"Wherever or whenever he [Paine] breathes his last," Cobbett wrote, "he will neither excite sorrow nor compassion. No friendly hand will close his eyes, and not a moan will be uttered, not a tear will be shed. Like Judas he will be remembered by posterity. Men will learn to express all that is base, malignant, treacherous, unnatural, and blasphemous, by one single monosyllable—Paine!"

After the articles had appeared in *Porcupine's Gazette*, Cobbett had the series issued as a pamphlet under the title *A Letter to the Infamous Tom Paine*. It was published in 1796.

During that same year Paine, then living in Paris, wrote and brought out *Decline and Fall of the English System of Finance*, which was one of the first studies of the evils of monetary inflation that had ever appeared in any language. The British treasury and the Bank of England were, at that time, pouring out a huge stream of paper money without taking even the most elementary measures to accumulate a fund of gold for its redemption, or to control the economic effect of so much paper money in circulation, a neglect which had its origin in pure ignorance on the part of those responsible. Paine had been in America during and after the Revolution, and had made a first-hand study here of inflation in its worst aspects, so he knew a great deal about the subject.

His book seems to have caused a sensation. It had a large circulation and was translated into all the European languages. As a result of his study of inflation and the disasters that were certain to follow it, Paine predicted in his pamphlet that the Bank of England would have to suspend payments. The great bank, head of the monetary system and the financial center of the British Empire, was considered as strong as the Rock of Gibraltar by the English people. Nevertheless, Paine's prediction came true; the bank did suspend payments, for there was not enough gold procurable to meet the incoming flood of paper currency.

Cobbett did not read the *Decline and Fall of the English System of Finance* when it was first published, for he thought that any book by Tom Paine would be worthless; but on his return to England he heard so much talk about the book that he read it and reread it. It became his constant companion and textbook. Until then he had known very little of Paine's work, but he began at once to read the *Rights of Man* and *The Age of*

Reason and other writings of the man he had abused so heartily. After he had read them he felt that he had been on the wrong road all his life. He became an admirer and a disciple of Tom Paine. He who had fought radical ideas in speech and in print underwent a change that might almost be compared to a religious conversion, and he became himself one of the leading radicals of his time.[6]

Cobbett liked to think of himself as Paine's successor and, after Paine's death in 1809, he wrote a eulogy in which he said: "Old age having laid his hand upon this truly great man, this truly philosophical politician, at his expiring flambeau I lighted my taper."

6

For the last five or six years of his life Tom Paine was the fixed and universal target of abuse in America. Preachers shouted sermons to frightened congregations on the subject of Tom Paine and the hellfire to which he was bound; mothers chided their disobedient children with a threat that, unless they mended their ways, "the devil and Tom Paine" would catch them; newspaper editors told their readers that the influence of Tom Paine and his religious heresy—unless it was checked—might eventually undermine civilization, and send the world back to primitive savagery.

John Inskeep, mayor of Philadelphia, refused to rent one of the city's wharves to Isaac Hall, a citizen who had bid fifty dollars more rent for the wharf than any other bidder had

[6] The short biography of William Cobbett in *Webster's Biographical Dictionary* says that he "published pamphlets attacking the French Revolution and any form of radicalism. . . . Left England in 1792 and came to America; settled in Philadelphia; published *Porcupine's Gazette*; was fined for libel. Returned to England in 1800; edited from 1802 the weekly *Political Register*, which was at first a Tory journal but in 1804 changed into a champion of radicalism, demanding parliamentary and social reform. Became a leader of discontented working classes after ending of the war in 1815; had to flee to America, where he lived on a Long Island farm until 1819, when he returned to England." He died in 1835.

offered, and the mayor's refusal—as he stated himself—was because *Mr. Hall was one of Paine's disciples*. The incident got into the papers and Paine read of it. Thereupon he wrote Mayor Inskeep a public letter (February 10, 1806) from which the following extract is taken:

If those whom you may choose to call my disciples follow my example in doing good to mankind, they will pass the confines of this world with a happy mind, while the hope of the hypocrite shall perish and delusion sink into despair. . . .

As I set too much value on my time to waste it on a man of so little consequence as yourself, I will close this short address with a declaration that puts hypocrisy and malevolence to defiance. Here it is:

My motive and object in all my political works, beginning with *Common Sense*, the first work I ever published, has been to rescue man from tyranny and false systems and false principles of government for himself; and I have borne my share of danger in Europe and America in every attempt I have made for this purpose.

And my motive and object in all my publications on religious subjects, beginning with the first part of *The Age to Reason*, has been to bring man to a right reason that God has given him; to impress on him the great principles of divine morality, justice, mercy, and a benevolent disposition to all men and to all creatures; and to excite in him a spirit of trust, confidence, and consolation in his creator, unshackled by the fable and fiction of books, by whatever invented name they may be called.

In New York City there was published during Paine's last years a daily newspaper called *The American Citizen*. Its editor was a young Englishman, James Cheetham, who had emigrated to the United States in 1798 from Manchester, where he had been a leading member of the local Constitutional Society, which was a reflex of the French Revolution. He was a radical at that time.

His New York newspaper, *The American Citizen*, was republican in politics and a supporter of Jefferson's administration. When Paine came to New York in 1803 Cheetham gave him a reception, followed by a dinner of seventy persons. He had read Paine's books and professed to have a great admiration for him. Would Paine send him some articles for publication?

Yes, Paine agreed, and thereafter he saw Cheetham and wrote an occasional article for him.

Then, a year or so after Paine's coming to New York, Cheetham declined his contributions and all intercourse between him and Paine came to an end. Paine never understood, to the last day of his life, why Cheetham had become his enemy, but the circumstances—as we see them now—seem to indicate that he received pay to turn against Paine. In other words, he was a venal, low-class literary prostitute who deliberately created situations from which he expected to profit, and there are fairly convincing reasons for believing that he became a radical in England in the hope of being bribed to desert the party, but it did not turn out that way, for the English authorities threatened to send him to jail for inciting labor troubles, so he ran away and emigrated to America.

Cheetham was the bitterest and most effective enemy that Paine had in America. His newspaper ran countless columns of abusive comments on Paine, his books and his beliefs.

Shortly after Paine's death Cheetham wrote a *Life of Thomas Paine* which was for years the only book-length biography of Paine published in America. In England there was the scurrilous life of Paine by George Chalmers (who wrote under the pen name of Oldys). Many of the lies about Paine made their first appearance in print in one or both of these volumes, and so gained a long start ahead of the truth. Some of them are current today and are implicitly believed by many people.

Here are a few extracts from Cheetham's book. They are brief, but their tone and falsity are fairly representative of the whole work:

The intention of Paine, and the intention only, both in politics and religion, constitutes a character entirely original. His intention was more completely destructive than that of any other author that perhaps ever lived. While conspiring to subvert all government, he meditated the overthrow of all religion. While planning devastation and blood on earth, he was hatching rebellion against heaven. With him, the mortal and the immortal parts were to sink together in the dust.

As a matter of record, it may be worth while to say again in this place that Paine was a firm believer in the immortality of the soul. His political ideas were not destructive, but just the opposite. He stood for the kind of government that would wipe out false distinctions and give opportunity, freedom and liberty to the greatest number of people.

He could not return to England, where he had been wisely outlawed, and he was aware that he was odious in the United States. Washington justly considered him an anarchist in government, and an infidel in religion. He had no country in the world, and it may truly be said that he had not a friend. Was ever man so wretched? Was ever enormous sinner so justly punished?

A few paragraphs further on Cheetham says that Paine, in France, associated with the lowest company and indulged to excess in liquor. "He became," says Cheetham, "so filthy in his person, so mean in his dress, and so notoriously a sot, that all men of decency in Paris avoided him."

It is a lie—that statement—without an atom of truth in it. Paine drank excessively only during his last three years—from around the beginning of 1806 until his death in 1809—and in that period his clothes were sometimes soiled because he was desperately ill, was dying slowly, and was too weak to keep himself clean. Today he would be sent to a hospital and looked after by capable nurses. He drank brandy with the idea (current at the time) that it would keep up his strength.

Twenty-odd pages of Cheetham's book are taken up by statements of William Carver as to Paine's bad temper, stinginess, whisky-drinking, lack of cleanliness and love of disorder and filth. These Carver revelations—contrasted with his later apologies to Paine and others, and his eagerness after Paine's death to pose as his friend—give a tone of gruesome comedy to the book, or perhaps it would be better to say that they make it seem as if it were produced in a lunatic asylum.

Cheetham wrote also that Paine had seduced Madame Bonneville and had her leave her husband and come to America as his mistress; and that her boy Thomas was Paine's illegitimate son. Madame Bonneville sued Cheetham for libel. There was no evidence whatever brought out that there had been any illicit relations between her and Paine. Moreover, he had not taken her from her husband, who remained on good terms with Paine. She had come to America with his consent, and he joined her and the family here as soon as he got permission to leave France.

Madame Bonneville won her case and Cheetham was found guilty of libel, but when he came up for sentence he was fined only one hundred and fifty dollars. The judge said that Cheetham's excellent book, in which the libel happened to be found, served the cause of religion and he did not want to impose a heavy fine on the author.

7

One of the interesting features of Paine's career is that hardly anyone who met him or had ever heard of him was indifferent to him. He was either liked or disliked and in this respect he was certainly unusual, for very few people arouse so much feeling in others.

Tom Paine had both friends and enemies, but during his last years in America the enemies were in a great majority. He was inexpressibly saddened by that situation, of which he was continually made aware. When we read between the lines that express his thought and feeling we gain a conviction that on his return to America he had hoped and expected to be welcomed as a national hero. But instead he was looked upon by many as a moral leper, as an outcast who was so lost to decency that he thrust himself on a nation that never wanted to see him again.

Nevertheless, Paine had friends—men of courage and of sound judgment—who realized his greatness and his ability and who never deserted him. Among them was the Irish patriot, Thomas Addis Emmet, brother of the martyred Robert Emmet. Because of his work on behalf of the United Irishmen and his part in the insurrection for which Robert was hanged, Thomas Addis Emmet was banished from the British Empire. He came to America in 1804, acquired citizenship and made his

BUST OF THOMAS PAINE

BY JOHN WESLEY JARVIS

This bust, which is owned by the New York Historical Society, was made by Jarvis when Paine was in his seventieth year. It shows his appearance when weakened by age and illness.

PAINE LIVED IN THIS HOUSE

The house that is depicted here stood at 309 Bleecker Street, New York City. It was demolished in 1932. Paine lived on the second floor from July, 1808, to April, 1809, when he was moved as an invalid to 59 Grove Street, where he died.

home here until his death in 1827. He had a distinguished career, not only as a lawyer in private practice, but also as attorney general of the State of New York. He became one of the executors of Thomas Paine's will.

Both Thomas Addis Emmet and his brother Robert had been inspired to take part in the Irish struggle for freedom by reading Paine's *Rights of Man*. Thomas made the acquaintance of Paine soon after he reached New York, and he became his staunch friend and adviser—a friendship that continued unbroken until Paine's death.

Another true friend was Colonel John Fellows, a well-known auctioneer, which was a calling that was highly esteemed in that era. Colonel Fellows was a confidant of Paine. Only a few of the letters written to him by Paine have been preserved, which is a pity, for they would have revealed, one must suppose, much about Paine that is now known only imperfectly. The following extract is from a letter by Paine to Fellows sent from the house at New Rochelle on July 31, 1805. It shows how Paine was living at that time:

I am master of an empty house, or nearly so. I have six chairs and a table, a straw-bed, a feather-bed, and a bag of straw for Thomas [Paine's godson], a tea kettle, an iron pot, an iron baking pan, a frying pan, a gridiron, cups, saucers, plates and dishes, knives and forks, two candlesticks and a pair of snuffers. I have a pair of fine oxen and an ox-cart, a good horse, a Chair, and a one-horse cart; a cow, and a sow and 9 pigs.

When you come you must take such fare as you meet with, for I live upon tea, milk, fruit-pies, plain dumplins, and a piece of meat when I get it; but I live with that retirement and quiet that suits me.

Mrs. Bonneville was an encumbrance upon me all the while she was here, for she would not do anything, not even make an apple dumplin for her own children. If you cannot make yourself up a straw-bed, I can let you have blankets, and you will have no occasion to go over to the tavern to sleep.

There was in New York City in the early years of the nineteenth century a group of rationalists who argued that no creed or religious dogma should be accepted unless it appealed to the reason, meaning that it must be logical, not merely traditional. The leader of the society was Elihu Palmer, a scholarly gentleman of the highest character. He was a native of Connecticut and a graduate of Dartmouth.

This group was always in close touch with Paine, and his relation to them was that of honored philosopher and adviser. He spoke occasionally at their meetings which were held in a hall owned by the society. Palmer also published a newspaper called *Prospect: or View of the Moral World,* and Paine was a contributor now and then. His first article in the paper was printed in the issue of February 18, 1804. The following quotation is taken from it:

Is it a fact that Jesus Christ died for the sins of the world, and how is it proved? If a God he could not die, and as a man he could not redeem: how then is this redemption proved to be fact?

It is said that Adam ate of the forbidden fruit, commonly called an apple, and thereby subjected himself and all his posterity forever to eternal damnation. This is worse than visiting the sins of the fathers upon the children unto the third and fourth generations.

But how was the death of Jesus Christ to affect or alter the case? Did God thirst for blood? If so, would it not have been better to have crucified Adam upon the forbidden tree, and made a new man?

Why do not the Christians, to be consistent, make saints of Judas and Pontius Pilate, for they were the persons who accomplished the act of salvation. The merit of a sacrifice, if there can be any merit in it, was never in the thing sacrificed, but in the persons offering up the sacrifice —and therefore Judas and Pilate ought to stand first in the calendar of saints.

8

On election day of the year 1806 Paine went to the voting place in New Rochelle to cast his vote. The supervisor of the balloting was Elisha Ward, a Federalist who had been a Tory during the Revolutionary War. Ward refused Paine's vote, declaring that he was not a citizen. There was considerable argument there at the polling place, for Paine insisted on his right to vote. Ward cited Gouverneur Morris as his authority for his attitude in the matter, as Morris had written from Paris to Washington during Paine's imprisonment and explained that he could not procure his release since he was not an American citizen.

After leaving the polls that day in 1806 Paine thought of suing Elisha Ward for refusing his vote, but his friends advised him to do nothing about it.

So America's godfather was thus disfranchised in the country whose independence he had helped to win. The blow was a mortal one. Paine had been in ill health for some time, and his rejection at the polls made him feel that he was an outcast and that life was no longer worth living. If he had possessed the means and had been in good health he would have left America at once and made his home somewhere else, no matter where. As it was, he made up his mind never to live again in New Rochelle, and he moved to New York.

It was during this year that his fatal illness began to develop. While he was a boarder at William Carver's house he had a "fit" and was unconscious for about an hour; and a few months later he suffered another attack. It occurred at the house of Wesley Jarvis, where Paine was living at the time. James Cheetham records these fainting spells in his malicious biography of Paine as evidences of his intemperance, but the physician summoned by Jarvis while Paine was lying in a coma diagnosed the attacks as apoplectic.

From that time until his death he was never really well, though he was up and about until a few months before the end came, and could take care of himself in the fumbling, half-hearted manner of those who are ill unto death and still refuse to accept it as a fact. In April, 1807, he left Jarvis's place and went to board on Broome Street with a Mr. Hill who owned a bakery. He lived there until February, 1808, when he took a room in a cheap lodging house at 63 Partition Street—it is now called Fulton Street—where he stayed for five months. He was too poor, or so he thought, to live in a more comfortable place.

The following July Madame Bonneville induced him to move to the home of a Mrs. Ryder, who lived in a small frame house that stood on the ground now occupied by a building at

309 Bleecker Street. There he had fairly comfortable quarters. Madame Bonneville lived in the neighborhood and she came in every day to see how he was getting along.

Another daily visitor was a Quaker watchmaker by the name of Willett Hicks. He was a gentle, kindly person and a never-failing friend of Tom Paine. From the brief accounts of him that have come down to us it does not appear that he was disturbed by Paine's disbelief in the myths of the Bible. He made no effort to convert Paine, nor did he argue with him.

In the latter part of January, 1809, most of Paine's remaining strength, such as it was, dwindled away, and from that time until his death he was so feeble that he had to be taken care of like a bedridden child. The stories about his filthy bed manners, which were magnified out of all sensible proportion by Cheetham and other lying biographers after his death, originated in this period of his fatal illness. It is true that on occasions he did perform the functions of nature in bed, but those who spread the story and embroidered it to suit their purpose failed to state that he was unconscious at the time. It was made to appear by his enemies that he took an unclean delight in turning his own bed into a privy. Had such been the case, Mrs. Ryder and her husband would certainly have had his friends take him away.

He made his last will and testament early in 1809. Besides a few minor bequests he directed that his land in New Rochelle be sold and that one-half of the proceeds be given to "Clio" Rickman, of London, a friend of Paine for many years; and that the remaining half should go to Nicolas and Marguerite Bonneville, to be held in trust for their children, their education and maintenance. In this document he said: "I know not if the society of people called Quakers admit a person to be buried in their burying ground who does not belong to their society, but if they do or will admit me, I would prefer being buried there. My father belonged to that profession and I was partly brought up in it. But if it is not consistent with their rules to do this, I desire to be buried in a square of twelve feet, to be enclosed with rows of trees, and a stone or post and rail fence, with a headstone with my name and age engraved upon it, author of *Common Sense.*"

On February 25, 1809, he developed a fever, and a doctor was called in. His landlady attributed his indisposition to his having ceased to take stimulants. The physician agreed with her and ordered the patient to have a certain quantity of brandy every day. A fortnight later symptoms of dropsy appeared.

Toward the end of April Paine was moved to a house on the present site of 59 Grove Street and Madame Bonneville took rooms there also in order to be near him and look after him. She employed a trained nurse, a Mrs. Hedden, to attend the invalid. Paine's physician was Dr. Romaine, a medical man of high standing in his profession and in the community, but Mrs. Hedden brought in also a Dr. Manly, later evidently the author of some of the false accounts of Paine's last days, though some of the stories were undoubtedly invented by Mrs. Hedden. In some of these yarns Paine is depicted as a repentant sinner; and in all of them his manners are deplorable and the description of his filthy habits unbelievable. These stories were told to James Cheetham and it is entirely probable he paid for them and was their inspiration in the first place. They appeared in his biography of Paine and have been handed down through the years.

It is a peculiar and interesting fact that the maligners of Paine always went too far in their stories. They overshot the mark in depicting his sinful ways, his debauchery, his bodily filth. Their lies would have been more credible if they had not been so absurdly overemphasized. In describing his alcoholic habits they made his liquor consumption and drunkenness so preposterous that, if it were true, he could never have written anything at all, and certainly not such powerful literary creations as *Common Sense*, the *Rights of Man* and *The Age of Reason*. Nor could he have lived to the ripe age of seventy-two.

They depicted his personal habits as being so unclean that, if the story were true, Paine would not have been tolerated for even a day as an associate of respectable people. As a matter of fact he had been a house guest in the homes of many people of distinction—in Paris for months with James Monroe and his wife; with Sir Robert Smythe and his lady; with Thomas Jefferson at the Executive Mansion in Washington; and with many other distinguished people here and abroad.

During his last year of life he would often sit without moving for hours, his eyes wide open, staring straight ahead, as if in some kind of trance, for although he seemed to be awake he would not reply when anyone spoke to him. There were other occasions when his speech was clear, sensible and very much to the point [7]—when, in short, he was the old Tom Paine.

About a week before he died Madame Bonneville called in Dr. Gouverneur Smith, a physician of much renown in New York at that time. Dr. Smith, after a study of the patient, agreed with the attending physicians that the case was hopeless.

His death occurred at eight o'clock in the morning of June 8, 1809.

I have looked through the files of the New York City newspapers—or the few of them that have been preserved—for a funeral notice. The only one I have been able to find appeared in the New York *Post* on Saturday, June 10, 1809. This is the way it reads:

Died on Thursday, the 8th instant, Thomas Paine, author of the *Crisis*, *Rights of Man*, etc. Mr. Paine had a desire to be interred in the Quaker burying ground and some days previous to his demise, had an interview with some Quaker gentlemen on the subject, but as he declined a renunciation of his deistical opinions his anxious wishes were not complied with. He was yesterday interred at New Rochelle, Westchester County, perhaps on his own farm. I am unacquainted with his age, but he had lived long, done some good, and much harm.

---

[7] While I was engaged in the research into Paine's life which preceded the writing of this book I consulted an eminent brain specialist and described the symptoms of Paine's illness. He considered the data I submitted and said that the patient was evidently a victim of arteriosclerosis of the brain. Paine was also afflicted with dropsy, but it was not fatal.

It was a bright, sunny day when the sad and shabby funeral procession left 59 Grove Street on the lower west side of New York City and made its way to the Paine farm at New Rochelle, a trip of about twenty-two miles.

The coffin was carried on a wagon. The only other vehicle was a carriage that had as its passengers Willett Hicks and Madame Bonneville, who was accompanied by two of her young sons. There were also two Negro men who rode on the wagon. They were to lift the coffin and dig the grave.

So Thomas Paine, one of the great patriots of the Revolutionary War, the godfather of the American nation, and the most widely read author of his time, went to his grave. Six people were there—a Quaker watchmaker, a Frenchwoman and her two little boys, and two Negroes. Not even one person of distinction took the time to pay his respects, to stand over the grave with uncovered head, or to say a few words at the funeral service.

9

To William Cobbett the thought of Paine lying under the ground of a country hillside was unendurable, for in Cobbett's world of fact and fancy Tom Paine was a saint and a martyr—a saint in the righteousness of his ideas, and a martyr in the suffering that had been inflicted upon him. He resolved to do something about it.

When Paine died Cobbett had been in England for seven years, and he remained there until 1817, when he came again to America and lived on his farm on Long Island.

Paine's grave was at the side of a road that runs north out of New Rochelle. The people who lived near by came to know William Cobbett by sight, for during 1818 and the following year he would visit the grave once or twice a month, and stand near it, bareheaded and bowed in an attitude of reverence, as if he were paying homage to the man buried there. His visits were a subject of comment in the neighborhood.

In 1819 Cobbett had to return to England. He made up his mind to take Paine's body with him and to put it in a shrine somewhere in England, so that it might become the object of pilgrimages among Paine's admirers. He knew that he could not get permission to remove the body, and he resolved to take it secretly.

One night in October of that year he drove to New Rochelle from New York in a wagon accompanied by a couple of men. They dug up Paine's body—in its coffin—and drove away in the direction of the city. These doings were observed by some of the people who lived near by, and they informed the local authorities. After a considerable delay a sheriff's posse set out on horseback to pursue the grave robbers, but it was too late; they had escaped. Evidently no further effort was made to capture Cobbett and those who assisted him, and soon thereafter he shipped Paine's body to England, concealed in an ordinary merchandise crate. The question is often asked what Cobbett wanted to do with Paine's remains. He has answered this question himself by saying:

I have done myself the honor to disinter his bones. I have removed them from New Rochelle . . . they are now on their way to England. When I myself return, I shall cause them to speak the common sense of the great man; I shall gather together the people of Liverpool and Manchester in one assembly with those of London, and those bones will effect the reformation of England in Church and State.

He hoped to raise money by popular subscription in England for the shrine, but his plans came to nothing. The news of his exploit was greeted with laughter and became the inspiration of grim jokes in the comic papers.

Cobbett kept the body—or skeleton—until his death in 1835, and left it to his son. That son went into bankruptcy and the skeleton was seized when his property was taken over, but the Lord Chancellor refused to consider it an asset. For several years the bones were kept by a day laborer, and then they passed into the hands of a furniture dealer. Where they are today is unknown.

PAINE COTTAGE AT NEW ROCHELLE

The State of New York gave Thomas Paine, in the early 1780's, a tract of land at New Rochelle, on which there stood a large and handsome dwelling. Paine lived there until he departed for France in 1787. While he was in Europe the house burned down and he had the cottage shown here built in 1793, to take its place. On his return in 1802 he lived in the cottage, off and on, for several years. The house is now kept open as a historical relic. It contains many of Paine's cherished possessions.

Thomas A. Edison breaking ground for the Paine Memorial
House at New Rochelle, New York, May 30, 1925. At Mr.
Edison's left is President Van der Weyde of the Paine Association
and at his right is Cyril Nast, the Treasurer of the Association.

10

At the time of his death Tom Paine had accomplished more for human freedom, for the abolition of physical and mental slavery, and for the brotherhood of mankind, than any other American then living. He did not die in a great house, surrounded by a host of grieving friends. He died in a shabby room in a lodging house where the foul smells of the back yard and the shrill noises of the street met and mingled.

No person of distinction attended his funeral or followed his body to its last resting place; and the leading newspaper of New York City had the bad grace to say in its obituary that "he had lived long, done some good, and much harm."

But his ill-wishers could not destroy his work or prevent his fame. His books are read today by millions of people of every race and nationality. They have been published in all the existing languages, and Thomas Paine is mentioned in the same breath as his famous contemporaries, George Washington, Thomas Jefferson, John Adams and James Madison.

He died in sadness and misery only to rise to a new life in the hearts and minds of men and women born long after Tom Paine had passed away. He has no grave, no last abiding place. His bones are lost. But his presence is still among us and his influence lives on.

The End

Bibliography

Adams, Randolph G., *Political Ideas of the American Revolution.* New York, 1939.

Becker, Carl, *The Eve of the Revolution.* New Haven, 1920.

Best, Mary Agnes, *Thomas Paine: Prophet and Martyr of Democracy.* New York, 1927.

Bowden, Witt, *Industrial Society in England Toward the End of the Eighteenth Century.* New York, 1925.

Bradford, Gamaliel, *Damaged Souls.* Boston, 1923.

Cheetham, James, *The Life of Thomas Paine.* New York, 1809.

Clark, George L., *Silas Deane, a Connecticut Leader in the American Revolution.* New York, 1913.

Cole, G. D. H., *The Life of William Cobbett.* New York, 1924.

Conway, Moncure D., *The Life of Thomas Paine* (2 vols.). New York, 1892.

Davidson, Philip, *Propaganda and the American Revolution (1763–1783).* Chapel Hill, N. C., 1941.

Durand, John, editor, *Documents of the American Revolution.* New York, 1889.

Fast, Howard, *Citizen Tom Paine* (a novel). New York, 1943.

Fisher, Sydney George, *The True History of the American Revolution.* Philadelphia, 1902.

Godfrey, Walter H., *At the Sign of the Bull.* London, n.d.

Hepburn, A. Barton, *A History of Currency in the United States.* New York, 1915.

Kronenberger, Louis, *Kings and Desperate Men.* New York, 1941.

Miller, John C., *Origins of the American Revolution.* Boston, 1943.

Minnegerode, Meade, *The Magnificent Comedy.* New York, 1931.

Morris, Gouverneur, *A Diary of the French Revolution* (2 vols.). Boston, 1939.

Oldys, Francis (pseudonym for George Chalmers), *Life of Thomas Pain.* London, 1793.

Padover, Saul K., *Jefferson.* New York, 1942.

Paine, Thomas, *The Life and Works of Thomas Paine* (10 vols.). New

Rochelle, N. Y., 1925. (This ten-volume edition of Paine's writing includes a biography of Thomas Paine by William M. Van der Weyde.)

Palmer, R. R., *Twelve Who Ruled* (The Committee of Public Safety During the Terror). Princeton, 1941.

Pearson, Hesketh, *Tom Paine, Friend of Mankind.* New York, 1937.

Postgate, R. W., *The Devil Wilkes.* New York, 1929.

Roosevelt, Theodore, *Gouverneur Morris.* Boston, 1888.

Smith, Frank, *Thomas Paine, Liberator.* New York, 1938.

Turner, Thomas, *The Diary of Thomas Turner (1754–1765).* London, 1925.

Tyler, Morris Coit, *The Literary History of the American Revolution.* New York, 1897.

Vale, G., *The Life of Thomas Paine.* New York, 1841.

Index

346 Index

The general design of this book is in the typographic style of the period in which Tom Paine lived. The title page is by Nathaniel Farmer.